An End to This Strife

The Politics of Gender
in African American Churches

Demetrius K. Williams

Fortress Press
Minneapolis

For African American women
past and present
who know what the vision is

And for the African American men
who have supported them

AN END TO THIS STRIFE
The Politics of Gender in African American Churches

Cover art: *400 Years of Our People* © 2004 Michael Escoffery / Artists Rights Society (ARS), New York. Used by permission.
Cover design: Marti Naughton
Interior design: Beth Wright

Library of Congress Cataloging-in-Publication Data
Williams, Demetrius K.
   An end to this strife : the politics of gender in African American churches / Demetrius K. Williams.
      p. cm.
   Includes bibliographical references and index.
   ISBN 0-8006-3637-6 (alk. paper)
   1. African American women—Religious life. 2. Sex role—Religious aspects—Christianity. 3. Bible. N.T. Galatians III, 28—Criticism, interpretation, etc. I. Title.
   BR563.N4W498 2004
   277.3'082--dc22
                                                                2004006957

Manufactured in the U.S.A.
08   07   06   05   04   1   2   3   4   5   6   7   8   9   10

Contents

Abbreviations

AAP	*The African American Pulpit*
AME	African Methodist Episcopal
AME Zion	African Methodist Episcopal Zion
ANBC	American National Baptist Convention
CME	Christian Methodist Episcopal
COGIC	Church of God in Christ
Col.	Colossians
Cor.	Corinthians
Eph.	Ephesians
Gal.	Galatians
Gen.	Genesis
HDR	Harvard Dissertations in Religion
HR	*History of Religions*
Isa.	Isaiah
JAAR	*Journal of the American Academy of Religion*
JITC	*Journal of the Interdenominational Theological Center*
JRT	*Journal of Religious Thought*
JSNT	*Journal for the Study of the New Testament*
KJV	King James Version
Matt.	Matthew
Mic.	Micah
NBC	National Baptist Convention
NBEC	National Baptist Educational Convention
NRSV	New Revised Standard Version
NTS	*New Testament Studies*
par.	parallel texts
1, 2 Pet.	1, 2 Peter
Rom.	Romans
RSV	Revised Standard Version
SBL	Society of Biblical Literature
1, 2 Tim.	1, 2 Timothy
v., vv.	verse, verses

Preface

It is truly amazing how quickly time flies. More than fifteen years ago I had an encounter, which I discuss in more detail in the introduction, that gave rise to the topic of this book. It began as a Harvard Divinity School Master of Divinity thesis entitled, "The Politics of Gender in African American Churches: Women in the Preaching and Pastoral Ministries," which was completed in May 1990. My fortuitous enrollment in two courses in the fall of 1988 and the fall of 1989—Elisabeth Schüssler Fiorenza's "Gospel Stories of Women" and Vincent L. Wimbush's "The Bible and African Americans"—significantly shaped the approach and content of the thesis, the present book, and the direction of my scholarly work. Schüssler Fiorenza's course and writings offered a historical reconstruction for understanding not only women's ministry in the Jesus movement and in Pauline churches but also how the egalitarian tradition in the church was domesticated and deradicalized toward the end of the first century in response to conservative trends in the early church. Wimbush's course and his writings introduced me to African American biblical hermeneutics—a signal experience in shaping my career choices. It was at this time, during the final year of the M.Div. degree, that I was trying to decide if my next academic pursuit would be a doctorate in theology focusing on black/liberation theology or a doctorate in New Testament and Christian origins. Before taking Wimbush's course, I thought that black theology was the most viable means of addressing the situation of African American people from an academically informed theological perspective. But Wimbush's course and writings exposed me to the possible contributions of New Testament studies—the area of my graduate training—for understanding and articulating the African American religious experience. Thus equipped with a feasible historical reconstruction of Christian origins and a practical interpretive perspective for engaging the African American religious tradition, I was able to make an initial formulation of this topic in the thesis. I had, however, much more to learn before a book-length study could be attempted.

In 1991 Fortress Press published *Stony the Road We Trod: African American Biblical Interpretation*, which introduced African American biblical hermeneutics to the general public. It was in this volume that I read Clarice Martin's "The *Haustafeln* (Household Codes) in African American Biblical Interpretation: 'Free Slaves' and 'Submissive Wives,'" which exposed the limitations of classical biblical appropriations of the Bible for addressing the plight of African American women. I recognized from her study that a viable paradigm was needed that could address the unique situation of black women and offer an alternative model for the African American religious tradition's understanding of the role of women in the church. Wimbush's contribution, "The Bible and African Americans: An Outline of an Interpretive History," supplied a historical framework for understanding the importance of Gal. 3:28 in the African American religious and protest tradition. I was able to explore the questions raised in Martin's work in my article "The Bible and Models of Liberation in the African American Experience," which proposed Gal. 3:28 as a potential paradigm for addressing the historical quests of liberation in the African American religious tradition in terms of race, class, and gender. From the framework supplied in Wimbush's article I was able to examine African Americans' rhetorical appropriations of Gal. 3:28 in sermons, speeches, and memoirs in "African American Churches and Galatians 3:28: A Brief Assessment of the Appropriation of an Egalitarian Paradigm." I must also mention another fortuitous course that was offered in 1992 by Richard A. Horsley, "Poverty and Servitude in the New Testament." This course introduced me to the ideological foundations of power relations in the ancient world. Equipped now with the two contributions by Martin and Wimbush and gaining important knowledge of ideologies of power and subjugation, I was able to establish the basis for a book-length project exploring issues of gender and women's ministry in black churches.

Although the opportunities and recognition of women in the preaching and pastoral ministries have been increasing in African American churches, I think that a book like this is necessary because there are still a number of churches and denominational bodies that do not recognize women's equality. I have heard stories about male pastors being dismissed or spurned from regional conventions and associations for ordaining or licensing women to ministry. In my own experience as a pastor, I remember participating as a preacher in a Good Friday service in which seven pastors were to preach the seven last words of Jesus (a staple of Good Friday services in the black church tradition). Two women pastors were included on the roster to preach, but when the pastor of the host church discovered that the two women pastors were to participate, he gave instructions (from his rest-home bed) to his young assistant pastor that they could "speak from the floor" but were not to enter his pulpit. Although this pastor was physically unable to serve as pastor to his church, he still wielded great influence over the congregation. Not surprisingly, however, the women pastors refused his offer to "speak from the floor." I am certain that stories like this can be told over and over again.

Thus I have undertaken to write this book in order to examine the biblical foundations of the black churches' understanding of gender relations in the church and in society. What I mean is that several persons with whom I have talked over the years, whether male or female, have said that while they have reluctantly accepted women ministers and pastors, they do not really believe that it is biblical—that is, it cannot be supported biblically because the Bible says that "women are to keep silence in the church." To me this is analogous to saying that although enslaved African Americans have been set free from slavery, it is not really biblical because the Bible states that "slaves are to be submissive to [their] masters." Not many people today would accept the latter statement as representing a socially acceptable position, although it has the weight of several biblical passages to support it. As a matter of fact, there are more injunctions related to slaves than to women in the New Testament. Therefore, just as the black religious tradition has dismantled the biblically supported argument for slavery and racism, this book seeks to attempt to do the same to the biblically supported arguments for sexism in the church. In this regard, this book is meant to be not contentious but instructive.

In the many years since beginning this work, I owe a debt of thanks to several individuals. For their assistance in guiding the initial thesis to completion, I thank Rev. Suzan Johnson Cook (many students knew her as "Sue-J" back then) who was a Dean's Fellow at Harvard Divinity School in 1990. She suggested exploring how African American preaching women have used the Bible to argue for the validity of their call to ministry. I was fortunate to have Lawrence Wills as thesis advisor. He also served as my Greek instructor and advisor for my earlier Master of Theological Studies degree. His kind and considerate guidance throughout my graduate work at Harvard is greatly appreciated. I must also mention and thank Elisabeth Schüssler Fiorenza and Vincent L. Wimbush. While neither individual read or offered suggestions for the project, both have been influential through their writings in how I approached the earlier thesis and the present book.

I also make grateful acknowledgment of the Center for Research at Tulane University for providing a summer research grant in 1997 for work undertaken in Part 1 of the book. In addition, I acknowledge the Newcomb Fellows Program of Sophie Newcomb College, Tulane University, for providing a summer research and travel grant in 2000 for research on Parts 2 and 3 of the book. I also thank Teresa Soufas, Dean of the Faculty of Liberal Arts and Sciences at Tulane University, for her support of my teaching and research, as well as my colleagues in the Department of Classical Studies.

I cannot forget the Fortress staff whose confidence in the project and editorial skills have brought this book to fruition. I am grateful to Michael

West, editor-in-chief at Fortress, who was very enthusiastic about the project from the beginning. I must also mention K. C. Hanson and Marshall Johnson. Thanks are also due to Beth Wright, whose editorial skills and interior design of the pages made this book a much better one than it otherwise would have been. Thank you all very much.

The present book has not benefited from the critical insight and scrutinizing eye of my colleagues in New Testament and African American biblical hermeneutics. For this I must apologize. This is a trend that I do not plan to continue. For any mistakes or oversights I ask the pardon of my peers and my other readers. My family, perhaps, will be more forgiving. Indeed they have been very supportive of my work from the beginning. I would not have been able to have a secure foundation, which has allowed me to pursue my career goals, without their love and support. It started in the cradle, when I was born the last child of my parents, Bessie and Timothy Williams Sr. My parents have served as an example for me of mutual cooperation and partnership in male-female relationships. Such a model has certainly influenced my thinking. Unfortunately, my father passed away before the completion of this project, but before his passing we had several conversations about its theme and content. The conversation with my mother continues. As for my siblings, all of whom are my seniors, I thank you all by name: Charles, Virginia Diane (my second "mother"), Tony, Ernest O'Neil (thanks for reading and commenting on the first draft of the introduction), Beverly, Jeffery (you and Caroline are great examples of spousal co-pastoral ministry), and James. To my brother Timothy Jr., a Master of Theological Studies candidate at Candler School of Theology, Emory University, who joins me as one of the two youngest, thanks for your helpful suggestions and critical reading of several chapters even in the midst of your own graduate studies. Keep up the good work!

Last but not least, to my wife, Robin: thank you for assuming the major responsibility of caring for our children, Taylor and Kelvin. This temporary division of labor allowed me the time to spend many evenings sitting at the desk and working. Having finished the book, I can now respond affirmatively to Taylor's constant inquiries of "Done working, Dad?" and spend more time with her and her new little brother playing at the park.

Introduction

Throughout their history African American people have struggled for the realization of full humanity, freedom, and equal opportunity regardless of race or class. In their struggles for these rights they discovered that the Bible could serve as an important source for their cause. Certain stories and themes in the Bible provided important paradigms (especially the exodus–wilderness–promised land saga) as well as a language and theology for articulating their hopes and aspirations for liberation. African Americans used the Bible to articulate messages of freedom and equality even while the Bible was used by the theological architects of American slavery to construct racially based oppression, which relegated black people to a status or class as slaves. Nevertheless, beginning with the "invisible institution" (slave religion before and during the rise of formal black churches) and into the emergence of institutional black churches, biblical paradigms of liberation and equality were used to support arguments against race and class oppression. An important element in black religion itself is its emphasis on social and religious protest. Hence one of the most important themes African Americans gleaned from the Bible was that "God is no respecter of persons" (Acts 10:34-35, KJV) or, in other words, "all people are equal before God" regardless of race, class, or sex (as expressed in Gal. 3:28). Even after emancipation from slavery in 1865, this biblical theme fueled the political-religious language of many black leaders, who in many cases were Christian ministers. Despite this biblical theme and the tradition of protest against racial and classist oppression, however, when the issue of sexism surfaced in the black church, particularly in the late nineteenth century on the heels of the emerging women's suffrage movement, the black churches did not see gender equality as a concern—or at least as a concern equal to that of race and class oppression.

The same African American churches that had found within the Bible models and paradigms of liberation from race and class oppression were not willing to explore the Bible to find equally liberative models to challenge the traditional roles and status of women, even black women, who suffered under the same harsh system of racial and classist oppression. *African American churches often uncritically accepted paradigms of gender oppression based on the same Bible that was used to support race and class liberation.* Support for sexism could be found in the creation narratives of Genesis 2 and 3, in 1 Cor. 14:33-36, in the household codes of 1 Pet. 2:13—3:7, and in the deutero-Pauline epistles (letters attributed to Paul: Col. 3:18—4:1; Eph. 5:21—6:9; 1 Tim. 2:8-15; 6:1-2). Instead of viewing these texts as supporting the oppression of and discrimination against women and hence incompatible with the principle of "the equality of all people before God," the African American religious tradition viewed biblical passages of this sort as establishing the "God-ordained place of women" in society and the church.

These texts have had such an effect on Christian religious tradition that even today the question of women's participation in leadership roles within Christian churches in general is far from resolved. More importantly for our purpose, there are still many African American churches and denominational bodies that limit or prohibit the participation of women in leadership roles, particularly in the preaching and pastoral ministries. The question of women's participation in leadership roles in the church is tied to the traditional biblical understanding of a "woman's place." This understanding has a particular nuance when considering a black woman's place in a society of racial, classist, and gender oppression. This means that African American women comprise the only group to date in North America to suffer "triple oppression"—because of their *race* (black), *class* (formerly as slaves and later as an oppressed economic group), and *gender* (female). For this reason, Gal. 3:28 can serve as a heuristic paradigm of liberation and as an important locus for exploring the issue of sexism in African American churches.

Prior Contributions to the Issue

Beginning in the 1970s, with the reemergence of the women's rights and liberation movements, African American scholars and theologians began to critically assess issues of gender, religion, and culture in the African American experience. Black feminist and womanist scholars in particular have done some creative work in reclaiming the humanity and contributions of black women and in critiquing the sexist practices of black religious institutions using a number of methodologies and from a variety of disciplines. Several of these early foundational articles are conveniently available in Gayraud Wilmore and James Cone's two-volume set, *Black Theology: A Documentary History*.[1] In more recent womanist articulation no one examining the question of sexism in black churches and black theologies of liberation can ignore Delores Williams's *Sisters in the Wilderness*.[2] In addition to arguing that black women's experience is more compatible with the wilderness motif than the exodus theme, she offers a stinging critique of the sexism and shortcomings of black theology and the gender-biased practices of black churches. She is not alone in this perspective. African American male scholars have also voiced critiques and challenges to black churches. In *Troubling Biblical Waters: Race, Class, and Family*, Cain Felder, an ordained minister and scholar, provides a chapter on women in ministry that offers new vistas for understanding this issue by pointing to liberative themes within the New Testament.[3] Likewise, Arthur Griffin, a pastor and scholar, offers in *By Your Traditions: A Theological Perspective on Women in the Gospel Ministry* a biblical-theological perspective on women's ministry that highly values the Pentecost prophecy of the prophet Joel: "and your sons and daughters shall prophesy." For Griffin, this is the key to opening wide the doors of ministry for women.[4] Clarice Martin, an early leading voice among a growing number of African American womanist New Testament scholars, has also contributed a number of salient articles that offer exegetical insights into problematical New Testament passages and language that support the subordination and silencing of women.[5]

Utilizing insights from sociological methodology, the works of Cheryl Townsend Gilkes have traced the ways in which black Christian women have found alternative avenues of power and praxis within the church and society to acclaim and reclaim black women's work and contributions to the black church and larger society. Several of these articles have recently been collected and published in a single volume, *If It Wasn't for the Women*.[6] Also employing sociological methodology, C. Eric Lincoln and Lawrence Mamiya have included an exploration of the roles and contributions of black women in the church in their classic work, *The Black Church in the African American Experience*.[7] The authors provide statistical data and brief historical overviews of early black Christian women preachers and evangelists. Their analysis is not exhaustive or essentially evaluative but is primarily descriptive.

In another vein, Ella Pearson Mitchell addresses the question of women preachers and sexism in the church homiletically, that is, through the medium of the sermon. She has offered two collections of sermons by black women preachers within a three-volume set titled *Those Preaching Women*.[8] The women featured in these collections, and others like them, have preached in some cases with denominational support or recognition and in others without any support. Her goal in these volumes is not to argue for the authenticity of women preachers but to allow the sermons of black women preachers to speak for themselves. Mitchell's latest collection of sermons, *Women to Preach or Not to Preach?*, includes both male and female preachers who answer the question of women's call to the gospel ministry positively. An introductory chapter directly addresses women's call to ministry.[9] More recently, Bettye Collier-Thomas, in *Daughters of Thunder: Black Women Preachers and Their Sermons*, has provided an important anthology of sermons and brief biographical sketches of black women preachers and evangelists, some of whom were

well-known in their time but whose significance may have been forgotten
with time.[10] Sheron C. Patterson's *New Faith* should be included here. She
does not use the sermon medium but a pastoral theology creatively informed
by womanist theology and black women's experience to address not only sexism but also strategies for healing the wounds black women have received
from sexism in the church and in relationships.[11]

Finally, historians Paula Giddings (*When and Where I Enter*) and Evelyn
Brooks Higginbotham (*Righteous Discontent*) have made major contributions
by recapturing the historic roles and work that black Christian women have
contributed to the black church and the black community.[12] And we should
not forget Angela Davis's *Women, Race, and Class*, which provides an overview
of black women's political and religious activism and social and religious
struggles from slavery to the early 1980s.[13] All of these works, and several
others that space limitations keep me from discussing, have made significant
contributions and helped to clarify important issues regarding religion, gender, and culture in the African American experience.

The Approach of This Book

I have benefited greatly from the previous yeoman work of others, and in this
book I seek to advance the discussion of sexism in African American churches
by incorporating it into the emerging field of African American biblical
hermeneutics. African American biblical hermeneutics means, in short, the
practice of interpreting the Bible in light of and through the history, culture,
and experience of African American people.[14] Another way of putting it is
that black folk have traditionally read their experience through the Bible and
the Bible through their experience.[15] This means that the biblically supported issue of sexism in the black church must be examined in light of the
interpretive traditions in black Christianity, which early on developed a
hermeneutic of liberation. This hermeneutic, represented most poignantly in
the phrase "the equality of all people before God," initiated and validated the
independent black church movement of the late eighteenth and early nineteenth centuries, and it provided the impetus for religious and social protest.
Therefore this study will go beyond other works by examining the issue of
sexism in the African American churches from the exegetical (interpretation
of scripture), historical, and theological perspectives. This combined tripar-
tite approach is important and necessary because all three areas must be
explored and examined in order to reclaim the liberative tradition in the New
Testament, the early Christian church, and the African American religious
tradition. These combined elements will help to foster a challenge against the
sexist practices of the black churches.

The thesis of this book rests upon a simple theoretical basis: since African American churches were organized and founded upon the biblical principle of "the equality of all people before God," which caused them to protest against slavery (classism) and race prejudice (racism), and in order for them to be faithful to their tradition as nonclassist and nonracist institutions (that is, their protest posture against race and class oppression), they must also become nonsexist institutions. This prophetic tradition, which was used to critique racism and classism perpetrated historically against African Americans, should be reversed to critique the sexist practices of the African American churches. The African American religious tradition of struggle against racism and classism is inconsistent and incomplete until it addresses sexism with the same vigor and attention. Galatians 3:28 will serve as an important paradigm for interpreting this issue in the African American context.

Galatians 3:28 as a Liberative Paradigm

African American political-religious appropriations of certain biblical passages and paradigms have supported arguments for liberation. These passages and paradigms were essential for constructing a hermeneutics of liberation or survival that could counter the oppressive passages and paradigms used by proslavery advocates. These passages and paradigms helped African Americans to interpret their situation and provided theological models to guide their praxis. The classical appropriations of the Bible—for example, exodus and promised land (hermeneutics of liberation) and exile and diaspora (hermeneutics of survival)—have been used to advocate liberation from race and class discrimination and therefore have been very important in the African American struggle for freedom and equality. They have fallen short, however, in providing a biblical paradigm that could also consistently challenge notions of gender oppression.

One biblical passage used in the early African American religious tradition applies to the holistic quest for historical liberation, namely, Gal. 3:28: "There is no longer Jew or Greek [abolition of racism], there is no longer slave or free [abolition of classism], there is no longer male and female [abolition of sexism]; but you are all one [equal] in Christ Jesus." This biblical passage or paradigm, unlike the classical appropriations, provides a model that can incorporate African Americans' tri-dimensional struggle against oppression with respect to race, class, and gender. Although this paradigm is commensurate with the traditional struggles of African Americans, the African American interpretive tradition has not fully explored its potential to alleviate gender/sex oppression. This book seeks to recover Gal. 3:28 as a model of liberation that can meet the challenges of the historical quest for freedom within the African American religious tradition, especially sexism, which continues to prevail in many African American churches and religious institutions, restricting women's opportunities for leadership.

The Black Church, Black Churches, or African American Churches?

Any work investigating the African American tradition—religious or nonreligious—has to contend with a number of descriptive terms. Various terms have been used to describe and identify people of African descent in America. In this introduction I have used "African American" and "black" interchangeably to describe people of African descent and their institutions without further explanation. I have done this intentionally to avoid a sense of redundancy and also to capture the richness of the descriptive terrain. The exclusive use of one term can deny the variety of ways that African American people have understood themselves.

Along with this issue of description is the question of whether a singular or plural should be used, particularly with respect to religious institutions— "*the* black church" or "black or African American church*es*." Gayraud Wilmore has addressed this issue:

> One frequently hears in popular lectures and discussions the ploy that there is no such thing as *the* Black Church—there are only "Black Churches." What is generally meant by "Black Church" is the plurality of formal institutions and networks of ethnic caucuses and congregations of Black Christians that seek to preserve some historic continuity with African American founders and forebears and some measure of separate identity, if not autonomy, from White controlled judicatories. . . . The designation "Black" is an attitudinal, theological, and ideological designation connoting the struggle against racism.[16]

It is apparent from the first line of the quote that Wilmore is opposing an attempt by some to deny a historical, theological, and ideological grounding that has traditionally united black religious institutions in their struggles against racism regardless of black religious denominational affiliation. Hence his preference for the singular, *the* black church, is understandable. However, it is my contention that it is possible to use the plural "black churches" or "African American churches" without losing view of the historical factors that have unified the vision and identity of African American religious institutions. Moreover, I prefer to use the plural because it represents to me the ambiguous legacy of the black churches in their stance regarding black women's liberation and freedom. To be sure, while there are a few African American denominations that have historically recognized and supported black women's ministry (AME and AME Zion), along with a number of individual churches within certain denominations, as a whole black churches have exhibited an ambiguous stance in this regard.

Overview: Structure, Methodologies, and Content

Part 1, on exegetical interpretation, examines the gospel message of Jesus and of Paul (chapter 1). Using current feminist-critical hermeneutics and social-historical analyses of biblical culture and texts, I explore how the teachings of Jesus and Paul are both arguably counter-hegemonic and entail not only the "salvation of souls" but also a critique of the current social and political conditions of their followers, Jew and Gentile, under Roman hegemony. Their messages of hope offered an alternative worldview and social vision of human relations that was countercultural and counter-hegemonic; their messages offered a new vision of human relationships that broke down the traditional barriers of race, class, and gender as expressed in Gal. 3:28, as well as economic exploitation.

Chapter 2 applies traditional historical-literary analysis to engage exegetically the prohibitions in 1 Cor. 14:33b-36 (a first-century Pauline letter) and to trace their connection with 1 Tim. 2:11-15 (a second-century deutero-Pauline letter written a generation later by an author in the Pauline tradition). Thus I will trace the effective role of Gal. 3:28 in early church history and show how this egalitarian vision was curtailed a generation later by a conservative movement within the early church toward the end of the first century C.E. This groundwork is important, because many contemporary male church leaders cite these passages as justification for closing the doors of leadership, preaching, and pastoral opportunities to women. I argue that in the original context of the Corinthian community, 1 Cor. 14:33b-36 does not prohibit women's speaking in church but is a statement against those in the community who desire to exclude women from full participation in the church. I show that the corruption of this passage was the work of second-century Paulinists who reformulated the text to read as a restriction against women's public speaking in church, intending to portray Paul as challenging women's leadership and preaching. The parallel statement in 1 Tim. 2:11-15 represents the perspective of the second-century Paulinists who took issue with women's leadership roles in the church. As I will show, the prohibitionist perspective carried the day.

Part 2, on historical interpretation, analyzes biblical hermeneutics in the African American religious tradition, showing that despite the use of the Bible to support slavery, the African American religious tradition is steeped in protest against race and class oppression. In addition, the tradition gleaned liberative biblical themes to counter proslavery and racist arguments and claims (chapter 3). This tradition of protest led African American churches to challenge America's stance in relation to their freedom and liberation. This chapter assesses how Gal. 3:28 and other passages were used to support the principle of the "equality of all people before God," which functioned not only as an impetus to found independent black congregations but also as a prophetic principle to critique American slavery and racism. Here I show how African Americans' engagement with the Bible's liberative paradigms caused them to reject oppressive passages of scripture that mitigated "the gospel of equality."

As in the early Christian churches, the effective history of this egalitarian vision of humanity became stifled in the African American religious tradition when it came to issues related to sex and gender. Thus the issues of the organization and power dynamics of African American churches will be explored (chapter 4). This exploration will focus on the question of why allowing women into the pastoral and preaching ministries is problematic in the African American context, especially for black males (and some black females too, but my main concern is black male leadership). I argue here that the oppressive social context of the black male in America historically caused him to seek within the black church a place of power and autonomy and, more importantly, his manhood. I contend that the principle of "the equality of all people before God" can and must be turned inward by African American churches to do self-critical evaluation of their own attitudes and practices with respect to leadership roles for women. In this process new directions for change and growth can be discovered.

The concluding Part 3, on theological interpretation, engages current feminist, womanist, and black theological perspectives to argue that all oppression—race, class, and gender—is interrelated (chapter 5). If the African American religious tradition has argued against race and class oppression, it must also challenge gender oppression and discrimination. Many African American women have realized this, despite the biblical prohibitions directed against women (or the church's accepted understanding of those prohibitions). Finally, this study will explore how several early and contemporary African American women have argued for women's "God-given right" to preach, act as pastor, and hold leadership roles according to their particular calling (chapter 6). It will become evident that the "equality of all people before God" is also operative in their arguments against sex discrimination in the church. Against the odds, African American women preached the gospel of the kingdom with power and conviction, a ministry that they have continued into the present day.

A brief conclusion summarizes the contemporary situation.

My Starting Point: An Eventful Encounter

The need to address sexism in African American churches became particularly evident for me while on a visit home to Milwaukee in the summer of 1988. On this particular visit a minister from the church in which I was reared invited me and three other ministers from our National Baptist tradition to his home for dinner and conversation. (I suspected that the real reason these ministers wanted to meet with me was to discuss how my studies were coming along at Harvard Divinity School—especially the possible influence of its "liberal tendencies" on my thinking!) We had a long, two- or three-hour discussion covering subjects from the impact of race on American social history and the role of the black church in the community to the importance of the study of biblical languages for exegesis and preaching. Up to this point, I was passing with flying colors. Our discussion was nearing a sweet denouement and we were beginning our pleasant farewells until I mentioned that I had recently purchased Ella P. Mitchell's *Those Preaching Women*. The mood of camaraderie and the demeanor of my fellow ministers suddenly changed. In response to my unwitting delight in having purchased what in their view seemed an "offensive" work, I was immediately interrogated with a stern question, begging a negative response: "You don't believe that women are called to preach, do you?" After gathering some emotional strength for the oral battle that I knew was about to ensue, I hesitantly answered, "Yes." Then the oral battle commenced, moving from cautious debate to open acrimony.

One minister accused me of being "indoctrinated" and "brainwashed" by secular biblical study, which has nothing to do with "really" understanding the scriptures. Then he offered this telling commentary: "That's what I figured would happen to you young boys when you got a little education." Despite his baffling comment, it seemed at first that the other ministers present might have been persuaded to see the issue of women in ministry differently when I quoted to them the passage from Acts 2:17-21 (a quotation from Joel 2:28-32): "In the last days, I will pour out my spirit upon all flesh . . . and your sons and your daughters shall prophesy" (which, I assured them means "to preach" or "forth tell"). However, when this particular minister made reference to the verses in 1 Cor. 14:33-36 (further elaborated in 1 Tim. 2:11-15), his argument for the sexist subordination of African American women in the church carried the day. While I was not successful in persuading the other ministers present at that time to view the issue as I did, I did not leave in defeat. I was determined to explore this issue further and find a sound historical, theological, and hermeneutical perspective for maintaining my position.

As I have reflected over the last fifteen years upon this event and the increasingly important issue of black churches and sexism, I have pondered whether this contemporary debate concerning women in ministry might reflect a similar situation in the early church. Does this issue represent a debate and conflict that invokes two opposing models or paradigms—one supporting an egalitarian, horizontal perspective ("*and* your daughters shall prophesy") and one supporting a hierarchical, vertical perspective ("let a woman keep silence in the church")? I think this is the case, because in the Bible one can find support for either perspective. The question is, which model or paradigm is in continuity with the black religious tradition and the African American churches' historical struggles for freedom and equality and their hermeneutical endeavors? This is perhaps the most salient question that I seek to address in the following pages.

It is my sincere hope that this book will contribute to the development of a better understanding of the biblical, theological, and historical basis of sexism and to the current issues of sex and gender discrimination in African American churches. I also hope that this book will show how the paradigm of Gal. 3:28 has been used within the African American interpretive tradition and has contributed to the principle of what Peter Paris has termed the "Black Christian tradition" or the principle of "the equality of all people before God."[17] This tradition and principle can still be used to root out oppression, not only from without African American churches but also from within them.

❧ Part One ❧

Early Christian Experience and Scripture

❧ 1 ❧
Jesus, Paul, and a New Paradigm

Mary [of Bethany] has chosen the better part, which will not be taken away from her. (Luke 10:42)

There is no longer Jew or Greek, there is no longer slave or free, there is no longer male and female; for all of you are one in Christ Jesus. (Gal. 3:28)

Richard Horsley and Neil Silberman have written a book whose title is quite telling for our purposes: *The Message and the Kingdom: How Jesus and Paul Ignited a Revolution and Transformed the Ancient World.*[1] The title and subject matter of this book unite two individuals whose messages and visions of human possibilities are important in the history of earliest Christianity and in Western culture—Jesus and Paul. Their messages were articulated in a world that was similar in some respects to that in which enslaved African Americans found themselves—a world of empire-building, patronage, slavery, and dominance, supported by a pervasive ruling-class ideology. On this note the authors explain that

> the movement that began with Jesus of Nazareth was primarily concerned with the way that people could somehow resist exploitation by the rich and powerful without either surrendering their traditions or resorting to violence. Likewise, the Apostle Paul—in his wide-ranging travels throughout the lands and peoples of the Eastern Empire—engaged in a career of confrontation with the forces of patronage and empire and died in the attempt.[2]

On some levels early Christianity might be considered a type of protest movement against the destructive forces of Roman social, political, and cultural hegemony. While some interpreters argue that there are significant differences between the proclamations of the two "founders of Christianity,"[3] they are connected in their common vision of new human relationships that challenge traditional notions of society and human relations. This point has often been overlooked, because traditional scholarship has seldom explored how the message of Jesus and Paul may have sounded to their hearers, who eked out a living in a world of Roman dominance and oppression. Heard in a different key, "Jesus of Nazareth offered desperate Galileans and Judeans a path to village revival; Paul of Tarsus sought to provide fragmented, aimless communities of Galatians, Greeks, and Macedonians a way to achieve the same ideals."[4] The nature of this revival lay in its *social vision*. This revolutionary vision of human relations is common to the messages of Jesus and Paul.

My focus in this chapter is to trace the development of this new vision of human relations in the preaching of Jesus and Paul. From this foundation I assess how this vision came to be formulated in the baptismal formula or confession of Gal. 3:28 and how it served as a paradigm for a new pattern of human relations for the early church. A related aim is to explore whether there is any evidence that Paul in his undisputed letters (Romans, 1 and 2 Corinthians, Galatians, Philippians, 1 Thessalonians, and Philemon) and the early Christian communities to which he preached took steps to actualize this egalitarian vision in a social reality.[5] To answer this question, I examine the passages in the Pauline corpus in which the issues of "Jew or Greek," "slave or free," and "male and female" are addressed. Finally, I analyze the data to determine how Pauline and later Christian communities "heard" his message that "all . . . are one in Christ."

The Ministry and Message of Jesus: The Beginnings of a Revolution

Jesus of Nazareth ignited a movement that had far-reaching religious, social, and political implications. Scholars are in general agreement that the movement that Jesus initiated can be termed a *revival* movement within Judaism.[6] To be sure, this was more than a "spiritual revival" concerned only with the souls of people and not with their political, social, and economic condition. As Ross Kraemer puts it, "The Jesus movement began as a *protest and renewal* movement wholly within Judaism, one of the many responses to the extraordinary conditions of political, social, economic, and religious crises experienced by Jews living in Roman Palestine in the first centuries B.C.E./C.E."[7] (emphasis added). Moreover, the recent investigations of scholars who employ social-historical and ideological analysis have explored Jesus' message of the kingdom of God as related more to this present world than that of a transcendent realm. For instance, it is surmised from this perspective that

> The mission of Jesus' disciples was an ambitious yet *down-to-earth attempt
> to overturn the accepted order through a revolution in the people's behavior*; it was
> not a program of purely spiritual conversion or even a well-intentioned
> tour of backcountry peasant villages by alienated young idealists seeking

to do good and find meaning in their lives. . . . Far from being a band with a purely spiritual mission of individual moral improvement, they were dispatched to promote a community-oriented political-religious program of renewal throughout the villages of Galilee.[8] (emphasis added)

In this way, social-historical readings indicate that Jesus had a revolutionary social message that probably also included a veiled critique of social, political, and economic conditions under Roman hegemony. In this reading, the message of Jesus takes seriously the systems of oppression and domination that create division and barriers among human beings. According to Horsley and Silberman,

In the New Testament and the early Christian tradition we may be able to catch a rare glimpse [of] the hopes, dreams, and utopian visions of those who suddenly find themselves at the bottom of a new civilization's social heap. . . . Earliest Christianity was a movement that boldly challenged the heartlessness and arrogance of a vast governmental bureaucracy—run on unfairly apportioned tax burdens and guided by cynical special interests—that preached about "opportunity," "self-reliance," and "personal achievement" while denying all three to the vast majority of men, women, and children over whom it presumed to rule. Christianity arose in a remote and poverty-stricken region of the vast Roman Empire, among the struggling farm families of a frontier province that could only be classed as "chronically underdeveloped" by modern economic criteria. Yet even after the movement's first great prophet was condemned as a threat to civil order and put to death for his preaching, his followers spread a coalescing gospel of resistance from the country to the city and from the eastern provinces of the empire to the far western edges of the Roman world. At the heart of this movement was the dream of a down-to-earth Kingdom first enunciated by the prophets of the tiny Land of Israel several hundred years before.[9]

It could therefore be argued that the kingdom message of Jesus represented for "those at the bottom of the social heap" a vision of "the praxis of inclusive wholeness."[10] In the ministry of Jesus, God is experienced within the community of followers as all-inclusive love (Matt. 5:45). God's love, graciousness, and goodness accepts *anyone* and *everyone* and brings about justice and well-being for everyone without exception, but there was a special concern for the poor, the marginal, and the outcast. Thus Jesus' preaching of the kingdom of God sought to reach three distinct groups of people: (1) the poor and destitute; (2) the sick and crippled; and (3) tax collectors, sinners, and prostitutes—those exploited by and on the fringe of society.[11] His message of the kingdom had far-reaching implications for those in these categories and was indeed heard as "good news." This good news of the kingdom was already emerging within his message and his community of followers:

> The Kingdom of God was indeed at hand if they believed it—not a dream, not a vision of heaven, not a spiritual state, but a *social transformation here and now* in the very fields they plowed and the very villages they lived in, if only they rejected injustice and heeded the commandments of God. Recalling the visions of ancient Israelite prophets that peace, prosperity, and well-being would come to the House of Israel when the laws of the Covenant were finally observed and justice honored, the hungry peasants and landless laborers of Israel looked toward the glorious period of God's restoration. . . .[12] (emphasis added)

In the following analysis I focus on two aspects of Jesus' teaching and ministry that stress the vision of a nontraditional social transformation: (1) an inclusive vision symbolized in an open table fellowship and the missionary activity of women and (2) the subversion of patriarchal social relations.

Jesus' Good News to the Poor, Gentiles, and Women: A Social Vision of Inclusive Wholeness

Elisabeth Schüssler Fiorenza's groundbreaking reconstruction of Christian origins, *In Memory of Her*, offers new perspectives for understanding the role of women in earliest Christianity. In the following paragraphs I touch on some of her important findings in this regard.

In her far-reaching analysis of the Jesus movement, Schüssler Fiorenza makes the observation that table fellowship was an important and inclusive aspect of Jesus' ministry and of the kingdom message. In the table fellowship practiced by Jesus, all people (initially, all of the people Israel) are welcome regardless of their social status, background, or sex. Through the collective memory of the early followers of the Jesus movement the evangelists of the Synoptic Gospels (Matthew, Mark, and Luke) assert that the Jesus movement invited into its table community not only women but also social outcasts and disreputable community sinners. Indeed, Jesus would even share a meal with some of his rivals, the Pharisees. Several Gospel stories and parables bear out this community table theme wherein Jesus is often portrayed as having an open policy toward anyone who wished to share a table. In addition, some parables with an end-time (eschatological) theme are filled with the symbolism of the banquet. For example, on the theme of an open community table, the evangelists depict Jesus sharing meals with common people, lepers (Simon the leper, Matt. 26:6-13; Mark 14:3-9), tax collectors (Levi and other tax collectors, Luke 5:27-32), and Pharisees (Luke 7:36-50; 11:37-44; 14:1-14). This gained Jesus the reputation of being "a friend of tax collectors and sinners" (Matt. 9:10; 11:18).

In some of Jesus' parables and in certain eschatological sayings the theme of the sumptuous end-time banquet emerges. While all of the Gospels reveal this motif of community meals, this theme is more prominent in Luke's Gospel. This is particularly evident in the parable of the rich man and the beggar (Lazarus). In Luke 16:19-30 Jesus tells the story about a rich man who dined sumptuously but refused to share the crumbs from his table with a poor beggar. The rich man was not willing to have an open table. While the story has some indications of Luke's personal concern for the rich to take up the welfare of the poor, the author is working with a well-known practice of the community table that goes back to the ministry of Jesus.

In Luke 14:1-14 Jesus is at the home of a particular leader of the Pharisees on the Sabbath and performs a miracle (heals a man with dropsy). After questions about the lawfulness of healing on the Sabbath, Jesus tells a parable about not sitting in places of honor at a marriage feast. He then speaks directly to his guest:

> When you give a luncheon or a dinner, do not invite your friends or your brothers or your relatives or rich neighbors, in case they may invite you in return, and you would be repaid. But when you give a banquet, invite the poor, the crippled, the lame, and the blind. And you will be blessed, because they cannot repay you, for you will be repaid at the resurrection of the righteous. (Luke 14:12-14)

Here again the theme of the common community table emerges. The placement of this story well before the parable of the rich man and the beggar might have been intended to emphasize the importance of welcoming anyone and everyone to the community table.

The symbol of a banquet is also used in Jesus' teaching for the eschatological future of the kingdom of God. In Luke 22:27-30 the disciples debated who would be the greatest in the coming rule of God. After Jesus instructs them on humility, he says, "You are those who have stood by me in my trials; and I confer on you, just as my Father has conferred on me, a kingdom, so that you may eat and drink at my table in my kingdom, and you will sit on thrones judging the twelve tribes of Israel." This banquet is not just for the disciples, however. In the story mentioned above (Luke 14:1-14), in which Jesus is at the home of a leader of the Pharisees, after he tells the host to invite all people, another invited guest remarks, "Blessed is anyone who will eat bread in the kingdom of God!" (Luke 14:15). Immediately following this comment, Jesus describes the kingdom of God in a simile (Luke 14:15-24; par. Matt. 22:1-14) in which someone (a king in Matthew) invites guests to come to his home to a great dinner, but the first guests make excuses and decline the offer. After several persons decline and the servant reports this to the host, he remarks:

"Go out at once into the streets and lanes of the town and bring in the poor, the crippled, the blind, and the lame." And the slave said, "Sir, what you ordered has been done, and there is still room." Then the master said to the slave, "Go out into the roads and lanes, and compel people to come in, so that my house may be filled. For I tell you, none of those who were invited will taste my dinner." (Luke 14:21-24)

It is apparent in this parable and the stories about Jesus' ministry that the common people—sinners, prostitutes, beggars, tax collectors, the ritually polluted, the crippled, the impoverished; in short, the disrespected of Palestinian society—constituted the majority of his followers. Table fellowship within the Jesus movement included individuals who represented the marginal element within ancient Palestinian society, thus tending to break down traditional barriers like status, degree of purity, and gender. All were welcome who responded positively to the message of the kingdom—even Gentiles—and many of Jesus' followers were women, who in turn helped to pave the way for the inclusion of Gentiles.[13]

Some early traditions embedded especially in Matthew attempt to limit the sphere of Jesus' ministry to the people of Israel, but the Galilean Jesus movement, on the other hand, seems to have accepted Gentiles at an early date. The issue to resolve seems to have been the question of inclusive table community with Gentiles in particular. This issue is addressed theologically in a Markan miracle story (7:24-30; par. Matt. 15:21-28) about the healing of the Syrophoenician (Gentile) woman's young daughter. The woman is a Gentile advocate for table sharing with Gentiles. She comes to Jesus to request healing for her demon-possessed daughter. But there is a problem. The problem is not necessarily that she is a woman but that she is a Gentile. After hearing her request for her daughter's healing, Jesus' parabolic response seems to speak against the admission of Gentiles to his community of followers: "Let the children be fed first, for it is not fair to take the children's food and throw it to the dogs" (that is, Gentiles). To this the woman responds with an equally provocative statement: "Sir, even the dogs under the table eat the children's crumbs." The woman wins Jesus' favor, because he is convinced by her argument and heals her daughter from the demon possession. She thus successfully uses her retort to argue for her inclusion within the sphere of Jesus' ministry. This story argues against those in the Jesus movement who would use the saying "Let the children be fed first, for it is not fair to take the children's food and throw it to the dogs," or any other like it—for example, Matt. 10:5-6, "Go nowhere among the Gentiles, and enter no town of the Samaritans, but go rather to the lost sheep of the house of Israel" (cf. Matt. 15:24)—to justify a strict prohibition against the Gentile mission. This indicates a new potential for Gentiles because the Jesus movement dismantled traditional societal and religious barriers.[14]

There should be little doubt today that women played a prominent role in spreading the gospel to Gentiles. The recovery of the historical role of women in missionary activity implanted in the Gospel traditions represents one of the most significant finds for understanding the beginnings of Christianity. While overlooked by the tradition, women not only supported Jesus' ministry with their goods and financial resources (Luke 8:1-3; 10:38-42; John 12:1-3) but also were leaders in expanding the Jesus movement in Galilee and in developing a theological argument from the Jesus traditions for why Gentiles should have access to the kingdom promises and a share in the messianic table community. These women advocated for and sought to protect the inclusive equality of discipleship called forth by Jesus. In this way, they challenged the Jesus movement to remain true to the new vision of human relations that Jesus initiated by extending its table fellowship, sharing the message of the coming kingdom (or rule) of God, and making the vision of the messianic future available also to Gentiles.

In John 4:1-42 there is another account about a Samaritan woman who initiates the beginnings of the Christian community in Samaria. This story also shows that there is evidence from the Gospel tradition that women participated in the extension of the Jesus movement to non-Jews. To be sure, it was Mary Magdala who first experienced and declared the message of the resurrection: "Jesus rose from the grave." This confession is based upon the experience of a woman who was a devout *disciple* of Jesus.[15] She was the first to *preach* the Gospel after Jesus' crucifixion, and there are a number of legends and noncanonical Gospels wherein her authority and apostleship are uncontested and unrivaled, even by those of Peter. It was thus probably Jewish Christian women who initiated a theological argument against limiting the inclusive messianic table community of Jesus to Israel alone and in this way opened up Jesus' movement and community to Gentiles.

It is possible to see then how women were decisive for the extension of the Jesus movement to Gentiles and also for the continuation of the movement after Jesus' arrest and crucifixion. They were the very ones to remain faithfully with Jesus at his crucifixion when the male disciples fled and hid themselves.

The Challenge to Patriarchal Structures

What can also be gleaned from the Gospel stories about women and Gentiles is that the Christian movement was inclusive of Gentiles' and women's leadership and can therefore be called *egalitarian*. "As a conflict movement within Palestine, Syria, Greece, Asia Minor, and Rome, it challenged and opposed the dominant patriarchal ethos through the praxis of equal discipleship."[16] Elisabeth Schüssler Fiorenza further clarifies this point:

> The assertion that liberation from patriarchal structures was not of primary concern to Jesus and his movement overlooks not only the androcentric tendencies that can be detected in the tradition and redaction of the Jesus materials, but also the "intrusion" of Jesus and his movement into the dominant religious ethos of the people. The prescription of the Holiness Code, as well as the scribal regulations, controlled women's lives even more than men's lives, and more stringently determined their access to God's presence in Temple and Torah. Jesus and his movement offered an alternative interpretation of the Torah that opened up access to God for everyone who was a member of the elect people of Israel, and especially for those who, because of their societal situation, had little chance to experience God's power in Temple and Torah.[17]

Thus Jesus' prophetic ministry shows not only his position on behalf of the poor but also his concern for the condition and status of women. However, it is important to note that his teachings "do not explicitly include or distinctly 'articulate' in either case a strategy for 'structural change.'"[18] Instead, the message of Jesus, while not addressing explicitly or critically the structures of ancient oppression, implicitly subverts them by envisioning a different future and different model for human relations on the grounds that all people are created and called by God. In this way, the Jesus movement and the later Christian community implicitly subverted the social and economic structures of ancient patriarchal society by creating an atmosphere of freedom for those who were dehumanized and subjugated to the structures of oppressive forces, even though the people involved in this process might not themselves have thought explicitly in these terms.

The new pattern of social relations among Jesus' community of followers was founded upon two examples that directly counter ancient social and patriarchal structures: one involving a child and the other a slave. In Mark 9:33-37 (par. Matt. 15:1-5; Luke 9:46-48) and 10:35-45 (par. Matt. 20:20-28; Luke 22:24-27) Jesus uses the example of a child (Who will be the greatest in the kingdom?) and a slave (James and John seeking a place of honor in the kingdom), respectively, as exemplars of humility and service among his followers. Each example is embedded in a long narrative regarding the nature of discipleship and greatness (chaps. 8–10). These examples reverse the social patterns of greatness found in the Greco-Roman world, which centered on the ideals and glamorization of independence, self-sufficiency, competition, and the man of power (divine man).[19] In the examples of the child and the slave—individuals without power, dependent, and lacking self-sufficient means—Jesus offers a counter-hegemonic model for his community of followers to that of the Gentiles (that is, Rome). In his model, service to others within the community is valued. Using the example of the slave, Jesus says:

> You know that among the Gentiles those whom they recognize as their rulers lord it over them, and their great ones are tyrants over them. But it is not so among you; but whoever wishes to become great among you must be your servant, and whoever wishes to be first among you must be slave of all. (Mark 10:42-44)

The rationale for this is based on Jesus' own self-understanding: "For the Son of Man came not to be served but to serve, and to give his life a ransom for many" (Mark 10:45). Here his critique of Greco-Roman social-political structures is not so subtle. Jesus intends his community to be counter-imperial and counter-hegemonic to that of the current political regime. This subversion of social norms and structures is also evident in his radical views of the patriarchal household because "the Jesus movement advocated a radical . . . ethic that had far-reaching ramifications for social roles including those associated with gender distinctions."[20]

The subversion of patriarchal structures can be seen indirectly in Jesus' saying about the disruption of the patriarchal household found in Matt. 10:34-36 (par. Luke 12:51-53). In this passage Jesus states that he has come to bring a "sword," not peace, to the patriarchal household, which is an example of the radical rupture of traditional familial relations that his message entails. The message of Jesus is that his movement "abrogates" natural family bonds, which sets son against father and father against son, daughter against mother and mother against daughter, daughter-in-law against mother-in-law and mother-in-law against daughter-in-law. His message incorporates an apocalyptic vision of the end times, wherein the destruction and dissolution of the family indicated the adumbration of the last days before the end of the world (see Mic. 7:6). For this reason Jesus' view of discipleship does not hold patriarchal family bonds in high esteem; instead it disrupts the "peace" of the patriarchal household. Jesus expresses a similar view of "natural" family bonds in Luke 11:27. An unnamed woman in the crowd cries out as Jesus passes by, "Blessed is the womb that bore you, and the breasts you sucked." But Jesus replies, "Blessed rather are those who hear the word of God and keep it." Faithful discipleship and commitment to God, therefore, is not biological, so the eschatological calling of men and women is rooted in a radical commitment to the word of God and the kingdom message.[21]

This interpretation is supported also by an account in the Gospel of Mark, which contrasts patriarchal family ties with that of discipleship in the Jesus movement. In Mark 3:31-35 can be found a story about the circle of disciples around Jesus that included men and women. In this account Jesus and his disciples are in a certain house and a disciple comes to Jesus and tells him that his family is outside and desires to see him. Jesus responds, "Who are my mother and my brothers? . . . Whoever does the will of God is my brother and sister and mother" (vv. 33, 35). Those who respond to the message of the kingdom of God are Jesus' true family, which includes brothers, sisters, and mothers, but, interestingly enough, not "fathers." According to Schüssler Fiorenza this is significant:

> This new "family" of equal discipleship . . . has no room for "fathers."
> Whereas "fathers" are mentioned among those left behind [Mark 10:29-
> 30], they are not included in the new kinship which the disciples
> acquire "already now in this time." Insofar as the new "family" of Jesus
> has no room for "fathers," it implicitly rejects their power and status and
> thus claims that in the messianic community all patriarchal structures
> are abolished. Rather than reproducing the patriarchal relationships of
> the "household," in antiquity, the Jesus movement demands a radical
> break from it.[22]

Such a break from patriarchal household norms is also evident in Luke's account of Mary and Martha (Luke 10:38-42; cf. John 11:1; 12:1-2). These two women may have been the most important and prominent women in Jesus' ministry. While some feminist scholars have detected a non-liberative strand within this account[23] and other exegetes in general have doubted its historicity, it still can positively highlight the abrogation of patriarchal household gender norms, and as to its historicity "it is more probable that this story has a sound basis in historical fact, even though Luke has written and presented the narrative in his own language and style."[24] In this story Jesus is at the home of Mary and Martha. While Martha is in the "kitchen," presumably preparing a meal to serve to her guests (in a woman's traditional "place" and gender role), Mary is at the feet of Jesus with the other disciples (a non-traditional "place" and gender role for a woman). As a matter of fact, "to sit at the feet" of a teacher means to be a disciple of someone (cf. Acts 22:3; Paul sat at the feet of Gamaliel). Martha comes to Jesus and chides Mary for not assisting her (or for not conforming to her expected role and place), fully expecting Jesus to support her. Contrary to her expectations, Jesus says, "Martha, Martha, you are worried and distracted by many things; there is need of only one thing. Mary has chosen the better part, which will not be taken away from her" (Luke 10:41-42). With this retort the story makes a remarkably telling point: in the community of Jesus' followers traditional patriarchal roles and expectations are abrogated in favor of the radical demands of the gospel and the kingdom of God.

According to Ben Witherington, "the story is really about Martha and what she must learn."[25] The lesson to be learned is that in Jesus' movement women were free to reject traditional gender roles in favor of the greater call of discipleship. It is apparent then that "the communities that coalesced first around the person and then the figure of Jesus of Nazareth were characterized by strong group identity coupled with a rejection of status distinctions, of hierarchical structure, of ritual purity, and of social conformity."[26] In this way, the ministry and message of Jesus challenged those within his movement to embrace a new vision of human relations—between men and women, between Jews and Gentiles, and among family members. It could be argued that "Jesus suggested that God was establishing [the] Kingdom by creating an alternative society."[27] This vision initiated by Jesus and continued by his faithful followers would inspire a movement after Jesus' crucifixion that would ignite the imagination of one Saul of Tarsus, who after an epiphany of the resurrected Christ, would enlarge upon this vision of human relations.

Paul's Gospel of the Cross: Justification by Faith in Christ Jesus

The crucifixion of Jesus around 30 C.E. in Jerusalem profoundly altered the nature of the movement. Its message and organization would be further developed by Paul and the other apostles as they carried the name and memory of Jesus throughout the world. Theirs was an age when the powers-that-be did not look kindly on anyone who would challenge Roman authority and power, yet that is precisely what the followers of Jesus did when they built their far-flung network of communities of "saints." . . . The continuing quest for the Kingdom of God by Jesus, Paul, and the earliest Christians should be understood as *both* a spiritual journey and an evolving political response to the mindless acts of violence, inequality, and injustice that characterized—and still all too often characterize—the kingdoms of men.[28]

After the death and resurrection of Jesus the women and men who were his faithful followers carried on and enlarged upon what he began. "In the power of the Spirit" they sought to take the message of the kingdom and salvation "to the ends of the earth." In this effort certain limitations of the movement had to be overcome: namely, what about the Gentiles? Should Jewish Christians allow Gentile converts to participate in the community table? This would become a pressing issue in the early decades of the church. The conservative Jerusalem faction would only allow Gentiles who were willing to be circumcised and conform to Torah observance. It was the diaspora Jewish

Christian community (those born and raised outside of Palestine in predominantly Gentile regions) that apparently sought to open the mission and community table to Gentile Christians without such regulations. The statement in Acts 11:26 that "it was in Antioch that the disciples were first called 'Christians'" is significant. Antioch was the first mission center to the Gentiles.

> The Church of Antioch was responsible for the missionary outreach, which demanded of pagan converts only faith in Jesus. It was in this spirit of freedom that Paul labored in Asia Minor and Greece. When Antioch later changed its stance and aligned itself with Jerusalem, which insisted on observance of the Law, the status of its churches to the north and west came under attack. The very nature of Gentile Christianity was put at risk. Paul was its main defender. For five or six years in the middle of the first century AD he invested every ounce of his energy, and every scintilla of his intelligence, in devising a response which was ultimately to prevail.[29]

Thus the vision of Jesus was mediated to Paul through the Jewish Christian missionary enterprise at Antioch. This was only after Saul, the "persecutor of the church," encountered the risen Christ on the road to Damascus (Acts 9). His experience of the risen Christ would involve a name change and also have profound implications for the early Christian movement. The combination of Paul's theological insight and indefatigable efforts to reach the Gentiles resulted in the rapid spread of Christianity throughout the Mediterranean world, especially after he lost the battle to keep the Antiochean mission true to its original stance of freedom for Gentiles (cf. Galatians 2). However, just as with Jesus, Paul's message had important consequences in the spiritual and *sociopolitical* lives of his converts. It is likely that intentionally or not Paul was founding alternative anti-imperial communities.[30]

> Early Christianity was, in fact, a down-to-earth response to an oppressive ideology of earthly power that had recently swept across continents, disrupted economies, and overturned ancient traditions. And this triumphant ideology of progress and development was expressed in many media: in the elegies of Latin poets, in the grandeur of Roman architecture, in Roman lawcourts and statutes, in the technological triumphs of Roman engineering, and in the majestic, fatherly wave of every emperor's hand. . . . *That* was why the early Christians were viewed as so subversive, for anyone who refused to pay homage to Caesar was both atheist and traitor.[31]

Such subversion comes through especially in the gospel of the cross, through which Paul believed he could unite both Jews and non-Jews into one eschatological messianic community.[32] To accomplish this, certain theological and social barriers had to be removed. For the Jews, Gentiles were impure and resided outside of the covenant promises to Israel; for Paul something new had happened with the advent of Christ—Gentiles were now a part of the end-time covenant promises. The Law and circumcision were no longer the canon to measure the relationship between God and humanity: now that relationship was based upon faith. In the last days, both Jew and Gentile are "justified by faith in Jesus Christ." It is this cardinal theological teaching with which Paul seeks to abrogate the Jewish identity symbols of circumcision and Torah observance that posed certain barriers for Gentiles. Within this doctrine lay also the continuation of an egalitarian vision of the unity of humanity, entailing a radical challenge to existing social structures. Galatians 3:28 represents an important outgrowth of this vision.

The Function of Galatians 3:28 in Paul's Argument on Justification

In the context of Paul's argument in Galatians 3, the egalitarian statement 3:26-28 appears at the end of an elaborate argument on "justification by faith" that is introduced at 2:15-21 (which recounts his conflict with Peter at Antioch—a debate that Paul lost, resulting in a new base of operations at Ephesus) and explicated in chapter 3. In Gal. 3:1-29, Paul grounds his teaching on justification by faith with the introduction of the theme of the crucified Christ (3:1), through whom the Galatians (and all those "in Christ") have received the promise of the Spirit (3:4-5).

Paul begins with the ancient father of faith, Abraham, to anchor his teaching on justification in the scriptures (3:6-18) because in the Abraham saga he could find support to argue that the fulfillment of the promise and blessing to many nations has been realized in his own missionary activity and in the life of the Galatian Christian community. In addition, it provided him with a means of including the Gentiles in the covenant people without recourse to circumcision and Torah observance. Moreover, the notion of the promise to many nations (especially 3:8-9) is not contingent upon the observance of the Law or circumcision but upon faith in what has been wrought by the cross of Christ: "For it is written, 'Cursed is everyone who hangs on a tree'—in order that in Christ Jesus the blessing of Abraham might be to the Gentiles, so that we might receive the promise of the Spirit through faith" (3:13-14). The gift of the Spirit to the Gentiles evinces the fulfillment of the promise made to Abraham and inaugurates the new era of God's grace upon all people indiscriminately (as in Joel 2:28-32; cf. Acts 2:17-21).

Finally, after a discussion of the purposes and limitations of the law in 3:19-22, Paul's argument on justification by faith culminates with the baptismal confession: "For in Christ Jesus you are all children of God through faith. As many of you as were baptized into Christ have clothed yourselves with Christ. There is no longer Jew or Greek, there is no longer slave or free, there is no longer male and female; for all of you are one in Christ Jesus" (Gal. 3:26-28). This baptismal confession has a particular function in Paul's argument: as a result of the crucifixion of Christ, which has wrought a new dispensation of faith ("Now that faith has come . . ."; 3:25), the promise of the Spirit and of blessing upon many nations is realized within the Christian community because those who have been baptized into Christ are the "true" heirs to the promise (v. 29). In this new era, all who have faith in Christ, whether Jew or Greek, slave or free, male or female, have equal access without distinction to the Spirit of God and the covenant promises. They are indeed a new covenant people (6:16). But is this as far as it goes? Is there a social dimension to the saying besides free access to grace and the formation of a new eschatological community? In other words, how is this new inclusive vision to be realized within the community of faith?

Galatians 3:28: New Spiritual Reality, New Social Paradigm, or Both?
Galatians 3:28 has received considerable attention in recent years. The probable reason is that in today's enlightened society we have come to recognize that the three traditional means of oppression and division among human beings can be categorized under the modern concepts of race/ethnicity ("Jew or Greek"), class/status ("slave or free"), and sex/gender ("male and female"). It appears that some early Christians believed that on the basis of the baptismal formula they had overcome or could overcome these categories of human oppression. Curiously enough, the scholarly study of Gal. 3:28 has depicted Paul as either a social conservative or a radical revolutionary. Those who represent the former argue that this saying is to be understood spiritually or sacramentally. Some interpreters in the past, presupposing their contemporary social relations, were certain that Paul could not have meant that blacks are equal to whites, the poor and homeless equal to the wealthy and well-to-do, and women equal to men. This was a "safe" interpretation for many scholars until recent decades, when other interpreters began to question and challenge such notions.

Moreover, Gal. 3:28 has also come to occupy center stage in the debate over the role of women within early Christianity,[33] perhaps because it appears to suggest that those who are "in Christ" have overcome the triple barriers of race, class, and gender that have been used historically to discriminate and deny human freedom and equality. And, although Paul's letter to the Galatians says a lot about slavery and freedom (2:4; 4:1-7, 21-31; 5:1, 13), it does not deal directly with a program for realizing freedom from these triple categories as a whole, nor does it spell out such an agenda in any significant way. An exploration of some contemporary perspectives will help to gain a better understanding of the issues involved in this debate.

Contemporary Interpretations of Galatians 3:28

There have been several contemporary interpretations of Paul's use and understanding of Gal. 3:28. First, it is argued that Gal. 3:26-28 supplies a paradigm for a revolutionary social program that represents Paul's ideal for Christian relations. Some even perceive that it has a political and social revolutionary dimension.[34] Most interpreters in this category argue that Gal. 3:28 represents Paul's own understanding of the liberating power of the gospel. The liberating implications of the gospel combined with "the Hellenistic desire for the One, which among other things produced an ideal of a universal human essence, beyond difference and hierarchy" were the motivating factors behind Paul's vision.[35] But this radical ideal was unsustainable in practice, because complete transformation and liberation from social norms is unattainable prior to the parousia. Therefore, since Paul had to curtail some of its overtly enthusiastic social appropriations—"for slaves because of the social unrest and suppression of Christianity that would result, for wives because of *porneia*—[he] settled for something else, something less than his vision called for."[36]

Second, it is argued that Gal. 3:28 does not entail an egalitarian social agenda at all. Paul does not advocate an abrogation of hierarchical structures but merely acknowledges that Jew and Greek, slave and free, women and men are equal in the sight of God and have equal access to grace because God is impartial.[37] The saying acknowledges the equal accessibility to God's grace but entails no revolutionary social agenda. This argument is based on 1 Corinthians 7, where Christians are commended to "remain in the condition in which you were called" (7:20; stated also in 7:17, where Paul adds—interestingly—"This is my rule in all the churches"; and 7:24). In 1 Corinthians 7, where the social implications of the three categories of the baptismal saying are addressed directly (vv. 17-19 = Jew/Greek; vv. 21-23 = slave/free; and vv. 27-39 [and earlier, in 7:1-16] = male/female [marriage]), Paul does not imply an overtly radical appropriation of the baptismal saying. On the contrary, as the argument goes, his advice is cautionary and conservative: do not disrupt the status quo but "remain as you are."[38]

Third, interpreters have argued that Gal. 3:28 is not Paul's own novel creation, but a quotation from early Christian baptismal liturgy: a pre-Pauline baptismal confession, expressing "the theological self-understanding of the

Christian missionary movement."[39] The notion of the radical equality of humankind through baptism into Christ is not a completely new invention of Paul but existed already in earliest pre-Pauline Christianity. To be precise, the Hellenistic Christian mission, apart from Paul, acknowledged the societal-leveling quality of baptism. Before baptism into Christ, the world was divided into Jew/Greek, slave/free, and male/female, but through baptism these distinctions are removed. This ideal would have significant implications for women in Pauline circles. As Scroggs states, "Paul is, so far from being a chauvinist, the only certain and consistent spokesman for the liberation and equality of women in the New Testament, although he probably inherited this affirmation of equality from the earliest church."[40] This view of Paul as a champion of feminism can be achieved only when the Paul of the seven uncontested letters (1 Thessalonians, 1–2 Corinthians, Galatians, Philippians, Philemon, and Romans) is divorced from the "Paul" of the Pastorals (1–2 Timothy and Titus) and the deutero-Pauline letters (Colossians and Ephesians [2 Thessalonians is not important in this matter]). Yet even within the uncontested Pauline correspondence, 1 Cor. 14:33-36 has to be pruned from the rest of the text, and 1 Cor. 11:2-16 must be positively evaluated in order to create "Paul the feminist." With these matters settled, the image of the Paul of female liberation can be created primarily from Romans 16 and Phil. 4:2-3 (where several women are mentioned as missionaries and coworkers).

Fourth, Gal. 3:28 has been viewed as both a traditional and an original formulation. Dennis MacDonald argues that Paul altered the wording of this confession, which profoundly affected its ethical consequences. In its present form, the denial of social divisions in Gal. 3:28 is Paul's "own original declaration and not an echo of a more socially egalitarian tradition still audible in spite of Paul's attempts to muffle it."[41] S. Scott Bartchy concurs, arguing that the three pairs of opposites represent actual social challenges to Paul's mission. Thus the three pair of opposites in Gal. 3:28 are the ones we should expect him to use.[42] The view that Paul is the creative redactor of the traditional baptismal saying is proffered against the previous position that Gal. 3:26-28 represents as a whole a pre-Pauline tradition. But, while Paul is no feminist, " 'There is no male and female' is Paul's vision of sexual equality in his communities as they *should* be, not a witness to conditions in these communities as they were in fact."[43] It is this reality of the "already and not yet" that Paul had to hold in creative tension because the new creation in Christ (2 Cor. 5:17) had already begun, but some patterns of the old creation must remain until the parousia.

A New Social Paradigm for the Church

While the debate within contemporary scholarship remains divided, Schüssler Fiorenza offers a persuasive proposal for the rhetorical-historical situation behind the letter of 1 Corinthians as a whole, which also touches significantly upon the debate regarding the social implications of Gal. 3:28. She suggests that the rhetorical situation of 1 Corinthians might be understood as follows:

> The Corinthian church had debates and discussions as to how their new self-understanding expressed in the pre-Pauline baptismal formula in Gal 3:28 could and should be realized in the midst of a society rooted in the patriarchal status divisions between Greeks and Jews, slave and free, men and women, rich and poor, wise and uneducated. Especially, [they discussed] the notion "no longer male and female."[44]

Notwithstanding the later Paulinist trajectory, which sought to curb women's leadership and participation in the churches, Gal. 3:28 was a liberating vision that arose within the Christian communities as an alternative model to the immediate social world in which the Christians lived. In my reading of the passage and understanding of early Christian history, the baptismal quotation used by Paul in Gal. 3:28, whether a pre-Pauline statement or a Pauline redaction (but more likely the former), represents an egalitarian vision to be realized in the present.

This theology of the egalitarian Christian missionary movement is rooted in the experiences of the Spirit. While the ministry and life of Jesus is fundamental for the Jesus movement and its vision, the experience of the power of the Spirit is basic for that of the Christian missionary movement. Even Jesus is raised "in power" so that he becomes "a life-giving Spirit" (1 Cor. 15:45). Like Jesus, whose ministry as described in Luke 4:1 is initiated in the power of the Spirit ("the Spirit of the Lord is upon me"), those who are "in Christ" are "filled with the Holy Spirit," possessed by God's Spirit for ministry. The expressions "full of the Holy Spirit," "full of the Holy Spirit and of faith," and "full of the Spirit and of wisdom" all appear in Acts. Those who "have called on the Lord" (Acts 2:21) or who have been "baptized into Christ" live by the Spirit (Gal. 5:25); they are pneumatics, Spirit-filled people (Gal. 6:1). What is of utmost importance is that "all flesh"—Jew and Gentile, slave and free, women and men—have access to and receive the Spirit.[45]

The early Christian missionary movement expressed this "equality" in the Spirit with the words of the prophet Joel (Acts 2:17ff.), and it is possible that it is summarized in Gal. 3:28. Another way of putting it is that Gal. 3:28 served as the motto or confession of the movement. As a matter of fact, equality in the Spirit and Gal. 3:28 compare quite tellingly in their emphases: the prophecy of Joel provides the conceptual framework for equality, and Gal. 3:28 serves as the simply stated confession of this movement. To clarify this point, compare the two passages:

Acts 2:16-21	Galatians 3
Prophecy	
this is what was spoken through the prophet Joel:	And the scripture, foreseeing that God would justify the Gentiles by faith, declared the gospel beforehand to Abraham, saying, "All the Gentiles shall be blessed in you." (v. 8)
Fulfillment	
"In the last days it will be, God declares,	But now that faith has come . . . in Christ Jesus you are all children of God through faith. (v. 25)
Abolition of Racial/Ethnic Barriers	
that I will pour out my Spirit upon all flesh,	As many of you as were baptized into Christ have clothed yourselves with Christ. There is no longer Jew or Greek,
Abolition of Sex/Gender Barriers	
and your sons and your daughters shall prophesy. . . .	there is no longer male and female,
Abolition of Class/Status Barriers	
Even upon my slaves, both men and women, in those days I will pour out my Spirit; and they shall prophesy. . . .	there is no longer slave or free,
Statement of Human Equality and Unity	
Then everyone who calls on the name of the Lord shall be saved."	for all of you are one in Christ Jesus.

These two passages exhibit several parallels. First, they have similar structures, although Acts includes more narrative details. Each includes a statement related to the realization of end-time promises and their fulfillment within the Christian community. Then there follows the abolition of traditional societal barriers—race, sex, and class—and a statement on the unity of humanity. Such structural parallels indicate the formation of a new paradigm based upon the advent and experience of the Spirit. Second, both passages are related to baptism. There is the "baptism in the Spirit" in Acts (1:4; 2:38, at the end of Peter's Pentecost sermon) and presumably water baptism in Galatians (Gal. 3:28 has been recognized as a baptismal confession). Both passages include a discussion of the presence of the Spirit within the community (Acts 2 and Gal. 3:2-3). The sum effect is that the creedal nature of Gal. 3:28 suggests its function as a confession based on the Joel prophecy of the Spirit, which democratizes human relationships. The old patterns of domination and separation have been overcome through the egalitarianism of the Spirit. What was promised in Isa. 43:18 or 65:17 is now realized in the community of the baptized: "Therefore if anyone is in Christ, they are a new creation. The old has passed away, behold the new has come" (2 Cor. 5:17). In Gal. 6:15 the expression "new creation" characterizes the Christian community. For those who have become a part of this new creation, Jewish concepts and rituals (circumcision or uncircumcision) have lost their meaning. Faith in Christ has become the decisive basis for salvation. Thus, armed with this new paradigm the early Christian missionaries sought to propagate this message in the Greco-Roman world.

Thus Paul appropriated and incorporated this vision into his gospel message; however, it is still important to examine and explore textually and contextually how Paul may have understood and sought to implement, if at all, the full implications of this egalitarian vision.

Race, Class, and Sex: Where Does Paul Really Stand?

In order to gain a clearer understanding of Paul's stance on the socially relevant implications of the paradigm of Gal. 3:28, it is necessary to examine the undisputed Pauline letters wherein such categories are addressed.

Paul on Jews and Greeks: The Race/Ethnicity Question and the Church

It can be said with confidence that Paul devoted most of his energy to the abolition of the social distinction of race/ethnicity (that is, Jews and Greeks). The distinctions that had customarily divided Jews and Greeks were related to religion or tradition. For the Jew it was the Law ("Torah," or instruction); for the Greek it was philosophy or human wisdom (cf. 1 Cor. 1:18-25). According to Rom. 3:1-20 and 9:3-5 the abolition of distinctions pertains to the religious prerogatives claimed by the Jews, symbolized by the ritual of circumcision (Romans 2; Gal. 5:6; 6:15; 1 Cor. 7:19). In other places and in various ways,

Paul used the slogan "neither Jew nor Greek."[46] "This formula . . . is most likely a variation of the well-known Hellenistic political slogan *Hellenes kai barbaroi*, 'Greeks and barbarians.' "[47] This formula, according to Hans Dieter Betz, had been circulating for several centuries before Paul's mission to the Gentiles and seems to point to Hellenistic Judaism as its source of origin. It proclaims both a universalizing and a Hellenizing of Judaism.

> This program seems to have been taken over by primitive Christianity, where in its mission the formerly exclusive Jewish prerogatives were extended to Gentile believers by simultaneously removing the Jewish external religious and social distinctions. In this program "mission" and "Hellenization" must necessarily have become one and the same thing, a fact which may have been a reason for the early opposition against Paul and his missionary effort.[48]

To be sure, when Paul and the Christian mission took over this slogan it was part of their socio-religious political program, claiming that in their midst it had become a reality accomplished through Christ and the gift of the Spirit (Gal. 3:28; 1 Cor. 8:14-15; 12:13).

Paul worked diligently and consistently to see that there was equality between Jews and Greeks: there were no exceptions! In the Christian community "there is no distinction between Jew and Greek; the same Lord is Lord of all" (Rom. 10:12). Another reason why Paul found no distinction was his view that both Jew and Greek are "under the law of sin," so the Jew is no better off. Thus he asks, "What advantage has the Jew? Or what is the value of circumcision?" (Rom. 3:1). For Paul there ultimately was none. And although Paul was not the first to have preached to Gentiles or to begin the Christian mission to them (according to Acts 8 and 10:1—11:18, Philip and Peter began it), he was the first we know to have consistently developed an ideology or theology of Gentile mission in the Christian movement.[49] He argued vehemently that Gentiles not be forced to conform to the customs of the Jews in order to become a part of the Christian church. He argued his position so thoroughly his Galatians correspondence has been called the "*Magna Carta* of Christian liberty."[50] That such "religious equality" had social and ecclesial consequences for the interrelationship between Jewish and Gentile Christians is apparent from the Antioch incident, which seems to have been well-known in the early church (cf. Gal. 2:11-21). Paul associated freely with Gentiles, being ardent in his missionary activity to see the social distinctions between Jew and Greek abolished *in reality*. He certainly realized that if the message of the gospel was to reach the world, the religious-cultural distinctions of Judaism (especially in terms of circumcision and the Law) had to be overcome. This effort on Paul's part is what made the Christian missionary movement more than just another sect of Judaism.

Finally, Paul was so ardently opposed to the social distinctions between Jews and Greeks because he was thoroughly convinced that the gospel was for all people, Jew and Gentile alike, and that he had been called to deliver that message. And in his attempt to fulfill his calling as "apostle to the Gentiles," he would allow no barriers to hinder him. Thus in his praxis he made no distinction between Jew and Greek. Paul's tenacious zeal was not carried out or argued as consistently, however, in the case of "no longer slave or free."

Paul and Slavery: The Question of Class/Status in the Church

Since the baptismal confession of Gal. 3:28 included a statement that appeared to offer an emancipated status for the one baptized, it was more than excessive enthusiasm.[51] Equality among all who call upon the Lord is based on the fact that they have all one and the same "master" to whom all humans are obligated (cf. also Rom. 3:22-23). That many early Christians believed that the "new creation" in Christ entailed a free status in society for slaves is apparent when one looks at the second set of opposites in the baptismal formula—"no longer slave or free." Betz informs us that the statement

> can be understood in two ways: (a) as a declaration of the abolishment of the social institution of slavery, or (b) as a declaration of the irrelevancy of the institution, which would include the possibility of its retainment. In the New Testament itself, and indeed in Paul's own letters, we find both positions in regard to slavery. The overwhelming evidence in early and later Christianity seems to recommend only the second option as viable.[52]

While there is no evidence that early Christianity advocated the abolition of slavery, there is evidence that slaves who became Christians were urged to seek freedom from their servile status. The clarion call for this assumption is Gal. 3:28. But is this the starting point for Paul's understanding of slavery? It is usually assumed that Paul's actual attitude concerning slavery is expressed in Philemon and in 1 Cor. 7:21-24, and that the literal understanding of Gal. 3:28 is a latter misunderstanding. Betz, however, rightly remarks that "it is more likely . . . that Gal. 3:28 was the cause of the confusion, rather than a confusion of the cause."[53] It seems that the baptismal message created problems unforeseen by Paul and the early church. A brief review of the aforementioned passages will bear this out.

Although the letter to Philemon was recognized early on as Pauline, it drew much less comment by early Christian writers than did Paul's other letters.[54] The traditional conjecture concerning Paul's correspondence to Philemon is that a slave had run away from his master, taking with him certain items belonging to his master. But Allen Callahan has offered an insightful

and creative reconstruction of Philemon that proposes that Onesimus is neither a runaway slave nor a slave at all but a blood brother of Philemon. In his
reading the letter has nothing to do with slavery at all but with the reconciliation of two estranged blood brothers.[55] His reading reinforces what
enslaved African Americans had suspected all along: Jesus, Paul, and the
Bible were being misused to support their unjust subjugation. However,
since the traditional hypothesis has had such an effective history in the interpretation of this letter and of North American slavery, it is necessary to give
it an obligatory hearing.

According to the traditional hypothesis, Onesimus ran away from his
master, taking several of his items with him. Under unknown circumstances
this slave came under the influence of Paul's teaching and preaching and was
converted while Paul was "a prisoner of [or 'for the sake of'] Jesus Christ,"
under house arrest at Rome (Acts 28:20, 30) or some other unknown locale.
Once Onesimus was converted, Paul persuaded him to return to his master,
Philemon, who also had become a Christian earlier under Paul in Asia Minor
(v. 19) and in whose house a Christian congregation met (or the house of
Apphia and Archippus). Paul wanted the slave to return to his master because
there were severe laws that punished those who interfered with the rights of
the slave-owner. Thus Paul goes to great pains, using every means possible to
ensure that Onesimus's return to his master does not incur the harsh treatment prescribed by Roman law for runaways.

First, Paul uses social and community pressure. He addresses the letter
not only to Philemon but also to Apphia,[56] Archippus, and the rest of the
congregation that meet at his house (vv. 1-2). Paul knew that if he had sent
the letter as a personal letter to Philemon there would not have been any
outside pressure to coerce him to follow through. Thus he addressed the letter to the entire congregation to make the congregation responsible for seeing that Philemon did what was right.[57] Then he uses a little *kolakeia*
(flattery) in vv. 4-7, mentioning how Philemon's faith and Christian witness
has benefited the church. Paul, then, abruptly breaks at v. 8 and makes a show
of authority: "I am bold enough in Christ to command you to do what is
required." But what does Paul require or want?

Norman Petersen, among other exegetes, argues that it is to manumit
Onesimus.[58] Peterson proposes that Paul and the church have accepted Gal.
3:28 as their new ideology, but if this is the case, why is it suggested that the
issue of slaves in the church becomes a problem only when Onesimus, as a
slave, becomes a believer?[59] Why did it not become a problem for Philemon
to have slaves when *he* first heard of the "freedom in Christ," before he and his
slave were estranged? This is a flaw in the logic of the early church, but it

shows that a slave-owner becoming a Christian did not necessarily mean the freeing of slaves and that slave-owners were not obliged to set them free.

Lloyd A. Lewis is a bit more cautious but suggests also that Gal. 3:28 governs Paul's reaction in Philemon and reveals that his sending Onesimus back to his master required that he handle the situation very delicately. Paul's elaborate and persuasive familial language in the letter shows how fragile the situation had become concerning slaves in the church. This new family of God abrogates status differences but Paul leaves it in Philemon's hand to do the right thing in light of this new family imagery. Therefore, Paul does not ask outright for Onesimus's freedom but makes appeals (vv. 9-14), promises to pay any debts incurred by Onesimus, and gives a vote of confidence that Philemon will receive Onesimus back as a brother, and not as a slave (v. 16).[60]

Paul addresses a slightly different situation in his Corinthian correspondence. It is almost certain that there were many persons in the Corinthian Christian community who were legally designated as slaves. Their presence in the early church receives no special notice in the New Testament except when servile status presents a problem.[61] But was there a problem in the community concerning slaves so that it became necessary for Paul to respond? Or did the Corinthians themselves ask him to respond to questions they had about the status of slaves in the community who became members of the church? On the surface this may seem to be the case, because nothing in the Pauline correspondence confirms that there was any problem in the community concerning slaves. "Indeed we have evidence in 1 Cor. 12:13 which strongly suggests that no 'unrest' was caused among those in legal slavery by their conversion."[62] The fact that slaves are mentioned and not women in 12:13 may support this conclusion, for in Gal. 3:28 both categories are mentioned and we know of no unrest with women or slaves in Galatia. On the basis of these observations, it seems unlikely that 1 Cor. 7:21f. was written to keep restless slaves in their place. If this is so, it is doubtful that Paul would have mentioned them in his illustration.

Paul's mention of slaves in 7:21 fits within the entire section of his exhortation for the Corinthians to live within their calling regardless of life's circumstances (7:17-24). S. Scott Bartchy suggests that "to walk" in 7:17 and "to remain" in 7:20, 24 refer to the same activity, that is, "walking according to God's calling" and "remaining in the calling in the sight of God."[63] This "theology of calling" is not a special call to a particular status in society, but an admonition to "live according to God's call to salvation." One should remain in this calling because "circumcision is nothing; uncircumcision is nothing; but keeping the commandments of God is everything" (7:19).

For Paul, however, the Corinthians had been boasting (3:21; 4:6-7) in their pneumatic (spiritual) experiences and in the wisdom and knowledge of human beings, not in the power of God (2:5). Thus in 7:21-24 Paul reminds them again that nothing is gained by status in the world or in the Christian community;[64] but they should live according to the calling of God. "There was no status that could be either the *content* of God's call or the *confirmation* of that call."[65] But what about those who are enslaved and have the opportunity to become free? Are they to remain slaves or accept that freedom, which would entail a new status? It seems that Paul leaves his illustration at 7:21, recognizing that some in the Corinthian community are slaves and may be manumitted. So he addresses them directly, encouraging them by stating, "if you can gain your freedom, by all means avail yourself of the opportunity."[66] He also reminds them, "You were bought with a price; do not become slaves of men"[67] (v. 23). Therefore, although Paul does not advocate the mass rebellion of slaves nor challenge the system of slavery directly, he does encourage slaves to take the opportunity of manumission if it arises. *Yet he provides no practical program to achieve such goals.* But this is not of central importance to Paul. He advises them not to fret: "In whatever state you were called, there remain with God" (v. 24). This seems to me to summarize Paul's position on slavery.

Paul and Women: The Question of Sex/Gender and Church

The third part of the baptismal saying—"no longer male and female"—had equally serious implications for Paul and the early church. But Paul displayed no evident consistency on this matter either. Paul seemed willing to make concessions on this point, unlike the firm position he took on the "Jew and Greek" category, for which there were no concessions. In order for this to be understood more clearly, 1 Corinthians 7; 11:1-16; and 14:33b-36 must be examined briefly (for a fuller examination see chapter 2). But it is important to understand something about the function of the "neither male and female" category in Gal. 3:28 before we consider how it was understood and practiced in the Corinthian community.

The second and third categories of the baptismal saying are not used in Paul's argument in Galatians because there was no particular problem with slaves or women at Galatia; the problem was with those who felt that the Galatians as Gentile converts had to be circumcised and keep the Torah in order to truly follow the gospel. The issue is thus related solely to the "no longer Jew or Greek" category. As explained above, Paul uses the baptismal saying in its entirety to remind the Galatians of their unity as one "people" in Christ through baptism and therefore quotes the saying as he had received it from the pre-Pauline Christian missionary tradition.[68] Whether Paul admits radical implications to be drawn from it, "he has obviously changed his position in 1 Corinthians [12:13], and it may not be accidental that the whole matter is dropped in Romans."[69] Thus in turning our discussion to 1 Corinthians, we will look briefly at the three places where Paul speaks concerning women.

First Corinthians 7; 11:2-16; and 14:33-36 undoubtedly reflect Paul's attempt to deal with women who were actualizing the emancipation of women proclaimed in Gal. 3:28. Instead of taking a firm stand on this issue, Paul makes concessions at the cost of female liberty. In 7:1 Paul states openly that he is responding to questions about which the Corinthians had written him. Here he is responding to questions concerning marriage and celibacy. In terms of marriage relations between wife and husband, he was very liberal. Paul made certain to stress that husband and wife have equal conjugal rights as well as the right to say no. A wife was not to be used as sexual property: "For the wife does not rule over her own body, but the husband does; likewise the husband does not rule over his own body, but the wife does" (v. 5). He interprets marriage as a relationship between two equal partners who must mutually agree and consent in their marital relationship. He also encouraged women who were not yet married to be celibate, which went against Roman marriage legislation.[70] "It is therefore important to note that Paul's advice to remain free from the marriage bond . . . stood over against the dominant cultural values of Greco-Roman society."[71] On this issue Paul takes a firm stand; however, 1 Cor. 11:2-16 and 14:33b-36 can be read as exceptions to the rule concerning female liberty for the sake of custom and tradition (11:16 and 14:33b).

In 11:2-16 Paul addresses women in the worship community who are praying and prophesying in the worship service. This, however, is not a problem. The problem is that they perform such activity with their head unveiled, which was not uncommon in Hellenistic cults.[72] The Corinthian women, some have argued, were following this pattern that they had already seen in the Isis cult, which had a major center at Corinth. Therefore Paul argues that women should cover their hair according to the custom of the churches (11:16). He reinforces gender differences by pointing to the Genesis account of creation and subordinates women's worship and the exercise of pneumatic gifts to the traditions and customs established by the church.[73] In fact, Antoinette Clark Wire has argued convincingly that the occasion for Paul's writing of 1 Corinthians may have been a veiled attack against these pneumatic women who were exercising great power and influence in Corinth.[74] That Paul does not mention women in 1 Cor. 12:13 is most likely intentional, because he has just finished speaking to the unrest caused by women in the congregation who understood themselves to be acting according to the message of equality in Christ (11:2-16). These women were probably exercising the freedom about which they heard Paul preach.

For several exegetes, if 1 Cor. 14:33b-36 is not an interpolation,[75] it is one of the most outright contradictions contained in any of Paul's letters. Here women are told to keep silence in the church. This contradicts 11:2-16, where it is presumed that women already prophesy and pray in the worship community. Schüssler Fiorenza has argued that Paul was speaking only to wives, not the single virgins spoken of in chapter 7, who have no husbands. Robert Allison argues that it is Pauline and the work of a redactor who either misunderstood or purposefully modified the saying so that it seems now as if Paul is arguing against women speaking in church.[76] Since this debate is far from settled and is not our primary concern in this chapter, the important point to make is that in regard to gender Paul was willing to make concessions for the sake of custom and church order (11:10; 14:33b, 36).

Galatians 3:28, the Myth of the Original Androgyne, and the Old and New Creation

As noted above, in 1 Corinthians 7 Paul had to address issues related to the baptismal confession. He may not have done this by choice; the Corinthians themselves may have thrust this upon him. In certain places in 1 Corinthians it is clear that Paul is responding to various questions that the Corinthians posed to him (1 Cor. 7:1, 25; 8:1; 12:1). It has been shown that Gal. 3:28 lay behind some of the Corinthians' questions and Paul's response in 1 Corinthians 7. For some in the Corinthian community the distinctions of race, class, and sex have been dissolved in the new creation that has occurred through baptism into Christ. Even the idea of patriarchal marriage is no longer constitutive of the new creation, which is represented by the saying "no longer male and female." One interesting aspect of the saying is that its form in the Greek renders "male" and "female" in the neuter gender (*arsēn* and *thēlu*, respectively). This has led some scholars to suggest that this saying may have been referring to the myth of androgyny or an adoption of Stoic anthropology.[77] Supporting this notion is the fact that there are no parallels elsewhere in the New Testament, although a large number of such sayings are found in Gnosticism.[78] Wayne Meeks argues that such notions in Corinth were strengthened by the myth of the "Original Androgyne."[79]

The myth of the Original or Adam-Androgyne was not uncommon in the ancient world. This myth refers to the idea that in the beginning humankind was created neither male nor female (or in some cases a unity of male and female), as it says in Gen. 1:27: "So God created humankind in his own image; in the image of God he created them; male and female he created them." For Philo (and others) the first Adam of Genesis 1 is a spiritual androgyne, neither male nor female.[80] Moreover, Philo believes that the division of humanity into male and female in Genesis 2 was the beginning of the fall (*On the Creation of the World* 134). Likewise, in Plato's *Symposium* the idea of the two sexes returning to their primordial unity is similar to the idea of "when the two become one," which equals "neither male nor female."[81] The notion of the eschatological reunification of the distorted image (of God) was also a part of the androgyne myth. For some in Corinth this truth had become a reality through baptism. Thus the combination of this myth with the baptismal confession joined together a powerful and revolutionary set of images:

> The reunification of male and female became a symbol for "metaphysical rebellion," an act of "cosmic audacity" attacking the conventional picture of what was real and what was properly human. . . . In baptism the Christian has put on again the image of the Creator, in whom "there is no male and female," then for him the old world has passed away and, behold! the new has come.[82]

The "new that has come" was a new order of creation, indeed, a "new creation" (2 Cor. 5:17; Gal. 6:15). Galatians 3:28 represents the order of the new creation that has overcome the old order of creation in Genesis. The old order divided humanity, but the new order unites it. To be sure, Paul and the Corinthians realized that the new creation implied radical social and political changes. But what was the nature of these radical changes? Did the new creation imply or entail the dissolution of the distinctions of race, class, and gender/sex,[83] or that the distinctions have been relativized,[84] which means that they remain but have lost their significance? The former position was most likely that of some of the Corinthians, while the latter was that of Paul. This situation is arguably reflected in Paul's discussion in 1 Cor. 11:2-16, in which the issue of women's wearing veils is addressed.

Although Paul used the baptismal formula in Gal. 3:28 and 1 Cor. 12:13, his use in 1 Corinthians 7 reflects an uneasiness with it because of the social implications being drawn by slaves and women in the Corinthian community. Moreover, 1 Cor. 11:2-16 reflects his uneasiness because of the ethical and ecclesial implications being drawn by women whose praxis was supported by the androgyne myth. But if Paul advocated the order of the new creation in his preaching and mission (as reflected in Gal. 3:28 and 1 Cor. 12:13), how could he then use the order of the old creation (that is, man as the head or source of woman as in Genesis 2) in 1 Cor. 11:2-16 to curtail the practice of women removing veils during worship?

The long and the short to this question is that Paul wanted to curtail some of the radical appropriations of the baptismal formula that resulted in some unexpected applications—wives and husbands were refusing one another conjugal rights (others were opting for celibacy and refusing to marry) and slaves were anxious for social emancipation (1 Corinthians 7). Even more, some women were removing their veils during worship as an ultimate display of returning to the divine image: they were behaving as if they were no longer female, but "neither male nor female," implying a restoration of the divine image at creation.[85] So Paul wanted to modify these (mis)applications of the baptismal confession by arguing that the distinctions of male and female have not been dissolved but relativized. The comments of Meeks and Scroggs may help to clarify this point. According to Meeks,

> Paul insists on the preservation of the *symbols* of the present, differentiated order. Women remain women and men remain men and dress accordingly, even though "the end of the ages has come upon them." Yet these symbols have lost their ultimate significance, for "the form of this world is passing away." Therefore Paul accepts and even insists upon the equality of role of man and woman. . . . The new order, the order of man in the image of God, was already taking form in the patterns of leadership of the new community.[86]

Scroggs agrees with this assessment, but he notes that Paul and the Gnostics share some of the same insights, with one crucial difference:

> Both agree in eliminating *value* judgments of man over against woman. The gnostics seem to have wanted to go further, however, to obliterate all *distinctions* between the sexes. Paul is . . . passionate about keeping the reality of the distinctions; he just will not suffer any value judgment to be drawn on the basis of the distinction.[87]

For Meeks, Paul reacted to the Gnostic appropriation because of their rejection of the created order. Paul, on the other hand, wanted to hold the symbols of the old and the new creation in eschatological tension. Paul insists, then, with much tension, that the current hierarchy is still in effect (1 Cor. 7; 11:1-16; Rom. 13:1-7)[88] but, as Scroggs suggests, a new evaluation of those differences is in order.

Contrary to these claims, Schüssler Fiorenza counters the androgyne notion because in her estimation:

> The pre-Pauline baptismal formula . . . does not yet reflect the same notion of anthropological unification and androcentric perspective that has determined the understanding of equality found in later Gnostic and

patristic writings. According to various Gnostic and patristic texts, becoming a disciple means for a woman becoming "male," "like man," and relinquishing her sexual powers of procreation, because the male principle stands for the heavenly, angelic, divine realm, whereas the female principle represents either human weakness or evil. While patristic and Gnostic writers could express the equality of Christian women with men only as "manliness" or as abandonment of her own sexual nature, Gal 3:28 does not extol maleness but the oneness of the body of Christ, the church, where all social, cultural, religious, national, and biological gender divisions and differences are overcome and all structures of domination are rejected. Not the love patriarchalism of the post-Pauline school, but this egalitarian ethos of "oneness in Christ" preached by the pre-Pauline and Pauline Christian missionary movement provided the occasion for Paul's injunction concerning the behavior of women prophets in the Christian community.[89]

Galatians 3:28 is therefore best understood as a communal Christian self-definition rather than a statement about the baptized individual. It proclaims that in the Christian community all distinctions of religion, race, class, nationality, and gender are insignificant. All those who are baptized are equal; they are one in Christ. Thus, taken at face value, the baptismal declaration of Gal. 3:28 does not express "excessive enthusiasm" or a "gnosticizing" devaluation of procreative capacities.

Galatians 3:28 and "No Longer Male and Female"

Paul did not write Gal. 3:26-28 necessarily as his declaration for sexual equality. The reference to "male and female" was a part of the traditional saying. Furthermore, this pair was omitted in 1 Cor. 12:13 because women were exercising their "freedom in Christ." But in Galatians Paul could use the saying in his argument unedited because there were no issues within the community related specifically to women. Thus in 1 Cor. 12:13 Paul does not say "all are one" (Gal. 3:28), which could imply a notion of equality, but instead he talks about the social unification implied by Christian rituals. In discussing baptism, he uses the image of "one body" and the language of "one Spirit." Furthermore, in Galatians Paul uses "neither . . . nor" to formulate the pairs of opposites, while in 1 Cor. 12:13 he uses the positive "whether . . . or." Paul's intention here is not to emphasize the abolition of social differences but the unity of these different groups into one body.[90] This indicates that Paul had an ambiguous stance with respect to the last pair of opposites. Later conservative Christian appropriation is also ambiguous on the application of this saying to social realities, although it expands upon the race/ethnic category. For example, Col. 3:11 says: "There is no longer Greek and Jew, circumcised and uncircumcised, barbarian, Scythian, slave and free; but Christ is all in all." It is interesting that while the saying enlarges the category of race/ethnicity, the aspect related to sex/gender—"no longer male and female"—is missing here, as in 1 Cor. 12:13. The reason for its omission in Colossians has to do with the development of the household codes (Col. 3:18—4:1), which sought to re-institute the patriarchal order of man over woman, curtailing women's free-dom. The very fact that the "neither male and female" pair was eliminated from the baptismal confession's liberative litany in 1 Cor. 12:13 and later in Colossians is a subtle indication of its potential for revolutionary social impli-cations for women and slaves.

This indicates further that the category related to sex/gender was the least important not only for Paul but also for the early church as it moved toward institutionalization. In fact the last two categories in Gal. 3:28 "came along for the ride because they are not a part of the rhetorical context—only the Jew/Greek pair."[91] It turns out that even though Paul does address all three categories in 1 Corinthians 7, the Jew/Greek category is again the most important *and the only category that Paul worked out theologically to support a pro-gram for the social realization of this vision prior to the parousia*. His teaching on justification by faith in Romans, Galatians, and Philippians was formulated to articulate and support his vision that Jew and Greek are equal and have equal access to the covenant promises (for Gentiles without recourse to the Jewish identity symbol of circumcision and the observance of certain parts of the Law). This ideal was sustained in Paul's theology and praxis even to the point of open conflict (as in his debate with Peter in Galatians 2). Thus Paul only fully worked out a sustained solution to the Jew/Greek question, not the woman and slave questions. But those who accepted the message of the gospel and heard at baptism the confession of Gal. 3:28 did not wait for a sus-tained argument in order to actualize this vision into social reality.

It is clear that some churches in the early Christian missionary movement believed that on the basis of the baptismal saying of Gal. 3:28, they had overcome the three categories of human oppression. The actions of women in the early church challenging their social roles and the attempts of slaves to gain freedom at all costs, even through the church,[92] show the great impact the message of freedom had for both women and slaves. While the use of Gal. 3:28 by Paul and by the emerging early church was ambiguous, it is not necessary to limit the liberating implications of this saying to Paul's or a seg-ment of the early church's position. It is the liberating applications of this say-ing in some early churches and beyond that we must consider. This saying radically challenged, although sparingly throughout Christian history, notions of race, class, and gender: the triple category of division among human beings. For this reason, even in the eighteenth and nineteenth centuries, Gal. 3:28 appealed to enslaved African Americans. It provided them with a model that envisioned unity and "equality of all people," regardless of social distinctions or physical characteristics. But even African American churches and interpretive traditions—like Paul's, whose legacy those churches have cautiously accepted—have not fully realized the egalitarian potential of Gal. 3:28, despite their historical rhetoric of freedom and equality for all.

Conclusion

I have traced the development of Jesus' revolutionary vision of human relations in the early church and have appraised Paul's response to the Gal. 3:28 paradigm. In doing so, I have tried to show that attempts at the social actualization of certain components of the paradigm resulted in serious problems for Paul. As a pastoral theologian he had to maintain unity and harmony for the sake of his mission and for the success of communities he had founded. Therefore, while all three aspects of the paradigm were challenged by both Jews and Greeks, Paul was willing to stand firm only on the "no longer Jew or Greek" question. The reason is clear: on this question hangs the very success of his mission to the Gentiles. But the other two aspects of the paradigm could await the eschaton for their fulfillment. Thus Paul was willing to make concessions "because of the time." This was not the case for others in the church to which Paul preached. It seems that many women and slaves in the church heard his message differently. For them it challenged and altered their present condition. It was this wing in the early church that sought to make the vision of Gal. 3:28 a new social paradigm.

❧ 2 ❧
Scripture, Subjugation, and Silence

33b As in all the churches of the saints, 34 the women should keep silence in the churches. For they are not permitted to speak, but should be subordinate, as even the law says. 35 If there is anything they desire to know, let them ask their husbands at home. For it is shameful for a woman to speak in church. 36 What! Did the word of God originate with you, or are you the only ones it has reached?
(1 Corinthians 14:33b-36, RSV)

11 Let a woman learn in silence with all submissiveness. 12 I permit no woman to teach or to have authority over men; she is to keep silent. 13 For Adam was formed first, then Eve; 14 and Adam was not deceived, but the woman was deceived and became a transgressor. 15 Yet woman will be saved through bearing children, if she continues in faith and love and holiness, with modesty.
(1 Timothy 2:11-15, RSV)

The two scriptures quoted above have had tremendous influence throughout Christian history upon the church's understanding of women's roles within society and the church. "These verses have been used in various ways to prevent women from full participation in church life. Sometimes only pulpit preaching is prohibited, but in some denominations . . . no woman may speak publicly in any capacity in a worship service."[1] It is important, therefore, to examine and explore the hermeneutical framework and historical contexts that fostered such commands, which will help us to understand who made such statements, why, and what they mean. This exegetical exercise is important because these verses have had such oppressive social and religious impact on the status and role of women throughout Christian history. Even today the accepted traditional understanding of these passages persuades many church leaders to curtail women's leadership in the church.

One resolution to the debate concerning women in ministry might be to explore the historical and theological dimensions of the paradigms used in the early church to support a conservative hierarchical form of human relations, on the one hand, and the egalitarian horizontal form, on the other. In the scripture itself evidence of both traditions has been preserved. I have already traced the development of the egalitarian paradigm based on Gal. 3:28, which suggests that in the early stages of the Christian movement both women and men experienced the Christian gospel as liberating, as the elimination of the old social order with its gender roles and system of stratified statuses. The New Testament scriptures and early Christian history provide a glimpse of the early church as a place where women indeed had an opportunity for greater freedom and participation in the ministry of the church than later Christian history admits. But as the early church moved toward institutionalization, the freedom and liberty "in Christ" proclaimed by the early church became domesticated. Instead of using the eschatological model of "all . . . are one in Christ" (Gal. 3:28),[2] the perspective that became the majority position in the early church followed the established social order of patriarchy: "Let women keep silence in the churches" (1 Cor. 14:34; cf. 1 Tim. 2:13).

An analysis of 1 Cor. 14:33b-36 will help us to determine whether the passage is Pauline (from Paul himself), an interpolation (a passage added by a later editor), a Paulinist redaction (the reworking of the passage by the second generation of Paul's students), or something else altogether. Once these exegetical matters are resolved, I will compare the implications of these two conflicting paradigms. The debate between me and my ministerial colleagues concerning women in the ministry in Milwaukee in 1988 has parallels to the debate of the early church (see the Introduction).

First Corinthians 14:33b-36:
"Let a Woman Keep Silence in the Church"

An Authentic Pauline Statement

Several interpreters of this passage argue that, despite its uncharacteristic tone and problematic injunction, it is an authentic Pauline statement. S. C. Barton, for example, supports the view that Paul, rather than a later redactor, wrote this prohibition because there is evidence that the tradition has been modified in terms expressive of Paul's own "sense of place."[3] For Barton, Paul's concern in this passage is to interject a regulation to the women of the Corinthian church to the effect that a distinction is to be made between church (the "place" of men) and home (the "place" of women). Women therefore must not confuse the two by engaging in speech or activity that expresses authority but are to remain submissive and silent, expressing subordination.[4] His argument has several problems, not the least of which is the fact that Paul allowed women to pray and prophesy as long as their heads were covered

(11:2-16). This means that they were engaging in speech and activity that was not the norm for a woman's "place."

Elisabeth Schüssler Fiorenza also understands the text to be from the historical Paul: "Since these verses cannot be excluded on textual critical grounds but are usually declared inauthentic on theological grounds, it is exegetically more sound to accept them as original Pauline statements and explain them within their present context."[5] She suggests that the context of 1 Corinthians 12–14 is the same as in 1 Corinthians 11. Paul seeks to persuade the Corinthian church that decency and order should be valued over spiritual status and the exercise of individual pneumatic inspiration. The Corinthians have rather esteemed "speaking in tongues" (glossolalia) above all. Paul interjects a command that is expressive of reason, order, and mission. Therefore 1 Cor. 14:26-36 should be understood as a concern for church order with rules for glossolalists (those who speak in tongues, 14:2-28), prophets (vv. 29-33), and wives (vv. 34-36).[6]

The issue in 1 Cor. 14:33-36, however, is not that *all* women are to keep silence, for this would contradict 11:2-16, which presupposes that women are pneumatics who pray and prophesy in the worship community. But the injunction pertains to the *wives of male Christians*. Schüssler Fiorenza asserts that "chapter 7 makes it clear that not all women in the community were married or had Christian spouses. They could not therefore ask their husbands at home."[7] She argues further that in 1 Corinthians 7 Paul acknowledges the equal status in Christ of both the husband and the wife but seems himself to have had a preference for the unmarried state. The married situation as Paul understood it divided one's loyalties between service to the Lord and the care of spouse and family. The unmarried woman and virgin, to whom Paul ascribes "a special holiness . . . because she has not been touched by a man" (cf. 7:1), can have single-minded dedication to the Lord (unlike the married woman).[8]

It therefore seems that Paul was able to accept the pneumatic (spiritual) participation of "holy" women in the worship service of the community but that he argues in 14:34-36 against such active participation by married women. Since Paul is assumed to be the author of the passage, the community rule presupposes that within the worship community married women questioned other women's husbands or pointed out mistakes during the congregational interpreting of the scriptures or of prophecy. This behavior was contrary to both custom and law. Thus Schüssler Fiorenza points out that in the text wives are to be *subordinate to their own husbands* in the worship community. But the text, in my opinion, is ambiguous; it simply asks women in general to keep silent in the community worship and does not specify married or single women.

Schüssler Fiorenza contends that it is only pneumatic single women who might speak during communal worship. Women, in general, are required to keep silence and to "cover their heads when praying." Barton, on the other hand, argues for Pauline authorship to make an erroneous case for the idea of "Paul's sense of place" and downplays the interconnectedness of 1 Cor. 14:33b-36 with 1 Tim. 2:11-5. In different ways, both Schüssler Fiorenza and Barton attempt to make sense of the passage within its context. I consider such positions untenable, because the passage seems to break the flow of the argument in chapter 14 and thus suggests interpolation.

First Corinthians 14:33-36: A Paulinist Interpolation

Hans Conzelmann argues unequivocally that 1 Cor. 14:33b-36 is an interpolation.[9] What he means by this is that a second-century editor inserted this passage into its present location to *use Pauline authority* to justify, in his own context and time period, the submission of women. Conzelmann notes that, if taken in the context of Paul's present correspondence with the Corinthian church, the injunction against women in 1 Cor. 14:33b-36 contradicts 11:2-16, in which the active participation of women is presupposed. The problem is that v. 37 does not link up with v. 36 but with v. 33a. Verse 37, he argues, returns to the subject of prophecy and its criteria. Verse 36 is unclear in the present context but seems to underscore the validity of the statement that *something* is practiced in "all the churches of the saints" (v. 33b). The *something*, which the text in its present condition seeks to advance, is the silencing and subordination of women in the church. In this effort to support the silencing of women, a later interpolationist unintentionally disrupted the literary flow of the text. When vv. 33b-36 are removed, the passage reads quite smoothly:

> 26 What should be done then, my friends? When you come together, each one has a hymn, a lesson, a revelation, a tongue, or an interpretation. Let all things be done for building up. 27 If anyone speaks in a tongue, let there be only two or at most three, and each in turn; and let one interpret. 28 But if there is no one to interpret, let them be silent in church and speak to themselves and to God. 29 Let two or three prophets speak, and let the others weigh what is said. 30 If a revelation is made to someone else sitting nearby, let the first person be silent. 31 For you can all prophesy one by one, so that all may learn and all be encouraged. 32 And the spirits of prophets are subject to the prophets, 33 for God is a God not of disorder but of peace. . . . 37 Anyone who claims to be a prophet, or to have spiritual powers, must acknowledge that what I am writing to you is a command of the Lord. 38 Anyone who does not recognize this is not to be recognized. 39 So, my friends, be eager to prophesy, and do not forbid speaking in tongues; 40 but all things should be done decently and in order.

With the interpolated text removed, the passage reads well. The context has to do with glossolalists and prophets. In each case Paul gives instructions that if one is "speaking" the others are "to remain silent" (vv. 28 and 30). The Paulinist author placed the injunction against women's speaking in this context because it seemed to include important verbal clues for his agenda, that is, a command to limit and control "speech" or speaking in the worship community. Reading this passage divorced from its canonical context indicates its uncharacteristic tone for Paul:

> 33b As in all the churches of the saints, 34 women should be silent in the churches. For they are not permitted to speak, but should be subordinate, as the law also says. 35 If there is anything they desire to know, let them ask their husbands at home. For it is shameful for a woman to speak in church. 36 Or did the word of God originate with you? Or are you the only ones it has reached?

Thus, according to Conzelmann, "in this regulation we have a reflection of the bourgeois consolidation of the church, roughly on the level of the Pastoral Epistles: it binds itself to the general custom. . . . This section is accordingly to be regarded as in interpolation."[10] William Walker agrees that this passage is an interpolation, and he argues that a common tradition can be found to support a Paulinist influence.[11] By *Paulinist* he means the tradition developed by Paul's later disciples. Walker's point is that the "authentic" or "historical" Paul advocated and supported a community where sexual roles and status distinctions were leveled under the sovereignty of Christ and God: "all . . . are one in Christ" (Gal. 3:28). Therefore, the passages supporting female subordination reflect one aspect of a post-Pauline reaction against what Walker has termed "radical egalitarianism." The passages in question, then, appear to conflict with Paul's attitude toward women as far as that can be gathered from his undisputed letters (Romans 16 and Phil. 4:2-3, where several female church leaders and coworkers are commended by Paul).

First Corinthians 14:33b-36: A Paulinist Redaction

Robert Allison advocates still another approach to this passage and the question of authorship.[12] He rejects both the interpolation theory as well as that of Pauline authorship because they do not address central questions best understood in sociological terms. He notes that there are textual problems, however, that could lend themselves to the theory of interpolation. All of the textual problems generally involve vv. 34-35. First, the repetition of "as in all the churches" (*en tais ecclesiais*) from v. 33b does not read smoothly in v. 34 as one continuous sentence. Second, vv. 34-35 is a bold contradiction of 11:3-16, in which women do pray and prophesy in the worship community. Third, the speaking (*lalein*) referred to in vv. 34-35 does not relate to prophetic or pneumatic (spiritual) speech as discussed in the context of chapters 11–14. Rather this passage opposes all talking, and "the authoritarian language is uncharacteristic of Paul, as validation by the Torah contradicts his teaching of freedom from the Jewish law" (v. 34, "as the law also says"; cf. Rom. 10:4, "*Christ is the end of the law*, that everyone who has faith may be justified").[13] Fourth, the words "Or did the word of God originate with you only?" (v. 36) form a rhetorically pointed antithesis with "in all the churches of the saints" (v. 33b), which seems to be interrupted by vv. 34-35. Therefore "a group of 'Western' manuscripts and medieval Western church writers give . . . [vv. 33b-35] after v. 40, a displacement which may reflect an attempt to smooth out the text."[14]

Despite these observations, Allison suggests that the view of interpolation is impossible. The omission of vv. 34-35 places v. 33b ("as in all the churches of the saints") with the preceding section beginning at v. 36 ("Or did the word of God originate with you?") In addition he argues that v. 33a and v. 33b do not read smoothly either. Therefore Allison suggests, "If v. 33b can be linked neither with the rhetorical question in v. 36, nor with Paul's assertion that God is a God of peace in v. 33a, then the theory that vv. 34-35 were inserted into their present context is not tenable; they must be taken with v. 33b. Nearly all scholars take the *Taceat* as a unit extending from vv. 33b to 36 on the grounds of smooth continuity of thought between v. 33a and 37."[15] If this is the case, Allison points out that there still remains to be found a resolution of the awkward redundancy in vv. 33b-34, as well as the problems raised by vv. 34-35. Therefore, exegesis that presumes the integrity of 14:33b-36 as Pauline must explain why v. 33b does not introduce this passage as a smooth continuation of Paul's preceding proposals that allow each person to speak; these proposals would now appear to be an exception.

The argument for Pauline authorship of this passage must show that it is consistent with Paul's other statements about women and account for its present location in 1 Corinthians. In 11:3-16 women are presumed to pray and prophesy in the worship community. One class of Pauline exegesis proposes that the presumed conflict between 11:3-16 and 14:33b-36 represents developments in Paul's thinking due to his change of mind over a period of time. This point is boldly rejected, because it does not do justice to the strong impression that 11:3-16 is not expressive of an exception but more likely the rule: Paul takes the praying and prophesying of women for granted in this passage.

Another attempt at resolving the discrepancy between 1 Cor. 14:33b-36 and 11:3-16 is the idea that 1 Corinthians is composed of two (or more) letters written at different times and later combined. The inconsistency between the two passages nonetheless remains, because both (or all) letters are presumably written to the same church and supporting two different notions of women's participation in worship. For Allison the problem with this approach is that if in the mixed company of the worship services disruptive talk had been a problem, it would most likely have been a problem among the men. "Even if Paul shared the prevailing view regarding women talking in public, he would hardly have attempted to impose order on the whole congregation by silencing only half of it."[16]

Allison argues that this is the work of a later redactor who in his editing of Paul's letter reshaped Paul's words to reflect the position of Paul's contemporary Corinthian opponents on male and female roles within the church. The editor reshaped the passage using Paul's authority to address the situation of the church in the second century. Allison's central thesis is that Paul vehemently opposed a group of pneumatics that was attempting to establish *exclusively male* leadership in the Corinthian church. Their ideas were derived from the synagogue model in which learning by explication of Torah was of central importance. In their understanding, women were expected to be silent and subordinate to male church leadership. Allison's rationale is based, like Walker's, on sociological grounds, taking into account Paul's assumed advocacy of a social order characterized as "eschatological egalitarianism." This perspective envisions that, upon the unfolding of the "last days," the entire social, economic, and political order of the old world will be eradicated. A new world order based upon peace and equality will be established. Many early Christians believed that, with God's promised Holy Spirit falling upon all flesh indiscriminately, they were living in the "last days" (cf. Acts 2). In the age of the Spirit all human relations are democratized.

First Corinthians 14:33b-36: A Rhetorical Rebuttal

One way to understand the meaning of this passage and who the author might have been is to examine Allison's theory in connection with Walker's. Allison's theory is that this passage should be understood as, originally, a rhetorical rebuttal of Paul:

> If we consider the *Taceat* apart from its present context . . . the force of the disjunctive ē ["or," v. 36] cannot be missed. Paul's rhetorical questions are his sarcastic rebuttal to his opponents' position, which he has summarized, in the authoritarian decree of vv. 33b-35. *The decree that women should remain silent in the church, then, must have been the assertion of an opposing group within the Corinthian church. The only words in the* Taceat *which express Paul's own views are the rhetorical questions following the disjunctive particle.*[17]

The problem with the received exegesis and interpretation of this passage is that it presumes that the entire passage—the decree and the rhetorical questions—is directed against the Corinthian custom of women speaking in the worship community. This reading has been the assumed meaning for centuries, namely, that women should be silent in church. This position is reinforced by the surrounding context of Paul's address to the Corinthian church regarding the problem of the disorderliness of their services of worship. "For these reasons, the antithesis required by the disjunctive *ē* (or) has been overlooked, regarded as awkward, but not awkward enough to raise questions about the status of women in church."[18]

Allison asserts that rhetorical questions introduced by the disjunctive *ē* are frequently used by Paul to counter the opposing view of his opponents (1 Cor. 6:2, 8). The use of the disjunctive *ē*, therefore, is a common grammatical feature of classical and Koine Greek, which introduces a rebuttal against a point of view implicit in the immediately proceeding clause presumably not perceived or recognized by its proponents.[19] Thus, Allison suggests that 1 Cor. 14:33b-36 is a fragment from another letter of Paul to the Corinthians. A later editor placed this fragment of another letter of Paul's into this present context because of linguistic and textual similarity. While doing this he shaped Paul's argument directed *against* the prohibition of women speaking in church, into the opposite, advocating the silencing of women, which one party in the Corinthian church supported. This thesis explains why this passage is in its present location and how it was manipulated in such a way as to make the injunction for female silence in the church appear to be Paul's position.

In my view, Allison's theory can be held without positing that the passage is a fragment; the later Paulinist editor could have simply reshaped the passage without using a different letter fragment. Nevertheless, if it is accepted that this passage is a fragment from another letter of Paul to the Corinthians, which was recast into its present location because of its linguistic and contextual similarity with the preceding section (order of worship, glossolalia, and prophecy), then the injunction in v. 33b concerning the silencing of women in the church was probably not a universal practice. "Paul's rhetorical questions presume that his readers will have to admit that no one has exclusive claim on mediating the Spirit to the church. Paul's sarcasm, moreover, is aimed directly at the Corinthian proponents of this exclusivist or elitist claim to divine inspiration."[20] Thus v. 33b, according to this theory, most certainly had to be a part of the argument of Paul's opponents, if it is kept in mind that Paul usually states his opponents' argument first in order to construct his own. His opponents were trying to make their argument a universal claim: "v. 33b, then, is an editorial transition intended to integrate the fragment smoothly into the preceding context."[21]

This makes it evident that Paul was addressing an adversarial situation (Paul had been doing this at other places throughout 1 Corinthians; for example, 4:9, 10; 5:6). According to Allison, this led to a faction in the Corinthian church whose views eventually prevailed. The adversarial reading of 1 Cor. 14:33b-36 reveals that the words "you only" (v. 36) imply a claim of exclusivity by Paul's opponents. This group opposed the participation of women in the worship services and attempted to silence them. Paul's rhetorical question in v. 36 challenged this group's notion that they had "exclusive mediation of the word of God." Allison proposes that those who composed this group were getting their ideas from Jewish influences, namely, the synagogue. These men wanted the church services to correspond to a Jewish synagogue model in which "knowing something" was a recognized focus of the service. In this service women could not speak, teach, or conduct any prayer. They even had to sit separately from the men and wait until they returned home to ask any questions about the service. "This group of men based its decree on Torah (*ho nomos*), referring to Gen. 3:16, and the order of creation derived from Genesis 2. Finally, the appeal to Torah was put into the form of a commonly used rabbinical formula for applying the Torah to contemporary life situations."[22] This trend represented a shift in the earlier egalitarian social patterns within many Pauline churches. This shift began as the churches confronted new and challenging situations near the end of the first century into the second century that sparked a move toward institutionalization to meet these challenges.

The Paulinist Tradition: The Move toward Institutionalization (or Proto-Orthodoxy)

The dynamic tradition of egalitarianism through the equality of the Spirit in pre-Pauline and Pauline Christianity became curtailed in the churches of the late first and early second centuries C.E. The churches during this period had to face several new problems and challenges.[23] One major problem in early Christianity was the delay of the parousia, which is evident already in 1 Thessalonians. By the 70s of the first century 2 Thessalonians (a deutero-Pauline epistle) sought to address difficulties related to this same issue. A second problem was the challenge of heterodoxy, especially that posed by Gnosticism. This challenge increased to a certain degree in the later decades of the first century and was addressed early on by Colossians and Ephesians. The threat and reality of persecution became an increasing challenge to the unity and integrity of the church. Finally, the post-Pauline churches sought to address the problem of church order and identity. On the question of identity, church leaders became increasingly conscious of how the larger society viewed the church, which resulted in placing emphasis on proper moral and ethical behavior that would not be perceived by the Roman populace as anti-patriotic or as a threat to Roman ethical views—hence the emergence of the household codes in Christian literature. The Pastorals (1–2 Timothy and Titus) especially represent the church at the beginning of the second century seeking to deal to some degree with all of these issues. This entire process is understood as the move toward proto-orthodoxy or the church moving toward institutionalization.

There is now a scholarly consensus on the origin of the canonical Pauline corpus:

Undisputed Pauline (49/50s C.E.)	*Early Pauline School* (70–90 C.E.)	*Later Pauline School* (100–125 C.E.)
1 Thessalonians	2 Thessalonians	1 Timothy
1 Corinthians	Colossians	2 Timothy
2 Corinthians	Ephesians	Titus
Philippians		
Philemon		
Galatians		
Romans		

Only seven letters are uncontestedly authentically Pauline. While 1 Thessalonians is most likely the first letter written by Paul and Romans was most certainly the last, the order of the remaining uncontested letters has been debated. What has been designated the "Pauline school" above is also known as "deutero-Pauline Christianity." This tradition or "school" shows the continuing influence of the apostle in the churches he founded. These Paulinists of the early school were probably taught by Paul (a strong case can be made for Colossians in this regard). After the death of the apostle and the vacuum of leadership and guidance, they collected and studied his letters, further developing some of his ideas. In the spirit and tradition of their teacher they carefully and conscientiously attempted to meet the challenges and needs of the churches and wrote formally in his name. Collecting Paul's letters and adding their own to his for circulation among the Pauline churches, they created literature that represents the authority and influence of Paul and his ideas a generation or two after his death.[24] According to Dennis Duling,

> The writers of some of these letters were most probably pupils of the apostle who consciously imitated their teacher, wrote in his name, and identified themselves with him. This means that we are in the presence of a Pauline School similar to the many schools of learning that existed

in the Greco-Roman world, from the rabbis to the Stoics. . . . It is well known, for example, that members of Platonic schools who imitated the life-style of Plato wrote works now called pseudo-Socratic and pseudo-Platonic.[25]

This school and the tradition built upon the memory and legacy of Paul sought to establish structure and "order" within the churches of the last decades of the first century and early second century C.E. This school, in its efforts to meet the challenges of internal order and external identity delineated above, sought also—perhaps contrary to the spirit of its teacher—to limit and prohibit women's leadership in the churches. This was not enough, however; they even attempted to *control* the tradition about early Christian women's leadership. In some ways their agenda entailed a reaction against their teacher even as they sought to reshape the tradition based upon his legacy and memory.

Post-Pauline Reaction to Christian Egalitarianism: 1 Timothy 2:11-15

Walker's theory can help us see more clearly the connection of 1 Cor. 14:33b-36 with 1 Tim. 2:11-15. Walker argues that it is possible to identify more precisely the *Sitz im Leben* (setting in life) of all New Testament passages supporting the principle of male dominance and female subordination. He offers the following points:

> (1) All of the New Testament passages supporting the principle of male dominance and female subordination (i.e., 1 Cor 11:3-16; 14:34-35; Col 3:18-19; Eph 5:22-33; 1 Tim 2:8-15; Titus 2:4-5; and 1 Pet 3:1-7) can be traced to a common source, origin, or tradition. (2) This common source, origin, or tradition is to be located, not in the apostolic period or widely read throughout the early church, but rather within one particular "wing" of early Christianity, namely, the "Paulinist" wing. (3) The passages in question reflect one aspect of a post-Pauline reaction against what can be termed the "radical egalitarianism" of Paul himself.[26]

Two points are of particular note: first, the idea of male dominance and female subordination is not a wide-ranging practice of the earliest strata of early Christianity; second, the passages in question reflect a common origin. On the second point, Walker observes that these passages written by Paulinist authors concerning women appeal heavily to the account of creation in Genesis 2 and the fall of humankind in Genesis 3 to construct their arguments about the place of women.[27] In my estimation, 1 Cor. 11:2-16 may also be related indirectly to the Paulinist writers' derivation of their argument from Paul for gender roles and the silencing of women in the church. But how could Paul have been used to support this position, which he seemed to oppose? It is possible to see conceptual similarities in 1 Cor. 14:33-36, 1 Tim. 2:8-15, and 1 Cor. 11:2-16. This development may be seen as an evolutionary progression because all three passages refer to Genesis 2 and/or 3 as the foundation of their arguments. On the contrary, Gal. 3:28, as we have seen, has a connection with Gen. 1:27, wherein male and female are created equally in the image of God. Such a view resulted in a new ordering of human relationships for several early churches. Already in the apostolic era the radical egalitarianism of pre-Pauline and Pauline Christianity was difficult to accept, stimulating debates in the Corinthian church and other churches on understanding this new reality against the backdrop of patriarchal society. However, "after Paul's death, when the Corinthian correspondence was edited, and [1 Cor. 14:33b-36] was integrated into its present context, it was easy to misunderstand the point of that short passage."[28] I suspect that here, then, in 1 Cor. 11:2-16 was laid the foundation upon which the Paulinist author of 1 Timothy could see in Paul an ideological companion and also the blueprint for 1 Cor. 14:33-36 and the construction of "woman's place" and "woman's silence." Paul, as it turns out, may have unwittingly supplied for his future disciples the groundwork for this perspective in his argument regarding women wearing veils in community worship.

Paul's argument in 1 Cor. 11:2-16 is puzzling and has been for centuries. While a number of modern interpretations have been offered, Ross Kraemer succinctly delineates the basic structure of Paul's argument:

> Paul proffers an ordered hierarchical classification in which the woman's head is man; the man's head is Christ; Christ's head is God. The next portion of Paul's argument here is tortuous and opaque. . . . Paul argues from the order of creation in Genesis 2:18-24, in which God creates the first male human, then the female from the rib of the male.[29]

From the creation account of Genesis 2, Paul argues that women should wear head coverings because they need a sign of *exousia* (authority) over their heads (since according to Genesis 2 they are subordinate to the male, being made from his rib). This notion of head coverings may also be related to the account in Gen. 6:1-4, in which angels copulated with the beautiful women who were "unattached" to a male. At any rate, whatever Paul may have had in mind, his use of the "order of creation" to argue for women's head coverings initiated (or validated) a trend, if nothing else, to regulate women's dress in the worship community. But several interpreters are certain that much more may be at stake.

As I discussed in chapter 1, the women in Corinth may have exercised their newfound freedom from male "authority" and patriarchal social expectations based upon Gen. 1:27, wherein both male and female are created in

the image of God (which may be related to the myth of the original androgyne). In this view, a "new creation" had taken place in Christ that overturned the order of the "old creation" (cf. 2 Cor. 5:17: "So if anyone is in
Christ, there is a *new creation*: everything old has passed away; see, everything
has become new!" And Gal. 6:15 is related to this issue too: "For neither circumcision nor uncircumcision is anything; but a *new creation* is everything!"
[emphasis added]). The "order of the new creation" expressed in Gal. 3:28
and Acts 2 resulted in a nonhierarchical democratization of human relations.
How then could Paul use the language of the "new creation" and at the same
time reinscribe the language of "the old creation"? My contention is that the
language of the new creation was useful for Paul so long as it validated the
unity of humanity before God; for in this way he could argue that the gospel
unifies both Jew and Greek. However, if the same concept is used to validate
slaves' emancipation or women's actualization of its radical implications
(which might disrupt the harmony and unity of Christian communities), it
has to be reevaluated and subordinated to the goal of unity. In Paul's reevaluation, the order of the old creation was used to counter that of the new creation in such cases. Thus a trend was set in motion within Pauline
communities that would have far-reaching repercussions.

It is possible to observe the evolving strictures and trend toward female
subordination in the three passages in question by noting their references to
Genesis 2 and/or 3. The important portion of 1 Cor. 11:2-16 reads:

> For a man ought not to have his head veiled, since he is the image and
> reflection of God; but woman is the reflection of man. Indeed, man was
> not made from woman, but woman from man. Neither was man created
> for the sake of woman, but woman for the sake of man. (1 Cor. 11:7-9)

Paul's use of the phrase "image and reflection" is based on Gen. 1:27. He
alludes to this passage without quoting it because this would have entailed
using the word *anthrōpos* (human being) rather than *arsēn* (male). Thus he
quickly moves to Genesis 2, where the male alone is the image and "glory" of
God. Paul usually refers to Christ as God's image and to us as reflecting
Christ. Here he changes the argument around to support his argument.[30]
Nevertheless, "even though Paul restricts women's activities in 1 Cor. 11:2-
16 by making reference to Genesis, nowhere in the undisputed letters do we
find such a blatant justification of women's inferiority."[31] The case for inferiority increases, however, in 1 Cor. 14:34, although it may not reflect Paul's
opinion but that of his later "school": "Women should be silent in the
churches. For they are not permitted to speak, but should be subordinate, as
the law also says." This passage, unlike the first, moves toward a more pronounced stricture of women's activity in the church and their subordina-

tion—if not inferiority—to the male. This passage finds support by an allusion to Eve's punishment after the fall; the text declares that because of Eve's
sin "he [her husband] shall rule over you" (Gen. 3:16). This clear reference to
what "the law says" is a bold step toward curbing women's full participation
and equality with males in the church. The passage in 1 Timothy brings this
notion to its logical conclusion:

> Let a woman learn in silence with full submission. I permit no woman
> to teach or to have authority over a man; she is to keep silent. For Adam
> was formed first, then Eve; and Adam was not deceived, but the woman
> was deceived and became a transgressor. Yet she will be saved through
> childbearing, provided they continue in faith and love and holiness,
> with modesty. (1 Tim. 2:11-15)

This text benefits from an allusion not only to the fall in Genesis 3 but also
to the creation narrative of Genesis 2, which clearly states that woman is subordinate to the male by virtue of her creation from him. As it turns out, then,
1 Tim. 2:8-15 is the only explicit prohibition in the entire Bible against
women not only speaking in church but also teaching and exercising any
kind of authority over males.[32] "In 1 Timothy, the proper sphere for Christian
women is carefully delineated. Good Christian women keep their mouths
shut, exercise authority only over their households and children and never
over men, and generally confine themselves to the private, domestic
sphere."[33] But what about the phrase, "Yet she will be saved through childbearing"? Does this mean that women who cannot or choose not to bear children cannot be saved? Interpretations abound, but two are of note.

The first is less encumbered by speculation. It simply suggest that the text
means by "saved through childbearing" that women will have a safe delivery
of their children, which is a relief from the woman's curse of bearing children
in great pain and danger, as in Gen. 3:16.[34] There is only limited relief from
the "curse," but no relief from female subordination and submission to the
husband. This is where the second interpretation finds its starting point, dis-
cerning the situation behind the text. The suggestion is that women in several
Christian communities used Gal. 3:28 and the notion "no longer male and
female" as referring to the end of patriarchal marriage and childbearing. Early
Christian history remarkably provides several instances where women chose
the ascetic life, disciplined lifestyles that renounced marriage and childbearing
and included dietary restrictions, in order to be wholeheartedly devoted to
Christ or even perhaps to avoid patriarchal domination (I consider below one
such woman, Thecla). The Pastorals have several injunctions against just such
practices, and the restrictions against married women and widows reveal that
such a threat was present in several early Christian communities. Hence the

force of the passage indicates that the author was saying to such radical, unruly women: "You will only be saved if you resume your 'proper place' under male authority and cease the practice of celibacy (non-marriage). This is indeed your place according to the order of creation!" In this reading, there is no relief from the "curse," only from the fall. Women can be restored and find salvation in Christ, but not liberation from the curse. The final result of this tradition finds completion in this passage. Such notions were also supported by the Greco-Roman household codes or duties.

The Emergence of the Household Codes (*Haustafeln*)

In the last decades of the first century, Christian texts emerged that sought to order relationships within the Christian family in terms of the Greco-Roman household and were articulated upon the order of creation.[35] Christian communities in this era appropriated a model of the household gleaned from Greco-Roman treatises on economics (household management) and politics that was already codified by Aristotle and the Greco-Roman philosophical and moralist schools of the first century C.E. Greco-Roman moralists sought to define a balance between the traditional demands of subordination and obedience to the *paterfamilias* (father of the family) and Hellenistic ideals of equality. What resulted was a code of household ordering that placed the male/father of the house at the top of the hierarchy. Such a view was also influenced by political theory.

In Aristotle's view, a union of "natural ruler and natural subject" defines human relations in the state.[36] Aristotle believed that

> The investigation of everything should begin with its smallest parts, and the smallest and primary parts of the household are master and slave, husband and wife, father and children. . . . We ought therefore to examine the proper constitution and character of each of the three relationships, I mean of mastership, that of marriage and thirdly the progenerative relationship. (*Politics* 1.1253b)[37]

For Aristotle human relationships are *ontologically* based, that is, relationships are ordered by what something or someone is *in essence*, its *is-ness*. In other words, certain people are by nature or *in essence* masters and others slaves, some leaders by nature and others subjects by nature (cf. *Politics* 1.1254b). Even in terms of sex, women and men are different by nature: "the male is by nature better fitted to command than the female. . . . Also as between the sexes, the male is by nature superior and the female inferior, the male the ruler and the female the subject. And the same must also necessarily apply in the case of humankind generally" (cf. *Politics* 1.1254b, 1.1259b).

These differences in essence must be properly structured and ordered so as to maintain harmony in society, so that the state may function properly—and every household is a microcosm of the state. If the household as the basic microcosm of the state is not ordered properly or if different forms of household governance are in existence at the same time, the very state itself is jeopardized.[38] Therefore the radical notion of "no longer male and female," which entails female liberation from patriarchal dominance, is a threat to the state. Aristotle speaks on this subject also:

> The freedom in regard to women is detrimental both in regard to the purpose of the *politea* [management of state] and in regard to the happiness of the state. For just as a man and wife are part of a household, it is clear that the state also is divided nearly in half into its male and female population, so that in all *politea* in which the position of women is badly regulated one half of the state must be deemed neglected in framing the law. (*Politics* 2.1296b)[39]

This was the position not only of Greco-Roman moral philosophy but also of Jewish moralizing about women and the household. Philo of Alexandria, first-century C.E. Jewish philosopher, saw a direct correlation between state management and the household:

> For the future statesman needed first to be trained and practiced in house management, for a house is a city compressed into small dimensions, and a household management may be called a kind of state management [*politea*]. . . . This shows clearly that the household manager is identical with the statesman. (*On Joseph* 38–39)[40]

Likewise, Josephus, Jewish historian of the first century C.E., addresses the role and position of women in Jewish law. In his work *Against Apion* Josephus discusses Moses' *politea* in comparison with that of the mythological founders of Rome, Romulus and Remus. Josephus argues apologetically that the Jews are exemplary upholders of the laws that Rome imposed on the entire empire: "The woman, says the Law, is in all things inferior to the man. Let her accordingly be submissive, not for her humiliation, but that she may be directed, for the authority has been given by God to the man" (*Against Apion* 2.201).[41] It is possible to see here that the Paulinist author's appeal to the law to support female submission in the construction of 1 Cor. 14:33-35 is quite at home among the ancient Jewish exegetes of scripture. It is also possible to see that, like Josephus, the early Christian leaders were also trying to make a case for Christians as law-biding citizens of the Roman Empire. In this effort, they appropriated for the church the morality and order of the Greco-Roman household.

The reasons for the emergence of Greco-Roman household codes are related in general to the problems and challenges (mentioned above) in which the post-Pauline churches sought to address the problem of church order and identity. This resulted in church leaders becoming increasingly self-conscious of how the larger society viewed the church. Thus church leaders placed greater emphasis on proper moral and ethical behavior that the Roman populace would not perceive as a threat to Roman ethical views. These texts have been seen as so counter-liberative that Frank Stagg has remarked that the household codes have been used to turn the "good news" into the "bad news" for women.[42]

While certain elements of the household codes appear in Col. 3:18-4:7; Eph. 5:21—6:9; 1 Tim. 2:8-15; 6:1-2; Titus 2:4-15; and 1 Peter 3:1-7, the brief discussion that follows will focus primarily upon Colossians and Ephesians, which represent a fuller appropriation of the codes than the fragmented uses in the other passages. In Colossians and Ephesians the household codes are presented in three pairs of reciprocal relationships: that of husbands and wives, fathers and children, and masters and slaves. The domestic duties are concerned primarily with the three subordinate groups under the male/master (wives, children, and slaves). The rationale for the Christian obligation to the household codes is out of "love for Christ." Hence Christian appropriation of the patriarchal household codes "out of love of Christ" has been termed "love patriarchalism." A comparison of the two sets of codes is instructive.

Colossians 3:18-4:7	Ephesians 5:22—6:9

Wives

18 Wives, be subject to your husbands, as is fitting in the Lord.	22 Wives, be subject to your husbands as you are to the Lord. 23 For the husband is the head of the wife just as Christ is the head of the church, the body of which he is the Savior. 24 Just as the church is subject to Christ, so also wives ought to be, in everything, to their husbands.

Husbands

19 Husbands, love your wives and never treat them harshly.	25 Husbands, love your wives, just as Christ loved the church and gave himself up for her, 26 in order to make her holy by cleansing her with the washing of water by the word, 27 so as to present the church to himself in splendor, without a spot or wrinkle or anything of the kind—yes, so that she may be holy and without blem-

ish. 28 In the same way, husbands should love their wives as they do their own bodies. He who loves his wife loves himself. 29 For no one ever hates his own body, but he nourishes and tenderly cares for it, just as Christ does for the church, 30 because we are members of his body. 31 "For this reason a man will leave his father and mother and be joined to his wife, and the two will become one flesh." 32 This is a great mystery, and I am applying it to Christ and the church. 33 Each of you, however, should love his wife as himself, and a wife should respect her husband.

Children

20 Children, obey your parents in everything, for this is your acceptable duty in the Lord.

6:1 Children, obey your parents in the Lord, for this is right. 2 "Honor your father and mother"—this is the first commandment with a promise: 3 "so that it may be well with you and you may live long on the earth."

Fathers

21 Fathers, do not provoke your children, or they may lose heart.

4 And, fathers, do not provoke your children to anger, but bring them up in the discipline and instruction of the Lord.

Slaves

22 Slaves, obey your earthly masters in everything, not only while being watched and in order to please them, but wholeheartedly, fearing the Lord. 23 Whatever your task, put yourselves into it, as done for the Lord and not for your masters, 24 since you know that from the Lord you will receive the inheritance as your reward; you serve the Lord Christ. 25 For the wrongdoer will be paid back for whatever wrong has been done, and *there is no partiality*.

5 Slaves, obey your earthly masters with fear and trembling, in singleness trembling, in singleness of heart, as you obey Christ; 6 not only while being watched, and in order to please them, but as slaves of Christ, doing the will of God from the heart. 7 Render service with enthusiasm, as to the Lord and not to men and women, 8 knowing that whatever good we do, we will receive the same again from the Lord, *whether we are slaves or free*.

Masters

4:1 Masters, treat your slaves justly and fairly, for you know that you also have a Master in heaven.	6:9 And, masters, do the same to them Stop threatening them, for you know that both of you have the same Master in heaven, and with him *there is no partiality*.

Scholarly consensus hypothesizes that Colossians was written first and that the author of Ephesians my have used Colossians as a source. This might explain why Ephesians provides more detailed elaboration and rationale for its codes, especially related to the duties of husband and wife. More important, however, is that Colossians quotes but changes Gal. 3:28. Colossians elaborates Gal. 3:28 with the household codes in mind. Since the relationship between Jew and Greek was no longer a problem, Col. 3:11 stresses the second pair ("no longer slave or free") to argue that in the new humanity in Christ national and cultural differences are overcome. In addition Colossians divides the slave-free polarization that defines the social-political stratifications of slavery. The "slave-free" juxtaposition of Gal. 3:28 is removed because Colossians adds them to the enumeration and elaboration of those who are uncircumcised—barbarians, Scythian, slave, freeborn—while the third pair of Gal. 3:28 ("male and female") are not mentioned at all. Now the restoration in Christ is no longer social but cosmic (2:1-4, 12, 20).[43] Therefore "in taking over the Greco-Roman ethic of the patriarchal household code, Colossians not only 'spiritualizes' and moralizes the baptismal community understanding expressed in Gal. 3:28 but also makes this Greco-Roman household ethic a part of 'Christian' social ethic." But the demand for submission of wives, children, and slaves is not an early (or genuine) Christian social ethic; it is a later interpretation of Gal. 3:28.[44]

Ephesians, on the other hand, is also concerned about the universal peace and unity brought about by Jesus Christ (2:14-18, esp. vv. 15-17; 4:1-6). This author's view is also informed by the baptismal formula in elaborating the household codes. This is evident in 6:8—"everyone *slave or free* will receive from the Lord." He maintains that now equality between slave and free (master) is eschatological. "The Colossians code clearly was interested in the patriarchally appropriate behavior of slaves, but the Ephesian code elaborates the relationship of wife and husband in patriarchal marriage." Ephesians compares the church with marriage using the church-bride paradigm, which does not spell out equality between the sexes.[45] Ephesians elaborates upon the aspects of the codes relating to husband and wife and provides an extensive theological justification for the appropriation of the codes for the Christian sacrament of marriage. Thus the codes have differing functions in various Christian communities.

There have been three primary proposals for the use and function of the household codes.[46] First, William Herzog argues that Christian groups represented a "minority community" trying to exist in a "majority culture."[47] In light of the delay of the parousia, Christian communities had to reassess their existence and learn how to settle down and live quietly and harmoniously with the larger world. Second, the adoption of the codes served as an *apologia* (defense) of the Christian faith to the outside world. This is particularly evident in 1 Peter 2:11—3:12. Christians have to maintain proper morality toward the outside world in order to show that they are not a threat in any way to the larger social world. They do this to avoid censure and persecution.[48] Third, Schüssler Fiorenza argues that the earlier egalitarian social vision, which overturned the social structure of the patriarchal household and society, was perceived as a threat to the Christian movement as it spread throughout the Greco-Roman world. Such radicalism had to be curtailed in light of a new situation in the church. In other words, the church appropriated the codes to lessen the tension between Christian churches and pagan patriarchal households.[49] Indeed even the church, the dynamic *ekklēsia* (assembly) of those who have been called to equality in Christ, becomes in the Pastorals the household of God. For example, 1 Tim. 3:4-5 states: "He [an aspiring bishop] must manage his own household well, keeping his children submissive and respectful in every way—for if someone does not know how to manage his own household, how can he take care of God's church?" (cf. 1 Tim. 3:15; Titus 2:5; 1 Pet. 4:17). Like Philo's counsel on the statesman's task as similar to that of the household manager, a church leader must now also manage the *household of God!* And this is all done in Paul's name.

Dennis R. MacDonald in a short but salient study, *The Legend and the Apostle: The Battle for Paul in Story and in Canon*, proposes correctly that the image of Paul was up for grabs by the second century.[50] Several Christian groups of differing theological perspectives and practices were attempting to claim the authority and legacy of Paul to validate their differing claims. This held true for validating not only doctrine, theology, ethics, and praxis (ascetic versus nonascetic, for example), but also the role and place of women within early Christianity. The author or authors of the Pastoral epistles (1–2 Timothy and Titus) attempt to recuperate the image and legacy of Paul to promote the agenda of the emerging proto-orthodox church. On the particular issue of the place and role of women in the proto-orthodox church, using the authority of Paul to silence and subordinate women into their "proper domestic sphere" becomes evident. The statements in 1 Tim. 2:11-15 clearly show that women had been doing the very opposite of that which is enjoined upon them. But even more than this, they received inspiration and validation for teaching and abrogating traditional roles from a different image and legacy of Paul. In the transmission of this legacy, Paul appeared in a role opposite from his role in the Pastorals. Far from prohibiting leadership positions in the Christian church for women, this "Paul" commissions women to preach and to baptize.

Incorporated within the apocryphal *Acts of Paul* is the story about a devout disciple named Thecla. In the *Acts of Thecla*, Thecla, a betrothed virgin, renounces marriage and male authority (upsetting the household) and renounces sex (and therefore reproduction) in order to pursue the gospel wholeheartedly. In this endeavor, she is commended and commissioned by none other than Paul. Thus MacDonald notes a connection between the regulation in 1 Tim. 2:11-15 supporting female subordination and the portrayal of Paul in the *Acts of Thecla*, which supports female teaching and preaching. Both traditions use Paul's authority to validate their perspectives on women. That the stories later incorporated in the *Acts of Thecla* were used to validate women's ministry is evident in a writing of the African church father Tertullian. He complained that some Christians were using Thecla's example to legitimate women's teaching and baptizing because, according to these individuals, she had been commissioned by Paul himself to do so. Tertullian says in rebuttal,

> But if they claim writings which are wrongly inscribed with Paul's name—I mean the example of Thecla—in support of women's freedom to teach and baptize, let them know that a presbyter in Asia, who put together that book, heaping up a narrative as it were from his own materials under Paul's name, when after conviction he confessed that he had done it from love of Paul, resigned his position. (*On Baptism* 1.7)[51]

Tertullian's statement admits of two things: the practice of individuals writing in Paul's name and that such an act had social and practical consequences—to legitimate a teaching or practice. Hence the Paul of the *Acts of Thecla* looks very much like the false teachers described in the Pastorals who forbid marriage, upset households, lead women from their proper duties, and eat a restricted diet (cf. 1 Tim. 4:1-3; 2 Tim. 3:6-7). Those who told these stories were most likely women who were also "upsetting" the stability of the patriarchal household (cf. 1 Tim. 4:1-5). Moreover, it may have been the widows, who are "unattached" to a husband (and male authority in the household), who told these stories.

First Timothy 5:13-15 is instructive in this regard:

> 13 Besides that, they [widows] learn to be idle, gadding about from house to house; and they are not merely idle, but also gossips and busybodies, saying what they should not say. 14 So I would have younger widows marry, bear children, and manage their households, so as to give the adversary no occasion to revile us. 15 For some have already turned away to follow Satan.

This statement includes three important points. First, widows, since they have no husband, exercise greater freedom to move about without restriction ("gadding from house to house"). Second, they exercise their freedom to speak their minds, which 1 Timothy finds problematic because they say "what they should not say." To some interpreters, this means telling the very stories about Paul and Thecla that validate women's freedom. For this reason, the author commands widows who are of marriageable age to marry and hence come under the authority of a husband (male). Third, the author characterizes widows in this manner because some women had already gone astray, while some others have already turned away or departed from the church to exercise their freedom!

It becomes clear that the church of the second century had to come to grips with two portrayals of Paul and two traditions or paradigms that supported each portrayal. This they did: the Pastorals eventually carried the day. So the legends were carried on underground.

The Egalitarian Vision in the Second and Third Centuries: Opposing Paradigms and Practices

Opposing Paradigms

The Pastorals represent the efforts of the proto-orthodox to curtail the egalitarian tradition embedded in early Christian history and in scripture. My goal in Part 1 is to trace the origin and development of the submerged, liberating voice. What results from this investigation is that by the end of the first and into the second century there were two opposing paradigms for the church. Kraemer succinctly spells this out:

> By the early second century, two distinctive interpretations of Christian life emerged that are reflected in the texts at hand. Those who wrote, read, and promulgated the Pastorals favored marriage, social conformity, hierarchy, and structure, and bitterly opposed any leadership roles on the part of women. Those who told stories like that of Thecla and ultimately committed them to writing and circulated them favored asceticism, rejected social conventions, denied the value of contemporary hierarchy, and believed that women could baptize and teach just as men. Both sought legitimation and conceivably even derived their positions from the same writings of Paul, even though the battle was hardly only an exegetical one. Both camps were equally willing to fabricate in defense of their positions, hoping to clarify once and for all what had proved incredibly ambiguous in Paul's letters to the Corinthians.[52]

Emerging in the early church are competing paradigms for the church and two competing images and interpretations of Paul. As is the case even today, exegesis alone is insufficient to understand this polarity in the tradition. But if one can determine the paradigms that support each position, it is at least possible to explain how the opposing positions are reached. In *The Structure of Scientific Revolutions*, Thomas Kuhn introduces and discusses the concept of competing paradigms in the realm of science in particular, but his analysis has significance in general for our study.

> The proponents of competing paradigms practice their trades in different worlds. . . . Practicing in different worlds, the two groups of scientists see different things when they look from the same point in the same direction. That is not to say they can see anything they please. . . . Both are looking at the world, and what they look at has not changed. But . . . they see different things, and see them in different relations one to the other.[53]

Kuhn's discussion of competing paradigms in science is quite apposite when applied to the study of religious and social phenomena. It is a known fact in religious studies that creation narratives function within cultures and societies to establish social and structural paradigms for a given society. These paradigms govern how the world and human relations are to be conceived. The way societies and cultures perceive their cosmic origins (creation) has a great deal to do with, among other things, how male and female relationships function in a given society. This is no less true for the early Christian communities. Both Christian groups have the Hebrew Scriptures (Old Testament) and the letters of Paul (the uncontested letters at first, then the canonical collection). Yet they arrive at two opposing interpretations of Christianity. Part of the reason, as Kuhn has pointed out, is that both groups "look from the same point in the same direction. . . . But . . . they see different things and see them in different relations one to the other." The same point from which they look is *creation*. From this point they come to very different conclusions because they perceive two different creation orders. Outlining this relationship and the scriptures that support each position can be instructive:

Gen. 1:27	Genesis 2 and 3
Acts 2	1 Cor. 11:2-16
Acts 10:34-35	1 Cor. 14:33b-36
Acts 17:26	1 Tim. 2:11-15
Gal. 3:28	The household codes

What can be gleaned from the above comparison is that within the New Testament itself is embedded the evidence of two opposing traditions. If one's starting point is Gen. 1:27, there is a tendency to perceive a less stratified, democratic pattern of human relationships. Moreover, if one's starting point is Genesis 2 and/or 3, patterns of human relationships are conceived in more structured, hierarchical ways. This trend developed into two opposing practices for the church: one supportive of and one severely curtailing women's leadership and ministry.

Opposing Practices

It is clear from the paradigms presented above that there is a correlation between religious theory (theology) and social practice. The way human relations are conceived depends on the paradigm to which one subscribes, and from this perception of human relations can be delineated a host of regulations. What I have argued in my examination of Jesus and Paul is that their vision of human relations was rooted in a worldview that sought to equalize human social structures and relationships. Their view opened the possibilities especially for women, who in several early churches were considered equal to men: some were revered as prophets, and others acted as teachers, traveling evangelists, healers, priests, and even apostles. This was rooted in a paradigm based on the saying "in Christ . . . there is neither male nor female."[54]

But after about 200 C.E. there is little or no evidence for women taking prophetic, priestly, and episcopal roles among proto-orthodox churches. This is an extraordinary transition from the earliest phase of Christian leadership patterns among women and men because, despite the previous public activity of Christian women, the majority of Christian churches in the second century aligned with the burgeoning wing of "middle-class" leadership in opposing the move toward equality. By the second century, an increasing number of Christian communities endorsed as canonical the Pastoral letters and household codes, which stressed willing subordination to oppressive trends in society "out of love for Christ." As I have argued, such views probably represented neither Jesus' nor Paul's views. Nevertheless, the views of the emerging proto-orthodox leaders were gaining ground and were finding support in many "orthodox" communities. Yet exceptions occurred.

Clement of Alexandria, whose writings date from about 180 C.E., is a noteworthy exception to the orthodox pattern and praxis. He identifies himself as proto-orthodox but also knows members of Gnostic groups and their writings well (too well for some). He could still at this time point to Gal. 3:28, perhaps filtered through his knowledge of Gnostic ideas, to offer a more egalitarian view of church leadership. To be sure, his works demonstrate several elements of what could be called a Gnostic pattern and how these ideas could be worked into orthodox teaching.

In his work *Pædagogus* (Instructor), which is addressed to new converts as a guide to morals, manners, and the formation and development of Christian character, Clement sets out to lay down the rules and regulations of the

Christian in all circumstances. Since the *Instructor* is the Word and Son of God who nourishes all Christians, he characterizes God in feminine as well as masculine terms:

> The Word is everything to the child, both father and mother, teacher and nurse. . . . The nutriment is the milk of the Father . . . and the Word alone supplies us children with the milk of love, and only those who suck at this breast are truly happy. For this reason, seeking is called sucking; to those infants who seek the Word, the Father's loving breasts supply milk.

It most certainly follows from this gendered imagery that since the Word can be described as both "father and mother" and has the power to "perfect" (make complete) equally, he insists that both women and men are to receive the same instruction because they share a common life: "Men and women share equally in perfection, and are to receive the same instruction and the same discipline. For the name 'humanity' is common to both men and women; and for us 'in Christ there is neither male nor female.'" It is important to see that both Gen. 1:27 and Gal. 3:28 are at work in his view of equality between the sexes. It is evident in his phrase "*humanity* is common to both men and women." He is referring to Gen. 1:27, which reads in part, "God created humankind in his image . . . male and female he created them." In this text the name *humankind* is common to both male and female. This is the starting point for his paradigm, which could then incorporate a positive assessment and practical application of Gal. 3:28 into the corporate and educational structures of the church. In this vein Clement continues: "For instruction leads to faith, and faith with baptism is trained by the Holy Spirit. For that faith is the one universal salvation of humanity, and that *there is the same equality before the righteous and loving God, and the same fellowship between Him and all*" (emphasis added). Clement believed that this view, based on Gen. 1:27 and Gal. 3:28, should be reflected in the praxis of the church. Therefore he urged women to participate equally with men in the community. "As a means of encouraging women, he offers a list, that is unique in orthodox tradition, of women whose achievements he admires."[55]

Clement's work demonstrates that even proto-orthodox Christians could affirm both masculine and feminine attributes of deity and also support the active participation of women in the church, but his view found little following. According to Pagels, "his perspective, formed in the cosmopolitan atmosphere of Alexandria and articulated among wealthy and educated members of Egyptian society, may have proved too alien for the majority of Western Christian communities, which were scattered from Asia Minor to Greece, Rome, and provincial Africa and Gaul."[56] The majority of Christian leaders opted instead for the position of Clement's conservative but equally intelligent provincial contemporary in North Africa, Tertullian.

As a trained jurist turned biblical theologian who had little patience for disorder or ambiguity, Tertullian wholeheartedly supported the growing trend toward institutional hierarchy. In his work *On the Veiling of Virgins* Tertullian addresses the issue of why some virgins refused to wear a veil that was required for other (married) women in the corporate worship. Although virgins are not under the authority of a husband, he argues, they are still required to wear a veil because they are female, and the rule of subordination thus applies to them by virtue of their sex. For this reason, a virgin is not to be accorded any special treatment: "nothing in the way of public honour is permitted to a *virgin*" (*On the Veiling of Virgins* 9). Indeed she, like all women, is to remain subordinate to male authority and to occupy no office that would jeopardize male authority. In driving home this point, Tertullian not only quotes but expands upon 1 Timothy's injunction against women: "It is not permitted for a woman to speak in the church, nor is it permitted for her to teach, nor to baptize, nor to offer [the eucharist], nor to claim for herself a share in any masculine function, least of all in priestly office."[57] Tertullian quotes only the first part of 1 Tim. 2:11. He leaves out the portion that appeals directly to Genesis 2 and 3 and expands upon the offices that in his view women are not to occupy. It is apparent that in his use of this text as a starting point—to chastise some virgins for their refusal to wear the veil as a sign of male headship or authority because they were not married—is designed to eliminate any vestige, hope, or display of female liberty. This is evident in his remark that follows directly the quote above:

> Let us inquire whether any of these [masculine functions] be lawful to a virgin. If it is not lawful to a virgin, but she is subjected on the self-same terms (as the woman), and *the necessity for humility is assigned her together with the woman,* whence will this one thing be lawful to her which is not lawful to any and every female?[58]

Perhaps through the allusion to 1 Tim. 2:11-15, Tertullian is making his case here with Gen. 3:16 in mind, in which the woman is "cursed" and instructed that her husband is to rule over her. This notion is apparent in his statement: "the *necessity of humility . . . assigned her* [the virgin] *together with the woman.*" This is the starting point for his paradigm, which could not incorporate a positive assessment and practical application of female leadership roles in the corporate and educational structures of the church. The final result of Tertullian's view, based on Gen. 3:16 and 1 Tim. 2:11-15, is that a hierarchical pattern should be reflected in the praxis of the church. Therefore he cannot support even a special class of holy women (virgins) to participate equally with men in the Christian community.

In line with my argument above, Pagels correctly determines that the opposing views are rooted in either of the Genesis paradigms of creation. The text used as a starting point determines the praxis for the church. She clarifies this in terms of Gnosticism (which influenced Clement and practiced an egalitarian social model) and proto-orthodoxy:

> We can see, then, two very different patterns or paradigms of sexual attitudes emerging in orthodox and Gnostic circles. In simplest form, many Gnostic Christians correlate their description of God in both masculine and feminine terms with a complementary description of human nature. Most often they refer to the creation account of Genesis 1, which suggests an equal or androgynous human creation. Gnostic Christians often take the principle of equality between men and women into the social and political structures of their communities. The orthodox pattern is strikingly different: it describes God in exclusively masculine terms, and typically refers to Genesis 2 to describe how Eve was created from Adam, and for his fulfillment. Like the Gnostic view, this translates into social practice: by the late second century, the orthodox community came to accept the domination of men over women as the divinely ordained order, not only for social and family life, but also for the Christian churches.[59]

History has demonstrated that Tertullian's position as representative of proto-orthodoxy ruled out Clement's position and has continued to dominate the view of the majority of Christian churches nearly two thousand years later. This view has been perceived as the "God-ordained" pattern for relations between the sexes. Thus by the end of the second century, women's participation and leadership in worship activities was explicitly condemned. For this reason, groups in which women continued in leadership were branded as heretical.[60] Despite this label, several women opted for heresy. It is no wonder that after 200 C.E. the connection between women and heresy, established in 1 Timothy, is amply manifested in a long list of historical instances. This led one modern scholar to describe "heresy as women's religion [and] women's religion as heresy."[61] The idea of women's leadership roles in the church as heresy has a long tradition. Even Jarena Lee, an African American woman who received and pursued a call to preach in the early nineteenth century, had to contend with such a notion. She argued,

> O how careful we ought to be, lest through our bylaws of church government and discipline, we bring into disrepute even the word of life. . . . *Why should it be thought impossible, heterodox,* or improper, for a woman to

preach? Seeing that the Savior died for the woman as well as the man.[62] (emphasis added)

Lee's statement makes it clear, however, that the tradition of struggle to challenge and resist such a claim of heterodoxy is equally as long.

Conclusion

In my reading, there are no hermeneutical or exegetical grounds to use 1 Cor. 14:33b-36 (or any passage of scripture, for that matter) to justify the silencing and elimination of women's voices and participation in the worship service or as ordained preachers and pastors. This view is what Paul argued vehemently against. The equality of all before God in Christ is not a Pauline invention. "He found it ready at hand in one of the key moments of earliest Christianity."[63] The place where Paul found it was in a baptismal formula (Gal. 3:27-28) where the elimination of value judgments between the sexes was eradicated. Within the Christian community male and female are equal.[64]

It seems clear then that within Pauline Christianity women claimed and exercised equality with men in the preaching and teaching of the gospel, but for some this was a problem. The egalitarian nature of the early Christian movement of which Paul was a proponent became unacceptable to the developing Hellenistic churches. Later writers and teachers had to "tone down" or "domesticate" this radical egalitarianism (as evidenced by 1 Tim. 2:11-15), just as a nonhierarchical egalitarian vision of human relations within the church was even yet rejected, and a subordinationist view followed. Thus I concur with Robin Scroggs's assertion that "the reluctance of the church even in modern times to read Paul afresh, unhampered by the distorted reflection of the Apostle in the deutero-Pauline mirror, simply suggests that the modern church has been as fearful as the early of the liberty inherent in the . . . gospel."[65]

Church leaders from various traditions still need to come to terms with this fear. African American churches can no longer advocate racial equality on biblical grounds and at the same time support sexism in the churches using the same Bible. They must have the courage to judge a person by the content of his or her character and abilities, especially in the church. Black churches in America emerged in reaction to oppression based upon the physical characteristics of African people—their race, ethnicity, and culture. The same gospel of liberty motivated black churches to form independent congregations and also supplied them with a critical hermeneutical principle with which to critique America's most egregious sin—racism combined with chattel slavery. The message of freedom and equality articulated in the

African American Christian religious tradition was the foundation for the black churches' most valued principles. These principles, like those of the early church, are rooted in the same paradigms, but this tradition must be excavated and exposed as such. This task will occupy Parts 2 and 3.

❧ Part Two ❧

African American Religious Experience and the Appropriation of Scripture

❧ 3 ❧
Proclamation, Protest, and a New Principle

For the word of God is living and active, sharper than any two-edged sword, piercing to the division of soul and spirit, of joints and marrow. (Hebrews 4:12, RSV)

Born in slavery, weaned in segregation and reared in discrimination, the religion of the Negro folk was chosen to bear the roles of both *protest* and *relief*. Thus, the uniqueness of black religion is the racial bond which seeks to risk its life for the elusive but *ultimate goal of freedom and equality by means of protest and action*. It does so through the only avenues to which its members have always been permitted a measure of access, religious convocations in the fields or in houses of worship.[1]

There is little debate today that the Bible has had an ambiguous career in the history of Western civilization. Far from being neutral on issues of human freedom and equality, the Bible has been used to support, in different places and at different times, both liberty and oppression. This ambiguous, "two-edged" position of the Bible on the issues of slavery and oppression and freedom and liberty has succeeded in the "piercing to the division of soul and spirit" of individuals as well as a nation, namely, the United States of America. The United States in the middle of the nineteenth century went to war to settle this debate over the issue of slavery—and all of the economic, social, political, and religious concerns that accompanied it. Before, during, and after the Civil War, the Bible was at center stage in the heated struggle between human freedom and human servitude. To be sure, the Bible could play this ambiguous role because it lent itself to either interpretation. This reality was characterized by correspondence between two professors in the early nineteenth century concerning the Bible and its position on slavery:

> Dr. Fisk, president of Wesleyan University, wrote in 1837 to the esteemed professor Moses Stuart of Andover Theological Seminary, hoping to get Professor Stuart to publicly oppose slavery. But professor Stuart responded with both *sic* and *non*, "yes and no," saying that "the theory

of slavery" stands opposed to the commandment "Love thy neighbor as thyself," but that Paul did not forbid slavery. When slaves and masters became Christians, Paul did not prescribe terminating the relationship, but urged slaves to give due respect to their masters (I Tim 6:2). Hence "the relation once constituted and continued is not such a *malum in se* [evil in itself] as calls for immediate and violent disrupture, at all hazards."[2]

Stuart's response shows that he was aware that the Bible was not unequivocally against slavery as an institution but could be interpreted to support or deny human oppression. Despite his deutero-Pauline[3] reference concerning slaves' respect toward their masters, the question still remains how the apostle Paul and the early Christian communities understood slavery. Is Stuart's assessment of Paul accurate? When slave and master became Christian (or one of them became a Christian), how did the new relationship with Christ affect the old relationship of slave and master in the Christian community and in the larger society, if at all? The ambiguous nature of the Bible on these issues is unquestionably the result of the nature and culture of the ancient world from which the Bible emerged and to which the Bible was responding. Many scholars agree that the ancient world could not imagine society without slavery and other systems of servitude and forced labor.[4] Nonetheless, there were some liberating visions that arose within the Christian communities that seemed to offer an alternative model to the immediate social world in which the Christians lived. One such vision is the baptismal quotation by Paul in Gal. 3:28: "There is neither Jew nor Greek, there is neither bond nor free, there is neither male nor female; for ye are all one in Christ" (KJV). This vision of human equality was significant for supporting arguments against racial, classist, and sexist oppression. It supported the principle of "the equality of all people before God." This came to be known as one of the most important principles in African Americans' religious and political quests for freedom and equality.

Proslavery Misappropriation of the Bible and the Evangelism of Enslaved Blacks

Chattel slavery in America was no different from any other system of human oppression that seeks to justify itself—its origins, traditions, and rationale. The institution of North American slavery between the years 1619 and 1865 pillaged science, history, literature, and religion in the quest of arguments to uphold the unjust system. Even after slavery's end, there was almost an exact parallel between the methods employed in support of slavery and those that were resorted to in justification of Jim Crow attitudes or "separate but equal" legislation before the Civil Rights Movement of the 1950s and 60s. This fact was so obvious that James Buswell could state in 1964 that "the Negro's slave status of yesterday find its parallels in modern 'caste' and color lines of today."[5] The longstanding argument for racial bigotry was that the separation of the races was "ordained by God," just as slavery at one time was called a "divine institution."[6] The supposed sanction for such an understanding of relations between African and Europeans was the Bible, "a classic of Western civilization." Biblical images, themes, motifs, and traditions have been found in all aspects of Western social, artistic, religious, legal, and political culture. For this reason those who sought to support arguments for slavery appealed to the Bible as the "word of God" and as the final court of appeal.[7]

The scriptural justification for slavery took several clearly defined forms, followed a predictable pattern, and used particular combinations of arguments. These arguments can be divided into four groups: (1) general assertions that the institution of slavery was natural or "ordained by God" and hence beneficial to the enslaved blacks; (2) appeals to examples of slavery described or alluded to in the Bible, particularly in the Old Testament; (3) the use of instructions and injunctions regarding the conduct of slaves and masters, primarily in the New Testament; and (4) beneath the whole structure of the system of slavery, the supposed teachings in the Bible regarding the African race based primarily upon elaborations on the story of Ham and the curse of Noah. These four points constitute the primary basis for the scriptural defense of North American slavery and postemancipation racial segregation.[8]

Slavery as a "Divine Institution" and Consistent with "Natural Law"

Proslavery advocates felt so strongly that their position was consistent with the Bible and Christian theology that the Society for the Advancement of Christianity in South Carolina published a tract that read: "No man or set of men in our day, unless they can produce a new revelation from Heaven, are entitled to pronounce slavery as wrong. Slavery as it exists at the present day is agreeable to the order of Divine providence."[9] In this view slavery was considered to be "by divine appointment" and "a divine institution." Some felt so strongly about the institution of slavery that they called it "God's institution." Slavery was not immoral but represented a legitimate "moral relation" between blacks and whites that was "founded in right." Not only was the institution of slavery given divine sanction, but the slave trade itself and the entire destiny of African peoples brought to America were considered "legal" and "licit," and "in accordance with humane principles and the laws of revealed religion"—even "a merciful visitation" because it was a means of bringing the gospel to the "heathen Africans."[10]

For this reason, slavery was considered consistent with the natural law, which was expressed and implied in the proslavery literature of the time. To add a veneer or validity to this view, examples from the natural world were employed. As one Dr. Cartwright expressed it:

> The same ordinance which keeps the spheres in their orbits and holds the satellites in subordination to the planets, is the ordinance that subjects the Negro race to the empire of the white man's will. Under that ordinance, our four millions of Negroes are as unalterably bound to obey the white man's will, as the four satellites of Jupiter the superior magnetism of that planet.[11]

The natural position of blacks under "the white man's will," unequal and subordinate to him in all things, was seen as natural and immutable. Therefore, support for slavery could be imagined as inscribed within the very structure of the cosmos and consistent within the plan and foreknowledge of God.

Slavery in the Old Testament as Justification of Its Compatibility with Scripture

Examples of slavery in the Bible could be detailed at length, from the time of Abraham to the case of Philemon, with arguments cited in support of each of them.[12] Suffice it to say that even after God liberated the Hebrew slaves from Egyptian slavery, their "God-given" law still contained statutes for the maintenance of the system (Exodus and Deuteronomy). But now it supported the Hebrews' status as slavemasters, with some amelioration of the system in terms of the treatment of slaves. This and other such items were fertile ground for proslavery advocates.

Slavery in the New Testament as Justification of Its Compatibility with Scripture

Slaveowners and proslavery clergy found support for slavery in the New Testament especially in nine places. These texts enjoined the obedience and subservience of slaves (Titus 2:9-10; Eph. 6:5-9; Col. 3:22-25; and 1 Pet. 2:18-25) with special regard for the master, rendering service to such as "unto the Lord" (1 Tim. 6:1-2; Eph. 6:5-9). From 1 Corinthians it could be argued that one "should remain in the condition in which you were called" (1 Cor. 7:20-24); therefore, slaves should not seek freedom at all, and if one encounters a runaway slave, that slave should be returned (Philemon). In order to justify such discrepancies in human social relations, it was argued that God intended such variety in human status (1 Cor. 12:13-26). Finally, there was an attempt to explain away Acts 17:24-26: "God . . . hath made of one blood all nations of men" (KJV). This passage had to be explained away because it could contribute to the notion of a common origin of all humankind, which would run counter to the intended aims of proslavery supporters. Nevertheless, with these few verses from the New Testament an ideological system was in place.[13]

Proslavery Biblical Teachings on the Black Race: The Curse of Ham

Many of the advocates of slavery never considered blacks to be human. If they considered them human beings, they based their opinion upon the confident assumption that the African race must be identified with the descendants of Noah's second son, Ham. Any and every mention of peoples inhabiting Egypt, Ethiopia, and the other lands occupied in the dispersal of Ham's progeny (Genesis 11) were assumed to refer to blacks. The length to which proslavery arguments tried to prove the association of blacks with Ham in order to justify the conclusion that blacks are under Noah's curse is staggering. A further assumption constantly made was that different traits, of racial character, correlated with Noah's three sons. It was further argued that these assumed traits could be ascertained by inference from scripture and that the God-given character instilled in each of these three sons was fated to be the character of their descendants for all future time. The idea that Noah's curse involved a future of servitude for the progeny of Ham's son was based upon such endless assumptions that the "logic" seemed impregnable. Some even believed that Noah spoke through the spirit of prophecy: "The fact that what was said by Noah of the descendants of Ham has actually come to pass is proof positive that he did not speak [for] himself, but by the spirit of prophecy."[14]

> The reasoning for the idea of the curse of Ham went something like this: Ham was a word which meant "black," not only referring to his skin color but also to "the very disposition of his mind." He was characterized as having always been wicked ("cursed Ham" not "cursed be Ham") with violence of temper, exceedingly prone to acts of ferocity and cruelty, involving murder, war, butcheries, and even cannibalism, including beastly lusts, and lasciviousness . . . dishonesty, treachery, lowmindedness, and malice. . . . This group of horrors . . . couched in the word "Ham" is all seen as . . . agreeing, in a most surprising manner, with the color of Ham's skin, as well as with his real character as a man, during his own life, as well as with that of his race, even now.[15]

The curse of servitude was thus the logical outcome of sin, and served as the "very first notice of slavery upon record." It was designed by God "to be perpetuated through all time, and was intended to cement and compact the whole human family, to establish the system of mutual relation and dependency, and to sustain the great chain of subordination, so essential to the divine, as well as all human governments."[16]

The Argument for Racial Segregation: Separate and Unequal

As with slavery, we find that the arguments from scripture in support of racial segregation fall easily into the same four categories. Of all New Testament references, the one most cited by defenders of segregation is Acts 17:26. The first half of this verse was, and is, used to support the argument for racial unity and equality: "And he made from one ['blood,' KJV] every nation of men." To this segregationists reply, "Yes, but you haven't quoted the rest of the verse. It ends with the words: "having determined allotted periods and the boundaries of their habitation." If God has set the boundaries for man's habitation, is it not violating God's program to mix populations together? The association of this verse with the dispersal of the progeny of Noah's sons was usually made.[17]

Proslavery advocates, having made the scriptural justification for the institution of slavery, gradually opened the door for evangelism. The slave regime, however, wanted to make it clear that enslaved "blacks could be 'saved by Christ,' but never 'free from their masters.'"[18]

Evangelism and the Conversion of Slaves

The slave trade and the institution of slavery were partially defended on the basis that the Africans were thus brought under the influence of the gospel in a Christian land. Church and missionary agencies did not seem to recognize that the increasing number of slaves, particularly in the New World, constituted a ready mission field of challenging proportions. However, a constant and demoralizing problem was repeatedly faced, namely, the widespread conviction that the message of Christianity was not intended for the inferior races. Such opinions were held in certain church circles where there was a marked preoccupation with purity of doctrine rather than missionary outreach. The reason for this situation is that the Anglican, Catholic, Episcopal, and Presbyterian denominations assumed a rather cerebral, sober, and nonemotional approach to religion and conversion. These denominations stressed conversion through the rites of the church: catechism, baptism, and sacraments.

Adding to this were the problems that the Christianization of the enslaved might entail. That is, inherent in Christian theology is that baptism and conversion of individuals would entail their humanity (Genesis 1), equality (Gal. 3:28), and freedom (Exodus), resulting in the fear of rebellions and a disruption to the slavocracy. These egalitarian elements could prove dangerous. In addition, faithfulness to the religion included religious instruction (catechism), which could be considered education.[19] Proslavery advocates posited a solution to these problems by arguing that Christianity would make better slaves; indeed, it would serve as a means of control and docility. To avoid educating their slaves, they would teach only certain parts of the catechism and the Bible orally. The basis of this catechism, among other things, would include certain passages from the Pauline corpus (as stated above), the curse of Ham, and fostering among the enslaved an otherworldly eschatology (that is, if they were faithful and accepted their lot in life, they would be rewarded in the next life).

Despite sentiments of this kind, gradual evangelization of slave populations had begun already in the early seventeenth century, but with few results. In 1673 Richard Baxter had laid the foundations for converting the slaves in his "Christian Directory," which "had an extensive circulation among the plantation owners." The Church of England began to take an active interest in converting the American slaves after 1679. One of its clergymen, Morgan Godwyn, before King James II "preached a sermon deploring the condition of the slaves and pleading that His Majesty use some endeavor toward having the Gospel ideas propagated in the Colonies." The king made a resolution the same year "that the Negroes in the Plantations should all be baptized."[20]

The response to this resolution and other appeals was not impressive because of not only a lack of manpower, enthusiasm, and resources but the problem of method in reaching the slaves. However, despite the slaves' own protracted acclimation to Christianity, something happened in the middle of the eighteenth century to make Christianity the most viable religious alternative (although they did not have a wide range of options) for life in the New World. This was the "dawn of a new day" in the history of the conversion of slaves to Christianity.[21] The protracted event has been called the "Great Awakening," because it seemed to awaken many regions of colonial life to a renewed religious piety. It represented the beginning of revivalistic piety in America. This revival or "awakening" led to enormous growth for the Baptists and prepared the way also for the Methodist movement as it spread south, because they accepted a more emotive style of worship. The cumulative effect is that it bridged the yawning cultural divide between blacks and whites. The Great Awakening began in Massachusetts in the 1730s and spread throughout the colonies into the 1770s. After the Revolutionary War, during the early 1800s the revivalistic impulse emerged anew in the frontier regions to the West. This new manifestation, "the Great Western Revival," included "camp meetings" held under tents and in the open air. Like the Great Awakening, these camp meetings embraced blacks who also participated in these events, which proved to be a powerful instrument in the rapid conversion of slaves.[22] Before the success of these revival movements there were only a few black Christians in some of the English colonies. Most of these black converts worshiped in the same congregations with their masters, and those who were free worshiped with their white neighbors—albeit under the conditions of racial segregation.[23] With the success of the Great Awakening and other revival movements a more integrated pattern of communal worship emerges. Albert Raboteau terms this *religious reciprocity*:

> When white sinners were awakened by black exhorters, when masters were converted by the singing, shouting, and praying of their slaves, when white congregations were pastored by black preachers, the logical extreme of revivalistic religion was reached. Certainly these incidents were rare, but that they occurred at all indicates the manner in which religious reciprocity was able to bend the seemingly inflexible positions of mater and slave.[24]

The Great Awakening and the later revival movements also significantly reshaped the sacred world of the slaves. These movements, emphasizing the *inward* experience of religion, *deemphasized* the *outward* social status of people. It had a universalizing effect, which stressed that *all* had to be saved—white and black, rich and poor, master and slave, male and female. It provided blacks with an experience of Christianity that allowed for their own personal contribution and ethos.[25] According to Gayraud Wilmore, however, the slaves' appropriation of Christianity was something more and something less than what is generally regarded as Christianity. Despite the universalizing effects of religious reciprocity in revivalistic piety, it was impossible for masters and slaves to share Christianity in the same way. The slaves' sacred world had to confront the present reality of bondage and suffering: theirs was a religion of the oppressed. The master's reality was motivated by economic and material gain and by maintaining social, economic, and political hegemony. The transmission of religion from one people to another cannot be wholly without change.[26] Thus these events initiated the beginning of the "invisible institution," that is, slave religion, out of which would be carved the hope and articulation for not only religious but also social freedom.

The notion of freedom was almost unavoidable in Christianity, and the slaves did not miss its implications. The doctrine of "the freedom of the Christian" was basic to the New Testament and the Reformation theology that heavily influenced various Protestant denominations. The rebellious colonial churches had no difficulty invoking this idea during the War of Independence. It was expected, however, that missionaries diligently avoid this idea in their instructions to blacks. Slaveowners already had been convinced that the religious conversion of their human property would not result in financial loss but greatly increase their profits. In this way, proslavery missionaries reduced Christian theology and ethics to their most simplistic and harmless affirmations.[27]

Despite this restriction, a few early Quakers and Baptist and Methodist preachers made attempts to sensitize black converts to the implications of Christianity for human justice and equality. We might add to this number Charles Colcock Jones, a Presbyterian plantation missionary who may have inadvertently passed along some subversive teachings against slavery. He reported some masters' accusations: "You teach them that 'God is no respecter of persons': that 'he hath made of one blood all the nations of men': 'thou shalt love thy neighbor as thyself': 'all whatsoever ye would that men should do to you, do ye even so to them.'"[28] The result throughout the South of these efforts was a fear and suspicion of strangers who came among the blacks with the professed purpose of evangelizing. For this reason, unsolicited preaching was either strictly forbidden or carefully regulated and kept under surveillance. Nevertheless, an indigenous cadre of black slave preachers emerged within the slave community.

The earliest religious practitioners (we might even call them preachers) to the slaves were not whites but former African priests or religious specialists of one sort or another who possessed unusual gifts of leadership and persuasion. It was not until after the Revolution that black preachers began to be licensed as exhorters by the Methodist and Baptist denominations (previously slave communities had most likely already recognized their gifts of leadership). Such individuals, licensed or unlicensed, with or without the master's permission, exercised their ministries whenever opportunity presented itself, and the slaves were able to assemble under their leadership.[29]

This did not mean, however, that slave preachers were able to exercise their ministry without restrictions. Many were illiterate, although some may have gained by various means the rudiments of literacy. This did not prevent them from sharing with their people the gospel of equality with eloquent preaching. They had to labor under a very difficult dichotomy. If they veered too closely to upholding the status quo, they were viewed as a mouthpiece of the master; if they verged too close to the gospel of equality, they were in trouble with the whites. Raboteau clarifies this situation:

> On the one hand, the slave preacher was criticized by former slaves as the "mouthpiece of the masters." On the other hand, some slave preachers preached and spoke freedom in secret. The weight of slave testimony suggests that the slaves knew and understood the restrictions under which the slave preacher labored, and that they accepted his authority not because it came from the master but because it came from God. They respected him because he was the messenger of the Gospel, one who

preached the word of God with power and authority, indeed with a power which sometimes humbled white folk and frequently uplifted slaves.[30]

In the final analysis, broaching the issue of human equality in the context of the gospel and the moral right of slaves to escape or resist enslavement was due in some measure to the agitation of a few courageous whites who transmitted the egalitarian spirit of the American Revolution and radical Christianity to the secret gatherings of slaves. The slaveowners' fears were in fact well founded. They were aware that any attempts to educate or indoctrinate enslaved blacks would eventually change the precarious relationship between master and slave. "For this reason many of them opposed any kind of religious instruction, preferring to maintain law and order by brute force rather than by a paternalistic Christian education."[31]

The Proslavery Response to Protestant Evangelicalism

It is not difficult now to understand the reaction of slaveholders who, for the better part of two hundred years, were in varying degrees hostile to the advances of Christianity toward their slaves. Attendant with this conviction were insistent denials that manumission was compulsory upon conversion or baptism. One Bishop Berkeley, before the Society for the Propagation of the Gospel in Foreign Parts in 1731, considered it "an erroneous notion." Indeed, so crucial was the nature of the question that specific legislation was enacted in an attempt to provide freedom of evangelism without freedom of the slave in order to put at ease the consciences of slaveowners. As early as 1667 the colony of Virginia passed a law stating that "the conferring of baptism doth not alter the condition of the person as to his bondage or freedom, to the end that masters, freed from this doubt, may more carefully endeavour the propagation of Christianity." In 1671 Maryland provided that "the conversion of the Holy Sacrament of Baptism does not alter the status of slaves or their issue." Other statutes to the same effect were passed in Virginia in 1682 and 1705, Maryland in 1699, New York in 1706, 1781, and 1801.[32]

One of the most detailed attempts to further the propagation of the gospel among American slaves without conferring freedom upon them was a lengthy letter prepared by the bishop of London. It was addressed "to the Masters and Mistresses of Families in the English Plantations abroad, exhorting them to encourage and promote the instruction of their Negroes in the Christian Faith." This letter, dated 1727 from London, explicitly addressed the question of whether slaves should be freed upon baptism:

> [To which it may be very truly reply'd, That] Christianity, and the embracing of the Gospel does not make the least alteration in civil property, or in any of the duties which belong to civil relations; but in all

these respects, it continues persons just in the same state as it found them. The freedom which Christianity gives is a freedom from the bondage of sin and satan, and from the domination of men's lusts and passions and inordinate desires; but as to their outward condition, whatever that was before, whether bond or free, their being baptized and becoming Christians, makes no manner of change in it. As St. Paul has expressly told us, I Cor. 7:20, where he is speaking directly to this point, "Let every man abide in the same calling wherein he was called": and at the 24th verse, "Let every man wherein he is called therein abide with God."

By spiritualizing and moralizing the notion of freedom and using Paul's authority to support it, this letter sought to initiate a trend that would, once and for all, settle the question of the slaves' status even after baptism. Although this and many other similar expressions were intended to ease the tension and provide official resolution to the dilemma, the anticipated results were not forthcoming. The great dilemma that faced the slaveholders is thus seen to have been not simply a legal matter, nor merely a matter to be decided by ecclesiastical authority. It was the *fundamental opposition of the Bible* to the very foundations of slavery and the pressing problem of its propagation to their slaves.[33] For the time being, they presented a skewed image of Jesus and believed that they had found an undaunted advocate in Paul, or rather a particular "reading" of his letters and Christian history. For this reason, enslaved and free blacks, literate and illiterate, were compelled to respond to proslavery misusage of the Bible to support oppression and also to provide assessments of both Jesus' and Paul's legacy.

Response to Proslavery Misuse of the Bible: The Emergence of the African American Protest Tradition

Responding to Proslavery Misuse of the Bible

It was nearly impossible to impart Christianity to the enslaved population without some mention or reference to its chief document, the Bible. Although in many cases slaves and slave preachers were illiterate, their sermons and songs were based on the cardinal stories, characters, images, and themes of the Bible. However, as one plantation minister remarked,

illiteracy proved less of an obstacle to knowledge of the Bible than might be thought, for biblical stories became a part of the oral tradition of the slaves. Oral instructions and Sunday School lessons were committed to memory. As one of the slaves reported: "To those who are ignorant of letters, *their memory is their book.* . . . In recent examination of one of the schools, I was forcibly struck with their remembrance of *passages of Scripture.*"[34]

As a matter of fact, slaves inculcated enough of scripture that they were mistrustful of whites' interpretation of the Bible, even though they could not ordinarily read it. It is not surprising that they began to differentiate their own experience of scripture from that of whites and to articulate how whites fell short of its themes of human unity and God's impartiality. While slave testimony attests to this, literate free blacks like David Walker and the former slave Frederick Douglass articulated the same message.

David Walker in his "Appeal to the Colored Citizens of the World," Article III, written in 1829, criticizes whites for their misuse of the Bible and for not preaching its message of human unity, harmony, and impartiality:

> Surely the Americans must believe that God is partial, notwithstanding his apostle Peter, declared before Cornelius and others that he has no respect to persons, but in every nation he that feareth God and worketh righteousness is accepted with him (Acts 10:36, KJV).[35]

As he develops this theme he goes on to included white preachers in his rebuke. He asks,

> How can the preachers and people of America believe the Bible? Does it teach them any distinction on account of a man's color? Hearken, Americans! to the injunctions of our Lord and master. . . . Go ye, therefore, and teach all nations, baptizing them in the name of the Father, and of the Son, and of the Holy Ghost. . . . Can the American preachers appeal to God, the Maker and Searcher of hearts, and tell him, with the Bible in their hands, that they make no distinction on account of men's color?[36]

It becomes clear that he is touching on an issue that frustrated blacks, who had imbibed enough of biblical knowledge to move from passively receiving its proclamation to forcefully employing it in protest.

Another articulate spokesman on this issue was Frederick Douglass, who touches on this theme of partiality in white Christianity in his "Slaveholding Religion and the Christianity of Christ." This article appeared in an appendix to his autobiography of 1845; he wanted to clarify that his stinging critique of slaveholding Christianity was not an attack against true Christianity.[37]

> What I have said respecting and against religion, I mean strictly to apply to the slaveholding religion of this land, and with no possible reference to Christianity proper; for, between the Christianity of this land, and the Christianity of Christ, I recognize the widest possible difference—so wide, that to receive the one as good, pure, and holy, is of necessity to reject the other as bad, corrupt, and wicked. . . . I love the pure, peaceable, and impartial Christianity of Christ: I therefore hate the corrupt, slaveholding, women-whipping, cradle-plundering, partial and

hypocritical Christianity of this land. Indeed, I can find no reason, but the most deceitful one, for calling the religion of this land Christianity.[38]

With this and other such critiques, blacks rejected the entire system of biblically based slavery and racism. Their understanding of the biblical God as impartial leveled directly and indirectly notions of their "God-ordained" enslavement (the curse of Ham) and inferiority. With and in the Bible they found a great ally in their struggle for freedom and wholeness.

The Pre-Scholarly Assessment of Jesus and the Apostle "Paul"

An assessment of the legacy of Jesus and Paul was not merely an option for enslaved African Americans; it was a necessity. Proslavery advocates constructed an image of Jesus and Paul that made them the pillar of slaveholding Christianity and the post of antebellum Southern values. To promote the docility of slaves, a distorted image of Jesus was gleaned from the Gospels that advocated subordination and willing submission to unmerited suffering. From the spirituals and slave testimony we see a different picture and appreciation of Jesus. Jesus is understood as the heavenly king who delivers humanity from suffering.[39] He is also the human-born Son of God. But in reality statements about God and Christ merge imperceptibly in slave Christology. It was the human Jesus, a man of suffering, with which the slaves could most identify. Yet they were not unaware of his redemption (resurrection) and ultimate vindication. This provided hope for blacks' own desire for redemption and vindication. On this note, James Cone says,

> black folks believed that Jesus could save them from the oppression of slavery because of his death and resurrection. They were deeply moved by the Passion story because they too had been rejected, beaten, and shot without a chance to say a word in defense of their humanity. . . . Through the experience of being slaves, they encountered the theological significance of Jesus' death: through crucifixion, Jesus makes an unqualified identification with the poor and helpless and takes their pain upon himself. . . . For black slaves, Jesus is God breaking into their historical present and transforming it according to divine expectations. Because of the revelation of Jesus Christ, there is no need to worry about the reality of liberation. It is already at hand in Jesus' own person and work, and it will be fully consummated in God's own ordained time.[40]

In this way, it is clear that for blacks Jesus was the ultimate source of their liberation, not the justifier of their oppression. They could identify with him in his humanity, because they saw in him their own predicament and its resolution. This was not, however, the case with Paul.

A portrayal of Paul as seen in the household codes, the Pastoral epistles, and, of course, the story of Philemon supplied the backbone for the construction of the image of the "proslavery Paul." This image created in the likeness of the slave-holding class to support their economic exploitation of black flesh mandated slaves to "obey your masters in everything" (Col. 3:22; cf. Eph. 6:5), while having little to say to masters. According to Clarice Martin, the Paul of proslavery hermeneutics never sought to question the social condition of the slave nor to threaten the privileged status of the master.[41] For this reason, Neil Elliott summarizes a consensus concerning Paul's letters: "The usefulness of the Pauline letters to systems of domination and oppression is . . . clear and palpable."[42] Accordingly, Brian Blount affirms that African American slaves swore out countless corroborations to this testimony. He states: "They found themes so supportive of the slave status quo that many vowed never to listen to Paul preached or, when and if they were so able, never to read Paul for themselves."[43] They believed that Paul religiously took away the freedom God and Jesus had so graciously offered. Amos Jones states further that "they held the apostle in righteous contempt. . . . Blacks in American slavery, though pitifully but understandably illiterate because of the prohibitions placed upon them by the white oppressor, discovered forceful themes of liberation in the Old Testament and New Testament; but they did not find these themes in Paul's writings."[44] The slaves and ex-slaves refused to accept and respect biblical passages that justified their exploitation and humiliation. This means that they did not simply interpret the biblical texts out of their experience; they also critiqued them out of and because of that experience.[45]

Despite the proslavery portrayal of Paul, several blacks developed a more nuanced understanding of him. Rather than outright rejection, they sought instead to "put Paul back together again."[46] Although Paul was used to support slavery and oppression, black abolitionists believed that a different image could be reconstructed to support slavery's abolition and win Paul over for the cause of freedom. Black abolitionists, then, sought to reconstruct Paul by several strategies: (1) use positive statements of Paul against those that were negative to critique slavery's mythological structures; (2) assume a typological correspondence between Paul and the abolitionist; and (3) seek the general "spirit" of Paul. These strategies were used to sustain a hermeneutic of liberation using a reconstructed Paul as a cornerstone. The African Americans' Paul of liberation could be seen most clearly through the egalitarian vision of Gal. 3:28, which provided them with a new principle for understanding God, humanity, and their social situation.

Galatians 3:28 and a New Principle:
"All Persons Are Equal before God"

The social cohesion of every society is based on a set of shared values that find significant expressions in various communal symbols, ideas, rituals, and pronouncements. Those values constitute the paramount cultural paradigm in which the people find their sense of identity and solidarity. More important, however, that root paradigm constitutes the ultimate authority for all moral obligation, legal enactment, social organization, and political association. . . . Further . . . the *black churches have always understood that paradigm to be grounded in the Judeo-Christian understanding of human society*.[47] (emphasis added)

It seems that the enslaved African Americans' encounter with the Christian religion confirmed within them the idea of "the equality of all people before God." Vincent Wimbush, one of the leading voices in African American biblical hermeneutics, in an insightful overview of the use of the Bible in the African American experience, has noted that during the late eighteenth and early nineteenth centuries—the period of the American Revolution and the rise of independent black churches—African Americans sought to institutionalize an ethical and moral principle that stressed the ideal of Christian unity:

African Americans seemed anxious to institutionalize as an ethical and moral principle one of the rare New Testament passages they found attractive and even identified as a *locus classicus* for Christian social teaching—"There is neither Jew nor Greek, there is neither slave nor free, there is neither male nor female; for you are all one in Christ Jesus" (Gal. 3:28). Ironically, this biblical verse stressing the principle of Christian unity was embraced and referred to over and over again as the separate church movements got under way. This and other passages were used to level prophetic judgment against a society that thought of itself as biblical in its foundation and ethic.[48]

Interestingly, despite the classic paradigms of liberation in the Old Testament (in particular, the exodus–promised land saga), they found a small selection of passages from the New Testament that embodied their aim. Wimbush elaborates further in another study:

The historical intent in the dramatic narratives of the Old Testament notwithstanding, there was a certain cluster of passages from the New Testament, especially Galatians 3:26-28 and Acts 2; 10:34-36, that provided the evocative rhetorical and visionary prophetic critique and the hermeneutical foundation for this dominant "mainstream" African

American "reading" of the Bible and American culture. These passages were important on account of their emphasis upon the hope for the realization of the universality of salvation. They were often quoted and paraphrased in efforts to relate them to the racial situation in the U.S. by generations of African Americans—from the famous to the unknown.[49]

To be sure, the passage from Gal. 3:28 and those from Acts[50] were used time and again to level protest against injustices in American religion and society, and to offer an alternative vision to the present state of affairs.[51] These select passages were also important because they confirmed within African Americans the idea of "the equality of all people before God." This idea was seized not only by literate blacks in the North but also by illiterate (and the small minority of literate) slaves in the South. The majority of enslaved blacks, lacking literary skills, were nevertheless exposed initially to the idea of the equality of all people before God in the form of prayers, sermons, and exhortations at camp and revival meetings. Through these means, evangelical Christianity impressed upon both master and slave that they were sinners equally in need of salvation. So impressive was idea of the equality of all people before God that it became African Americans' basic source of authority, and they have been unreservedly committed to this biblical anthropology.[52] According to Peter Paris, who has explored this idea in some detail, this notion represents

> that tradition governed by the principle of non-racism, which [is called] the black Christian tradition. The fundamental principle of the black Christian tradition is depicted most adequately in the biblical doctrine of the parenthood of God and the kinship of all peoples—which is a version of the traditional sexist expression "the fatherhood of God and the brotherhood of men."[53]

The black Christian tradition's most useful function was to give African Americans not only a fundamental principle with which to critique American oppression and society, but more importantly a means of justifying and motivating the endeavors for survival and the social transformation of society. "Thus the black Christian tradition has exercised both priestly and prophetic functions, the former aiding and abetting the race in its capacity to endure the effects of racism, the latter utilizing all available means to effect religious and moral reform in the society at large."[54] In effect, the black Christian tradition posited the most stinging moral and religious dilemma to the souls of white America and Christianity and was born in opposition to that problem. The discovery of this principle revealed to African Americans the contradictions implicit in the religion of white Americans, whose practice of racism and oppression over their fellow human beings contradicted this biblical understanding of humanity. Thus the black Christian tradition used all available means to effect religious and moral reform in the society at large. For this reason the black Christian principle has been employed by oppressed African Americans in their efforts to urge America to live up to its rhetoric of "freedom, liberty, and justice for all." Paris states that the principle of "the equality of all people before God" was so important that "apart from [this] tradition it is doubtful that blacks would have been able to survive the dehumanizing force of chattel slavery and its legacy of racial oppression."[55]

In accordance with their endeavors for survival, African Americans seized this understanding of God and humanity as a revolutionary hermeneutic for understanding scripture, starting with the slaves and continuing into subsequent generations.[56] Moreover, based upon this understanding of God, enslaved African Americans were able to practice a nascent "hermeneutics of suspicion" long before this idea was articulated as a modern hermeneutical method.[57] They were suspicious of whites' interpretation of the Bible and their practice of Christianity, both of which were used to support slavery and racism. Blacks felt so strongly about this notion that they set out to form religious organizations where they could actualize this idea of equality and freedom, even if it could only be realized within the confines of independent black churches. In this way, the principle of the equality of all people before God became institutionalized within the emergent independent black churches.[58] Galatians 3:28 and Acts 2; 10:34-36; and 17:26 provide important biblical authority and rhetorical foci through which this principle could find expression in their political and religious rhetoric for freedom and equality.

This principle of the equality of all people before God served as an arbiter and judge—or better, a balance in which America was weighted and found wanting. The great dilemma for America, and especially for African Americans, was that the United States, which boasted of being a righteous and Christian nation of freedom and liberty, did not practice this central teaching of the religion it espoused.

African American Scholarly Assessments of Jesus and Paul

Like their forbears, African American liberation and womanist theologians and biblical scholars have been compelled to appraise the legacies of Jesus and Paul. Contemporary black thought regarding Jesus is strikingly similar to that of earlier black religious tradition: Jesus is the ultimate liberator. This idea found early theological articulation during the rise of black theology in the United States in Joseph A. Johnson's essay "Jesus the Liberator." Johnson explains,

> The black Jesus is deeply embedded in the black man's experience in this
> country. The black man's introduction to the white Jesus was a catastro-
> phe! . . . The Blacks encountered the American white Christ first on the
> slave ships that brought them to these shores. Blacks on the slave ship
> heard his name sung in hymns of praise while they died chained in
> stinky holes beneath the decks, locked in terror and disease. When
> Blacks leaped from the decks of the slave ships they saw his name carved
> on the side of the ship. When the black women were raped in the cabins
> by white racists, they must have noticed the Holy Bible on the shelves.[59]

In contrast to the white image, both early and contemporary black thought
envisioned a different Christ, or better Jesus who is the liberator of all human
kind, but especially the poor and oppressed:

> The Christians of the first century saw in Jesus, the Liberator, the answer
> to their most distressing problems. Jesus in his ministry identifies him-
> self with all men. . . . The people of all races, because of his service, are
> able to identify with him and to see in his humanity, a reflection of their
> own images. Today the black man looks at Jesus, observes his ministry
> of love and liberation and considers him the black Messiah who fights
> oppression and set captives free.[60]

Jesus is the liberator: this theme is constant within the tradition, and in some
ways Paul's assessment is too.

Some contemporary black biblical scholars and theologians have perceived
almost unequivocal liberating potential in Paul's thought (Jones), while some
have taken a *via media* with respect to the liberating potential of Paul's
thought, recognizing his ambivalence and ambiguity in the matters of class
and sex.[61] Others have viewed Paul's thought, at best, as conservative and useless to the cause of human freedom and hence to be dispensed without further
ado.[62] This modern assessment of Paul is similar to that in the earlier African
American interpretive tradition. In both cases, one has to confront Paul's
ambivalence on the important matters of human freedom and oppression.

On this point, Delores Williams wonders how biblically derived messages
of liberation, especially from the Exodus and Paul, "can be taken seriously by
today's masses of poor, homeless African Americans, female and male, who
consider themselves to be experiencing a form of slavery—economic enslavement by the capitalistic American economy."[63] For Williams, Paul's ambiguity is insurmountable for those today in oppressive situations who need to
hear a clear and unequivocal voice for liberation. While her point is well
taken, the suggestion of Cain Felder must also be considered:

> Does this mean that we simply ignore today those many New Testa-
> ment passages that are patently conservative or, by modern standards,
> repressive on the status of women? Does the Christian in our time seek

only to ascertain the probable stance of Jesus and Paul, discarding the rest of the New Testament? To both questions, the response must be in the negative.[64]

Felder raises a fundamental conceptual issue for our concerns: even if the position of Paul on various issues is unascertainable or unacceptable, his position alone does not determine a particular reading, hearing, or appropriation (regardless of authorial intent). Just like women and slaves in the early church, enslaved Africans gleaned liberating potential from Paul's gospel message, coined especially in Gal. 3:28. To be sure, Paul had an ambiguous stance with respect to Gal. 3:28. But his position alone does not limit the liberating potential of the paradigm. Contemporary African American interpreters of Paul who anguish about Paul's ambiguity may well take note of Callahan's reflections: "In the modulation of activism and accommodation African Americans appreciated with ambivalence, and, rarely, with hostility, Paul's canonical ambiguity. . . . It is this profound ambiguity that black folks have not only appreciated in Paul, but, perhaps, have shared with him."[65] Callahan's statement raises important questions: Has Paul been fairly assessed in the African American religious tradition? Can black churches claim that with respect to the baptismal saying they have fared better than Paul has? A brief examination of the African American religious tradition's track record, as it were, will help us to evaluate its success in upholding the potentially revolutionary baptismal saying.

Galatians 3:28: Where Do Black Churches Stand?[66]

The egalitarian vision of Gal. 3:28 certainly did not escape the attention of African Americans as they combed the scriptures to find biblical support in their quest for freedom and equality. African Americans, faced with the realities of racism and class oppression centuries later, found a biblical statement such as Gal. 3:28 quite appealing. Although African Americans, like the ancient Corinthians, have had to deal with Paul's ambiguity on the social implications of this saying, they did not cast him aside as totally useless. To be sure, the vision of human unity and equality that Gal. 3:28 espoused had enormous impact upon enslaved blacks. Although this apparent fact has been stated and acknowledged by several contemporary African American scholars, theologians, and interpreters of the Bible,[67] no adequate elaboration of the political-religious uses of Gal. 3:28 in African Americans' discourses of unity and equality has been made.[68]

In order to fill this lacuna, in the following overview I explore Gal. 3:28 (and in some instances selected passages from Acts) under three rubrics: issues related to the unity of humanity, issues related to race, and issues related to class (issues related to sex will be taken up in chapter 6). It will be apparent that Gal. 3:28 in some cases can be used in the same breath with one of the kindred passages from Acts. The reason is clear: all of the passages support the central theme of human equality and unity under God. Nevertheless, the use of Gal. 3:28 in African Americans' political-religious discourses, while governed by this general theme, is not by any means monolithic.

Galatians 3:28 and Issues Relating to the Unity of Humanity

The equalitarian vision of Gal. 3:28 provided a powerful means for African Americans to argue for a universalism that included them unequivocally within the human family regardless of their race, class, or social status. God is, they argued, the common "father" and creator of all humanity and shows no partiality among his creation. An ex-slave, G. W. Offley, expressed this reality by claiming "that he learned from his mother and father the potentially revolutionary doctrine 'that God is no respecter of persons, but gave his son to die for all, bond or free, black or white, rich or poor,' and that 'God protects those whom he chooses to sanctify for some task.' "[69] Offley, or the tradition he received, elaborates upon the categories that are relevant to the contemporary situation. The unique aspect of this saying is that it combines two important passages together that were significant elements of the building block for the notion of human equality for African Americans—Gal. 3:28 and Acts 10:34 ("God is no respecter of persons"). First, God's impartiality is addressed. Second, the gospel relates that Jesus' death was "for all," which again underscores God's impartiality. Finally, Offley expresses the categories that are relevant to the American social situation: "bond or free, black or white, rich or poor." Interestingly enough, the statement "neither male and female" is missing! Nevertheless, it would seem that in the same way as in the deutero-Pauline tradition (cf. Col. 3:13), this saying was so versatile that it could be modified to fit various contextualized visions of unity and equality.[70]

Offley's use of this saying combines a trope of Gal. 3:28 in connection with Acts 10:24. However, the Reverend Reverdy C. Ransom, the eloquent and influential bishop of the AME Church from 1924 to 1952, in his sermon "Golden Candlesticks Shall Illuminate Darkest Africa,"[71] emphasizes the unity and equality of humanity through the declaration of Acts 17:26 that all humanity stems from "one blood." Important for him is the connection of the principle of the equality of all people before God with American democratic principles, which are not based upon race, creed, or any other factor. For Ransom the idea of the equality of all people before God has concrete political implications—equal opportunity for all regardless of race, creed, color, or nationality:

> American democracy is founded upon the Bible; its chief cornerstone
> rests upon the fact that God is the common father of all mankind. All
> men are brothers; if brothers, then all men are equal. This is the very
> foundation upon which American democracy stands. Upon this concep-
> tion we have established our American democracy. We do not seek by
> force of arms to dominate the world, but to give equal opportunity and
> freedom to each and all, to achieve without limit of legal handicaps, to
> the extent . . . of their capacity and ability. Our democracy is not based
> upon race, creed, color, wealth, or nationality, but upon cooperation in
> the spirit of brotherhood.[72]

After stating his case for the biblical foundation of American democracy
based upon the notion of the equality of all under God, Ransom alludes to
Acts 17:26 in order to impress upon his hearers the social and political implications of this familiar passage: "God hath made of one blood all peoples to
dwell upon the earth."

> Since all the families of the earth are now one through their daily con-
> tacts upon the land, sea, and the air, they are in a position now to receive
> and accept the "One Blood Doctrine," as a final link in a chain that not
> only reveals the sovereignty of God, but also unites all the peoples of the
> earth by affirmation of the "One Blood Doctrine," which means the
> brotherhood, freedom, and equality of all mankind.[73]

The "one blood doctrine," as Ransom termed it, was another important means
of underscoring the central theme of the unity of humanity, as well as the
equality of all people before God.

Dr. E. C. Morris, in his presidential address before the 42nd Annual Ses-
sion of the National Baptist Convention in St. Louis, in December 1922, clarified further how black Baptists understood and justified their separate
existence and what was at stake:

> We early imbibed the religion of the white man; we believed in it; we
> believe in it now . . . but if that religion does not mean what it says, if
> God did not make of one blood all nations of men to dwell on the face
> of the earth, and if we are not to be counted as a part of that generation,
> by those who handed the oracle down to us, the sooner we abandon
> them or it, the sooner we will find our place in a religious sect in the
> world.[74]

It is important to note that these and countless other expressions reveal that
black Christian communities understood and explained their existence not
through exclusive theological propositions or dogma but chiefly on account of
social—including political, economic, and educational—realities. Black Baptists and Methodists did not bolt from their respective white ecclesiastical

counterparts on account of differences in dogma; those who bolted did so on account of the racism of white Christians.[75]

In Howard Thurman's work we find a further development of the theme of human unity and equality. He takes the theme to its logical conclusion: not only are all physical characteristics insignificant, but all racial, ethnic, cultural, religious, and sex distinctions are eradicated before God. Only the human spirit is important. He says: "It is my belief that in the Presence of God there is neither male nor female, white nor black, Gentile nor Jew, Protestant nor Catholic, Hindu, Buddhist, nor Moslem, but a human spirit stripped to the literal substance of itself before God."[76] Thurman, to his credit, did not delete the aspect of Gal. 3:28 that is related to sex and gender, but placed it first in his elaboration. Thurman was the consummate mystic and philosopher and perceived all seeming physical, religious, or cultural differences as facile. His trope of Gal. 3:28 advanced both traditional and personal themes for him. What is important to him is the human *spirit*: his spiritualizing of the saying fits well with this philosophy and ministerial aspirations. Beneath the guise of corporeal differences lies the true essence of the unity of humanity—the human spirit.

Galatians 3:28 and Issues Relating to Race

Not only did African Americans find it necessary to argue for their inclusion in the human family as free and equal members to be treated with civility and fairness, but they also were forced to address racism and a constellation of arguments for their inferiority. In this cause, too, the egalitarian themes of Gal. 3:28 could find expression in their discourses. Along these lines, J. W. C. Pennington, the black abolitionist and preacher, delivered a speech at Exeter Hall, London, before the British Foreign Anti-Slavery Society on June 21, 1843, in which he evoked Col. 3:11 (already an early modification and elaboration of Gal. 3:28 by a deutero-Pauline author).[77] A variety of participants attended the gathering, since the World's Anti-Slavery Convention had closed in London one day before. Included were "political leaders, a few colonial administrators from the West Indies, and a sprinkling of European anti-slavery activists. The gathering was notable for the 'large party of ladies' present . . . [and] several 'gentlemen of color' attended."[78]

Before an audience so composed, Pennington delivered his ad hoc speech, in which he protested in particular England's sanction of emigration from Africa to the West Indies but in general slavery as a whole.[79] After touching upon the injustice of England's policy, he concluded:

> Though I have a country that has never done me justice, yet I must return to it, and I shall not recriminate. It has pleased God to make me

black and you white, but let us remember, that whatever be our complexion, we are all by nature laboring under the degradation of sin, and
without the grace of God are black at heart. (Hear, hear.) I know of no
difference between the depraved heart of a Briton, an American, or an
African. There is no difference between its colour, its disposition, and its
self-will. There is only one mode of emancipation from the slavery of sin,
from blackness of heart, and that is by the blood of the Son of God.
(Hear, hear.) Whatever be our complexion, whatever our kindred and
people, we need to be emancipated from sin, and to be cleansed from our
pollution by the all-prevailing grace of God. I bless his name, that in
Christ there is neither Jew nor Greek, Barbarian nor Scythian, bond nor
free, but all are one.[80]

Pennington in his conclusion, according to Abraham Smith, "relegates all
persons—whether black or white—to a common bondage of sin and exploits
Gal. 3:28 to support his claim of the common humanity of all persons despite
the societal labels of bond persons and free persons."[81] He also universalizes
the concept of "blackness." While Pennington and his kindred people were
created black in complexion, all of humankind labor under the "blackness of
heart" on account of sin. Although it is unfortunate that Pennington adopts
the pejorative connotation of blackness, as is common in Western culture, he
at least universalizes this notion to all people. It might also have been rhetorically advantageous for him to trope this theme in order to address racial attitudes concerning "blackness" that were prevalent in his day. In this way,
through the lens of Col. 3:11 and its reformulation of Gal. 3:28, he can claim
a common humanity of all people and at the same time covertly attack racist
attitudes about black humanity.

Zilpha Elaw, an early woman preacher of the nineteenth century, used Acts
2 and 17:26 to attack the racist notions of white Christians who "refused to
admit into their seminaries" this bright female of color.

The pride of a white skin is a bauble of great value with many in some
parts of the United States, who readily sacrifice their intelligence to their
prejudices, and possess more knowledge than wisdom. The Almighty
accounts not the black races of man either in the order of nature or spiritual capacity as inferior to the white; for He bestows his Holy Spirit on,
and dwells in them as readily as in persons of whiter complexion: the
Ethiopian eunuch was adopted as a son and heir of God; and when
Ethiopia shall stretch forth her hands unto him [Ps. 68:31], their submission and worship will be graciously accepted. This prejudice was far
less prevalent in that part of the country where I resided in my infancy;
for when a child, I was not prohibited from any school on account of the
colour of my skin. Oh! That men would outgrow their nursery prejudices

and learn that "God hath made of one blood all the nations of men that dwell upon all the face of the earth." Acts xvii.26.[82]

One of the best-known black preaching women during the late nineteenth century, Amanda Berry Smith, won international acclaim as a leader in the Holiness movement. She made a rather unusual appropriation of Gal. 3:28. Born a slave in Long Green, Maryland, on January 23, 1837, she later affiliated with the Sullivan Street AME Church in New York. One Sunday morning in September 1868, however, she attended a predominantly white church and heard the Reverend John Inskip preach about "instantaneous sanctification." On that day, she testified to being sanctified and distinctly heard the words, "There is neither Jew nor Greek, there is neither bond nor free, there is neither male nor female, for ye are all one in Christ Jesus" (Gal. 3:28; KJV). These words took on new meaning for her. For the first time in her life, she confronted her fear of whites. Smith said, "Somehow I always had a fear of white people—that is, I was not afraid of them in the sense of doing me harm . . . but a kind of fear because they were white, and were there, and I was black and was here!"[83] But her new understanding of Gal. 3:28 delivered her from a sense of inferiority.

Florence Spearing Randolph, born in Charleston, South Carolina, on August 9, 1866, was a renowned AME Zion minister, missionary, suffragist, lecturer, organizer, and temperance worker. She would emerge as one of a handful of women affiliated with a mainline black denomination to hold a regular pastorate of a church. In her sermon, "If I Were White,"[84] she speaks out directly against racist attitudes. In this sermon she posits that, if she were white and believed in God, Jesus, and the Bible, she would prove her "true race superiority" by her willingness to live out the principles of the equality of all people under God as delineated in the Bible. This would mean taking up the cause of the oppressed and marginalized. She grounds her attack against racism upon the "one blood" saying of Acts 17:26:

> If I were white and believed in God, in His Son Jesus Christ, and the Holy Bible, I would speak in no uncertain words against Race Prejudice, Hate, Oppression, and Injustice. I would prove my race superiority by my attitude towards minority races; towards oppressed people. I would remember that of one blood God made all nations of men to dwell upon the face of the earth.[85]

In the final analysis, Randolph infers that race really means nothing in the sight of God. All humanity shares a common ancestry. Randolph also offers a challenge to those white Americans who want to claim a racial superiority: if such a thing exists, it would be based upon how one treated those who are oppressed and on the fringes of society, because all are equal before God through a common origin by the plan of God.

Rev. Reverdy Ransom uses several passages from the book of Acts again to address the specific issue of race in his sermon "The Race Problem in a Christian State, 1906." While racism is his theme, he articulates his message through the biblical notion of the equality of all people before God and the kinship of humanity. This for him is the hermeneutical key to interpret all of scripture and Christianity.

> There should be no race problem in a Christian State. When Christianity received its Pentecostal baptism and seal from heaven, it is recorded that, "there were dwelling in Jerusalem Jews, devout men, out of every nation under heaven" [Acts 2:5]. . . . St. Paul, standing in the Areopagus, declared to the Athenians that, "God hath made of one blood all nations of men for to dwell on the face of the earth" [Acts 17:26].
>
> Jesus Christ founded Christianity in the midst of the most bitter and intense antagonisms of race and class. Yet he ignored them all, dealing alike with Jew, Samaritan, Syro-Phoenician, Greek and Roman. . . . God, through the Jew, was educating the world, and laying a moral and spiritual foundation. That foundation was the establishment of the one God idea. Upon this foundation Jesus Christ built the superstructure of "the Fatherhood of God," and its corollary, "The Brotherhood of Man."
>
> The crowning object at which Jesus Christ aimed was, "to break down the middle wall of partition," between man and man, and to take away all the Old Testament laws and ordinances that prevented Jew and Gentile from approaching God on an equal plane. And this He did, "that He might reconcile both unto God in one body by the cross, having slain the enmity thereby, so making peace" [Eph. 2:14-15].[86]

Ransom, like other African Americans, could see in Acts that the theme of human unity and equality was being worked out in the early Christian message and communities. In this text they could see a Paul who was also a liberator, unlike the portrayal of Paul in the Pastorals and the household codes. This Paul, as in the undisputed letters, preached impartiality and equality. Two other points are of note in Ransom's speech. First, he argues that Jesus himself had to contend with the two issues that, according to Ransom, were most pressing in America—race and class. (But Ransom does not see sex as a problem. The issue of the tradition's blindness to sex will be taken up later.) Second, he attributes the ultimate work of Paul in breaking down the division between Jew and Gentile to Jesus! We shall see in our evaluation below that this motif is almost constant within the black religious tradition.

Mary McLeod Bethune, the indefatigable educator and founder of Bethune-Cookman College, touches upon this well-established theme of the equality of all people before God in her argument against racism and its accompanying evil—black inferiority. In recounting her early childhood realization of self-worth, she relates the account of her teacher who read to her of

God's love from John 3:16. In recounting her moment of enlightenment she tropes Acts 9 and Paul's "Damascus Road experience."[87] In this same narrative, she also tropes Gal. 3:28 when, in her moment of self-discovery, she realizes that "[her] sense of inferiority, [and her] fear of handicaps, dropped away."[88] It was the phrase "whosoever . . ." through which she saw herself joined to a common humanity through God's love that ignited her determination and passion: "'Whosoever,' it said. No Jew nor Gentile, no Catholic nor Protestant, no black nor white; just 'whosoever.' It meant that I, a humble Negro girl, had just as much chance as anybody in the sight and love of God. These words stored up a battery of faith and confidence and determination in my heart."[89] Like those before her, Bethune sought to validate her aspirations for self-realization and equal opportunity through the essential principle of human equality under God, using Gal. 3:28 as the focal point. Although she does not include the "neither male and female" reference so important for black women's arguments for preaching and pulpit ministry, it can be inferred through her reference to herself, "a humble Negro girl," who had not even reached womanhood but "had just as much chance as any body" in God's sight. Thus, like Pennington, Ransom, and Randolph, Bethune also combats racist notions using the vision of human unity and equality as espoused in Gal. 3:28.

Galatians 3:28 and Issues Relating to Class

Enslaved blacks were not convinced that it was God's will for them to be slaves, no matter what the Bible, their masters, or proslavery preachers told them. This point can be most adequately depicted in a now commonly related incident that Charles Colcock Jones, the white Presbyterian plantation missionary mentioned above, recalled in his memoirs. Describing a sermon he gave before a slave congregation in 1833, he wrote:

> I was preaching to a large congregation on the Epistle of Philemon: and when I insisted upon fidelity and obedience as Christian virtues in servants and upon the authority of Paul, condemned the practice of running away, one half of my audience deliberately rose up and walked off with themselves, and those that remained looked anything but satisfied, either with the preacher or his doctrine. After dismission, there was no small stir among them; some solemnly declared "that there was no such an Epistle in the Bible"; others, "that they did not care if they ever heard me preach again." . . . There were some too, who had strong objections against me as a Preacher, because I was a master, and said, "his people have to work as well as we."[90]

This incident reveals that blacks did not and could not accept as "word of God" any scripture that upheld their oppression in any way. "Slaves distinguished the hypocritical religion of their masters from true Christianity and rejected the slaveholder's gospel of obedience to master and mistress."[91] Because of this they would eventually set out to form religious organizations in which they could actualize freedom, even if only in the confines of the churches.

Other whites found out too that a gospel of obedience to earthly master and mistress did not go over well with enslaved Africans, no matter how much "biblical" or "Pauline" authority was mixed in with it. An ex-slave, Lunsford Lane, recounted an incident in which a white clergyman who was favored by the slaves made the mistake of preaching a sermon in which he argued from the Bible that it was the will of God from eternity that blacks should be the slaves of whites. Despite their fondness for him, many left him without a word or question.[92] Other blacks believed that there existed somewhere a real Bible from God, because they were convinced that the Bible used by the master was *his* Bible, "since all they heard from it was 'Servants, obey your masters.'"[93]

Blacks were using the fundamental principle of the equality of all people before God or the "gospel of equality" as a hermeneutical method to understand scripture. They knew that the God of justice, peace, deliverance, and freedom could not be in agreement with their brutal sufferings regardless of what white preachers claimed that the Bible said. Their hermeneutic was based in their existential reality: even if the scripture said, "Slaves, obey your masters," it could not be the "word of God" because it justified the suffering of human beings, which challenged the very essence of the Godhead as righteous and just. Thus the black Christian tradition served not only to inspire independent congregations but also to challenge America to repent from its unjust practices. As far as the black churches were concerned, race and class oppression was evil and against the will of God.

In due time, Marxist and socialist thought began to influence the African American consciousness and surfaced in their political-religious discourse in the early decades of the twentieth century.[94] A small cadre of African Americans believed that the idea of a classless society was one solution to American racism and classism. Even socialist idealism could be bolstered by reference to Gal. 3:28. I turn again to Rev. Reverdy Ransom. In his speech "The Paraclete of God the Only Hope for Brotherhood and Peace,"[95] he argues that since all humanity is the creation of God, they should be free not only to marry whom they please, but also to have access to the freedoms outlined in the Declaration of Independence. The problem has been that America has not lived up to the principle of the equality of all people under God as outlined in its charter document and in the biblical account of creation, which declares that all humanity is created in the image of God (Gen. 1:27). Therefore, "the progress of African Americans in the United States is necessary in order to bring about the truth of the declaration and its connection to Scripture."[96]

In its ancient context Gal. 3:28 represented the Hellenistic Jewish missionary vision that embraced certain traditional ideals of Greco-Roman society. Religious and social visions merge. The same is the case in the African American situation: the vision of Gal. 3:28 merges with American idealism expressed in the Declaration of Independence. On the idea of a common human origin in creation and its connection with the Declaration of Independence, Ransom says,

> From the marriage of one man to one woman stem families, tribes, nations, states, and empires. But these do not invalidate the fact that "all men are created equal," equal in the sense of having a common origin and fatherhood by the creative act of God. There is but one race, the human race. It follows then, there can be no such thing as "mixed marriages." More than that, they are endowed with certain unalienable rights, among which are "life, liberty and the pursuit of happiness." Thomas Jefferson was inspired in his choice of words when he said, "created equal." This was an act of the Creator—God. Now this does not mean equal in the sense of equally wise, equally endowed or equally powerful and resourceful.[97]

Interestingly, he has to clarify what he means by "created equal." He clarifies this point above in the negative, by explaining what he feels equality is not—not equally wise, endowed, powerful, or resourceful. What he means positively by "created equal" is the freedom to pursue life, liberty, and happiness without the restrictions of laws and customs that unduly thwart these "God-given" pursuits. Ransom alludes to Gal. 3:28 to underscore the idea in terms of a classless society. He declares:

> Our chief weapon is that we have here in America a "classless" society. There is neither Jew, Gentile, white, black, consumer, producer, farmer, labor, or capitalist but because he is a man and possesses the personal God-given integrity of each free man in the American "classless" society.
>
> For added emphasis I declare that God created all men free to develop, achieve, and pursue any line of human activity [they] may desire. No human law is valid that seeks to divide or to segregate mankind into "classes," "minority groups," "labor," "industry," "white," or "black."[98]

Ransom recasts Gal. 3:28 to reflect the themes of socialism: "neither . . . consumer, producer, farmer, labor, or capitalist" but also to reflect that of a race conscious society: "neither . . . 'white' [nor] 'black.'" These points emphasize that "Ransom's reading of the world was class- and race-specific."[99] To be sure, while he seeks to emphasize the issue of classism, class and race have always been unified partners in the American socio-religious and political contexts. This reality has been equally true for racism and sexism, as we shall see; African American women in particular employ Gal. 3:28 in their arguments for equality and open access within the church and larger society for all people regardless of sex.

A Summary Evaluation of African Americans' Use of Galatians 3:28

This survey of African Americans' writings reveals a telling trend and a curious motif: *rarely do the African American writers refer to Paul as the author of Gal. 3:28, and in other cases, liberative motifs in Paul's letters are squarely attributed to Jesus.* Galatians 3:28 or some other liberating theme in Paul can be quoted, alluded to, or paraphrased—but seldom with ascription to Paul. I discovered no introductory formula such as, "according to the apostle," "as Paul says," "as Paul says in his letter to . . . ," or even, "as it says in Galatians." The passage or saying can, however, be ascribed to God or Jesus or the scriptures in general. Why might this have been the case? I suspect that there was some tension with Paul vis-à-vis the proslavery and racist portrayal and construction of Paul. In order to appropriate liberative paradigms and motifs in Paul as useful, Pauline authorship and authority had to be wrested from Paul and alternatively ascribed to God, Jesus, or scripture. This meant that the paradigm of Gal. 3:28 and other liberative themes could be appropriated without addressing the issues or problems related to Paul's negative injunctions or proslavery portrayals of Paul. Another reason may be that they perceived such liberating themes as coming directly from God in the first place.

Thus in their quest for freedom from slavery and in their hermeneutic of liberation, the early African American religious tradition—whether of free blacks, slaves, or subsequent generations—were able to use the liberative vision of Gal. 3:28 to support the fundamental principle of "the equality of all people before God" or the "gospel of equality" as a hermeneutical key to understand both scripture and their social situation. They also used it as a rhetorical strategy in their discourses against racism and classism (and sexism) and to argue for an inclusiveness and universality that embraced them also within the human family. A critique of sexism in the African American churches, however, has not yet fully benefited from this tradition; but this question must be bracketed for the moment.

In terms of the baptismal saying, then, it is clear that the most important aspects for African Americans historically have been "no longer Jew or Greek, . . . slave or free," that is, issues related to *race* and *class* (their status as slaves and "second class" citizens). This has been evident in their religious and political history. For it was from the crucible of racial injustice and class oppression (slavery) that independent black congregations arose to institutionalize a nonracist and nonclassist appropriation of the Christian faith as they had come to know it.

The Rise of Independent Black Churches
and Other Institutions of Resistance

The independent church movement among blacks, during and following the period of the Revolutionary War, must be regarded as the prime expression of resistance to slavery. It was in every sense the first freedom movement, a form of rebellion against the most accessible and institutional racism in the nation: the American churches.[100]

The Rise of Independent Black Churches

America's practice of racial oppression through the institution of slavery and Jim Crow pervaded every aspect of its society and its social institutions, including the churches. This is not surprising, since the church in all ages and in every culture in which it took root has tended to support the status quo. The white church in America was no different. Not only did the enslavement and oppression of Africans forcefully taken from their homeland have the support of the church, but many preachers and theologians of the church put the stamp of divine approval on the institution of slavery by employing theological and scriptural manipulations. The ideology of the day even questioned whether the Africans were indeed human or even had souls in need of salvation. This debate lasted for some time, but it was finally resolved, and efforts to convert the enslaved Africans began. They were human beings but of a presumed physiologically and sociologically inferior status to that of whites.

The purported inferior status of enslaved Africans was reflected in church services wherein blacks and whites worshiped together. "During the eighteenth century there were more black and white Christians worshiping in the same congregations, proportionate to their numbers as baptized Christians, than there are today."[101] This is not to imply, however, that the churches were egalitarian and both blacks and whites shared equally of ecclesiastical opportunities. It did not occur to many white Christians that the equality of human beings inherent in the gospel, which was denied to their African brothers and sisters in civil society, should at least be made available to them within the church. Indeed, the fact remained that the church sustained the status quo, and "the relationship pattern of whites and blacks in the household of God made it difficult for Americans to perceive that there was anything wrong with inequity in the household of Caesar."[102]

The inequality in the household of God is what led may blacks to form independent congregations in the latter decades of the eighteenth and beginning of the nineteenth centuries. In this respect, they functioned as nonracist institutions, that is, they were formed as institutions given to the principle of human equality, regardless of one's race. Thus this reaction to racism "had the advantage of being carried on under the cloak of ecclesiastical affairs rather than as an affair of the state or the economy."[103] The establishment of independent black congregations was carried on in the North as well as the South, in cities and on plantations, by free as well as enslaved blacks.

It is important to note that reaction to racism is not the only cause for the rise of independent black churches. Just as the children of Israel requested of Pharaoh an opportunity to worship their God freely in the desert, so too the enslaved Africans desired a place where they would have their own space and the freedom to pray, praise, and dance according to the dictates of their own hearts. "The movement, therefore, could [also] pass as representing the more or less legitimate desire of the slaves to have 'a place of their own in which to worship God.'"[104]

Finally, a probable subconscious reason for the rise of independent black congregations was perhaps the basic human desire for autonomy. The slaves desired ultimate freedom, but this was not realistically accessible to them at the time. The church, however, could offer an adequate substitute for the time being, and history has shown that no better institution in America could have been chosen. The engagement of the Bible and its powerful imagery and symbols sustained the enslaved Africans' conviction that the argument proffered by their oppressors that God ordained their enslavement was a lie. "And they knew too that whatever could be done by black preachers to hasten the demise of slavery—whether in the open pulpit or in secret— was a part of their commitment to the ministry."[105] Consequently the black church became a religious, social, and protest institution, serving the various needs of an oppressed people.

The Rise of Resistance Institutions to Combat Slavery and Racism

While perhaps the first institutions of resistance, the churches were not the only ones that claimed the allegiance of blacks. Two other institutions served to advance their cause, the abolitionist movement and later the National Association for the Advancement of Colored People (NAACP). Both of these "institutions" were integrated in leadership (to some degree) and operation. The beginning of abolitionist sentiment can be said to have emerged in 1688 in Germantown, Pennsylvania, when Quakers raised their famous questions against slavery.[106] This was only the start of a movement against slavery that would even involve English abolitionists. Many free blacks and black ex-slaves participated in and gave voice to this movement, which came to an end after the Civil War in 1865, putting an end to the question of slavery or class as such. The NAACP was the next institution to emerge to address the practice of racism and Jim Crow social and political policies. Organized in 1909 and 1910, the NAACP would become the dominant protest organization prior to the outbreak of the Civil Rights Movement of the 50s and 60s.[107] Thus there have been institutions beside the churches that have protested against classism and racism, and they had the support of the churches. When, however, have black churches supported institutions to combat sexism? The evidence on this issue is nil: the black churches as a whole have not found it within their orbit to lend similar support to movements or organizations to address sexism. This is most certainly due to their own misunderstanding and partial appreciation of the principle of the equality of all people before God. A new appreciation of this principle, we can hope, might generate different results.

Conclusion

The commitment to the struggle for freedom and equality was at the molecular level, as it were, of the black religious tradition and churches. Their reaction against racism, the desire to worship freely, and the desire of their members to have some autonomy as human beings led the black churches to adopt a nonracist and nonclassist ideology as their foundational principle. All people are equal before God, they held, and as such should not be unjustly treated on the basis of the color of their skin.

Enslaved African Americans and subsequent generations appropriated this understanding of God and humanity. As far as African Americans were concerned, race and class oppression were evil and against the will of God. What the African American religious tradition has never done is to apply this very same principle to a consistent analysis of sexism. This is where African American religious tradition has failed in the actualization of Gal. 3:28, for, like Paul, it too has had a limited agenda that has neglected to address fully the concerns of women (the "no longer male and female" aspect of Gal. 3:28). In the following chapter I examine how this neglect has produced a history of black patriarchy and male chauvinism. Yet African American women have found the means to resist and carve out an alternative vision of human wholeness that could include them wholly within its purview.

❧ 4 ❧
Pulpit, Power, and Prohibitions

We [black women] are the slaves of slaves; we are exploited more ruthlessly than men.[1]

Subordination and subservience were evident problems, but not silence, isolation, and exclusion.[2]

The "proper" place of women in the church is an age-old debate and from all appearances, it seems that it perhaps will be an eternal one—for most mortals at least. This is because too often humanity has looked to the misty heights of theory rather than the lowly foothills of practice and necessary human service.[3]

The previous chapter charted the African American political and religious protest tradition against racism and classism. This tradition, supported by the concept of the equality of all people before God, has been at the root of African American religious experience. As such, this tradition had the potential to influence the African American churches' views regarding gender equality. When it came to the issue of church order and the roles of men and women in the church and society, however, black male church leaders adopted and instituted the patriarchal order of the white church and its reading of the Bible.

This should not surprise us. The patriarchal domination of men over women, children, and other forms of *property* was not peculiar to American (or European) society: "Black male sexism existed long before American slavery. The sexist politics of white-ruled and colonized America merely reinforced in the minds of enslaved black people existing beliefs that men were the superiors of women."[4] The problem, however, was that this social order was oppressive and contradicted the principles upon which the black churches were founded. Apparently this escaped the notice of many black men (and black women too), but it must be considered that American racism was the primary issue and that the patriarchal social order was just taken for granted. What this affirmed was that "men of all races in America [could] bond on the basis of their common belief that a patriarchal social order is the only viable foundation for society."[5]

The patriarchal social order of America and the church subjugated women into the rigid and limited roles of homemaker, wife, and mother. The home and the rearing of children was their primary function, and for them to attempt to enter the domain of males—the public domain—was a threat to their reputations as "good" wives and mothers. In the church this amounted to certain roles and duties, which were extensions of their motherly and wifely duties, namely, nurturing, cooking, and cleaning. They were allowed to lead prayer or sing but only in very rare instances to preach or administer the ordinances (or sacraments) of the church, for this would threaten the domain of male power and authority. Women of color did much, even in their proscribed gender roles, to advance the mission and increase the growth of black churches. The recognition of these valiant efforts caused many to acknowledge that black "women are the backbone of the church."

The truth of the matter, as Theresa Hoover realized, was that black women were not only the backbone but also

> truly the glue that held the churches together. The women worked, yet found time to be Sunday School teachers, sing in the choir, and support the church's program in every way. The women found time and energy to be active in the women's missionary societies and to serve as counselors or sponsors for the youth group. . . . The church was their "home away from home," the social orbit in which they met the right people.[6]

Women performed these functions and could have done more in leadership positions had they been given the opportunity. The work that they did, however, bespeaks the leadership and organizational capabilities of many women. Yet, they rarely had any voice in decision-making processes in many mainline churches.

In response to this state of affairs Jacquelyn Grant provides an insightful addendum to Hoover's statement about women as the backbone of the church. Grant discovered that

> on the surface this may appear to be a compliment, especially when one considers the function of the backbone in the human anatomy. . . . In any case, the telling portion of the word backbone is "back." It has become apparent to me that most of the ministers who use this term have reference to location rather that function. What they really mean is that women are in the "background" and should be kept there. They are merely support workers.[7]

The truth of Grant's statement cannot be denied. The facts of history and indeed the present state of affairs in many black churches support her statement. While black women have been the backbone of the church, they have remained in the background in many instances. While they are permitted to do the manual labor, men do the "thinking" for the church and make the decisions related to its program. The inequity of such a policy is that "women are consistently given responsibilities in the kitchen, while men are elected or appointed to the important boards and leadership positions. While decisions and policies may be discussed in the kitchen, they are certainly not made there."[8] Decision-making in the church is the black male's domain. In fact, the black church itself has functioned historically as the only place where black males could actualize their "manhood."

Black Churches and the Struggle for Black "Manhood" in a Racist Society

To say that *the* black church has functioned as the black male's domain and the place where he could actualize the "manhood" that was so long denied him needs some qualification. First, Gilkes with her usual insight reminds us that at present

> the distorted images of African-American women's professional and economic successes provide further fuel to many men's belief that the ministry is still the only place where African-American men have access to influence and authority. As a result, resistance to women's ordination is still quite fierce among many African-American ministers.[9]

Second, qualification is needed "because 'the church' is still in a certain sense 'the people.'"[10] As a result of the elimination of blacks historically from the political and social life of the American mainstream community, the black church became the arena of their political and most of their social activities.[11] Both black men and black women found in the church "the social life where ambitious individuals could achieve distinction and the symbol of status."[12] C. Eric Lincoln succinctly expresses the "universal" significance of the black church for the entire black community. As he says, "the Black church . . . is in some sense a 'universal church,' claiming and representing all Blacks out of a tradition that looks back to the time when there was only the Black church to bear witness to 'who' and 'what' a man was as he stood at the bar of his community."[13] I am certain that Lincoln would want to include women in this assessment of the universal significance of the black church, although he uses gender-specific language. Insofar as the church functioned as a place of community, an opportunity for status, and a place where the lust for power could be satisfied, to a certain degree, women were included in these processes. But the church was a place where the struggle for power *as men* was especially important for black men "who had never been able to assert themselves and assume the dominant male role, even in family relations, as defined by American culture."[14] Consider the statement of two black Southern women in the 1960s:

> [Woman one] Here the church is all a man's domain and the women really don't have much to say. They do a lot of the work, they cook for picnics and socials, and they raise the most money and they kind of keep the church going, but when you get to policy, the men have it all tied up. They don't want a woman in any kind of power.
>
> [Woman two] Well, for one thing that [the church] is the only place a colored man can be strong. He doesn't have any power, any place else. This movement [civil rights movement] is changing things but it will be many a year before you see a colored man with influence, generally speaking, in this world. So he'll swing it all into the church where he can order all the people around and put down the law the way he wants.[15]

To this extent, the black church became the domain of the black male's quest for manhood, status, and power. The black church was an institution, and black men could enjoy this "power" so long as it offered no threat to the racial status quo in economic and social relations. On the whole, the black church was not a threat to white domination, and it assisted blacks' accommodation to an inferior status prior to the Civil Rights Movement. Before this time (and beyond) the church also assisted in the maintenance of sexism.

The Civil War and emancipation destroyed whatever stability and order had developed among blacks under the slave regime.[16] The emphasis on the sexist definition of the male role as protector of and provider for his wife and children caused many problems for black males. The damaging impact of slavery and racism was that black males in particular were not allowed to assume the traditional role that was held as the norm for all males.[17] Therefore, it could be argued that,

> in a sense, Black men's acceptance of the patriarchal model is logical and to be expected. Black male slaves were unable to reap the benefits of patriarchy. Before emancipation they were not given the opportunity to serve as protector and provider for black women and children, as white men were able to do for their women and children. Much of what was considered "manhood" had to do with how well one performed these functions.[18]

It seems only natural, then, that postemancipation black men would consider as primary importance the reclaiming of their *property*—their women and their children. "Moreover, it is natural that Black men would claim their 'natural' right to the 'man's world.'"[19]

This process began early on with the fusion of the "invisible institution" of slave religion and the institutional church that had grown up among the blacks who were free before the Civil War. The most obvious result of this merger was the rapid growth of the black church. Another much more important result was the structuring and organization of black life to an unprecedented extent. According to Frazier,

> this becomes clear when we recall that organized social life among the transplanted Negroes had been destroyed by slavery. . . . Among the slaves themselves one may note the germs of stratification based upon their different roles in the plantation, but no system of stratification ever came into existence that became the basis of an organized social existence. . . . This was all changed when the Negro became free, and . . . an organized religious life became the chief means by which a structured or organized social life came into existence among the Negro masses. The process by which the "invisible institution" of the slaves merged with the institutional churches built by the free Negroes had to overcome many difficulties.[20]

Despite the difficulties, the integration of the "invisible institution" into the mainline black church organization established by the free blacks provided an organization and structuring of black life that had enormous implications. A critical situation confronted black churches after emancipation. According to Frazier, under slavery the black family was essentially an amorphous group gathered around the mother or some other female on the plantation. The father was a visitor to the household without any legal or recognized status in family relations. In these circumstances, sexual relations under the slave regime were constantly under the supervision of the whites. While Frazier's assessment of slave family life as solely headed by women has been clarified and corrected by later scholars, his point that sex relations between blacks was highly monitored remains.

The removal of the authority of masters as the result of the Civil War and emancipation made it necessary for the church to step in and assume the role of governing and maintaining order and control of black life. The problem of creating a stable family life was one of the most vexing challenges that confronted northern white missionaries and free blacks in the North who undertook the task of assisting the newly liberated blacks in adjusting to their new status. These missionaries and free blacks undertook to legalize and formalize the marriages that were informally established under slavery. In accomplishing these goals, the church served as the primary agency of social control over the ideology of the black family and sexual life during the years following emancipation.

Certain role changes took place after emancipation that placed larger responsibility upon the black male than was the case under the slave regime.

New economic conditions tended to place the black man in a position of authority in family relations. Free black males refused to work in gangs as they had done during slavery; instead, a man, with his wife and children, would rent and operate a farm on his own account. In this new system of sharecropping, a man of the family was required to sign the rent or work agreements. Sometimes wives were also required to sign, but the husband or father was always held responsible for the behavior of his family. Certain individuals among freed blacks who had been in a position to assimilate the sentiments and ideas of their former masters soon undertook to buy land. This new situation gave the man an interest in his wife and children, a responsibility that was supported by black preachers and white missionaries. It is important to recognize the extent to which the new economic position of the man was affirmed by the moral support of the black church.[21]

Black churches, in fact, served to integrate the black family into the Western patriarchal norm, using the Bible as validation.[22] Moral support for a patriarchal family structure could also be found in the Bible (especially Genesis 2–3 and the household codes), which conferred divine sanction on the new authority of the black man in the family. However, there were more important ways in which the black church gave support to black family life with the father in a position of authority. As stated above, after emancipation the newly freed slaves had to create a new communal life or become integrated into existing communities created by the blacks who were free before the Civil War. This integration resulted in the expansion and complete transformation of these communities. The leaders in creating a new community life were men who with their families worked the land or began to buy land or worked as skilled artisans. These pioneers, many of whom were preachers, generally built churches as well as homes, gathering their communicants about them. There was a close relationship between the newly structured life of blacks and church organizations.[23] It must also be kept in mind that the control in black churches was exercised by dominating personalities. In many cases they were preachers who had become leaders of black communities because of their talents and ability to govern and organize. They were self-motivated men who found in the Baptist and Methodist churches, in which the majority of the blacks were concentrated, great opportunity for self-assertion and the assumption of leadership. This naturally resulted in a pattern of autocratic leadership that spilled over into most aspects of organized black religious and social life, "especially in as much as many forms of organized social life have grown out of the church and have come under the dominant leadership of [black] preachers."[24]

Because of the elimination of blacks from the political life of the larger American community, the church was the main arena of political life in which blacks could aspire to become leaders. The church was the place where the struggle for power and the thirst for power could be satisfied. This was especially important to black men, who had never been able to assert themselves and become dominant in politics or assume the traditional male role even in family relations, as defined by American culture. In the Baptist churches, with their democratic local autonomy, individual preachers could rule their churches in an arbitrary manner, while the leaders in the hierarchy of the various Methodist denominations (AME and AME Zion), which had episcopal governance, exercised almost absolute authority. Moreover, the monetary rewards that went with this power and control were quite considerable when the contributions of millions of blacks and the various business activities of the churches are taken into account.[25]

Thus, for black men in America the church was usually the most viable access into a man's world, and in the church they found limited fulfillment. But it came at the expense of gender inequality. The highest place of authority and prestige in the Protestant black church ministry, that of preacher and pastor, was denied to women. Moreover, many black males found great status and acclaim through preaching the word of God. The "Black Fathers of Preaching"[26] advanced the cause and mission of the church through their eloquent oratory, and we must not forget that deacons and trustees have wielded a powerful sway in black churches too. The need to restrict these roles to males alone by appeal to custom and scripture attests to the notion that these positions carried power and authority.

An important parallel now emerges between the early Christian churches and African American churches. Faced with new and difficult challenges of northern migration, pervasive racist repression, and the need for ecclesiastical maintenance, Paul's letters (especially the deutero-Paulines, the Pastorals) and legacy, along with the household codes, receive a second life, that is, a new assessment and appreciation in black churches. As in the early church these texts are used in the process of institution building. Black churches, like early Christian churches, required a source or body of writings that could serve as a model for its institutional endeavors. In addition, black churches were also trying to make a favorable showing to those on the outside (cf. 1 Tim. 3:7; 1 Pet. 2:12). While there were egalitarian trends in early Christianity and in the early black religious tradition that the black church could have appropriated, they instead opted for a patriarchal model for their ecclesiastical structure; authority in the church and family rested squarely within the domain of males.

Women in the preaching and pastoral ministries can still be a problem for some men. It is a threat to a hard-won status and to who they are as black males, as men. Black women who claim rights to the preaching and pastoral ministry are encroaching on the sphere of the black male's place of power in the church. The man is the God-appointed head of the family and the pastor the God-appointed leader of the church. This notion of God-ordained authority for the male leader of the church means that

> the preacher in the black church *is* more directive, authoritarian, and singular in his administration. The degree to which he uses his position selfishly marks the amount of personal privilege and reward he enjoys at the expense of a "not so well endowed" membership—the majority of which are women.[27]

The traditional black preacher thus enjoyed his privileged status at the expense of his primarily female support base.

Thus the struggle over women in the pulpit is not just a biblical issue but is deeply rooted in the black male's identity as a man—and not just any man, but as a black man whose identity the dominant culture has so often defined. The autonomy of black churches, however, gave black men an opportunity to redefine their manhood on their own terms—or did it? It seems that instead of redefining manhood based upon certain egalitarian trends within slave culture, black males opted for the patriarchal pattern of their white counterparts. This pattern spawned a history of black patriarchy in the church and society.

Patriarchal Foundations of African American Male Sexism: The Return of Black Manhood

African American religious and social history has been until recently profoundly patriarchal.[28] Black male scholars have accepted the sexist framework of American white history. Their research on the black church dealt primarily with the leadership of the church, which has traditionally been male. Moreover, the scholarly reconstruction of the African American religious past has too long overlooked black women. There may be general references to "outstanding women" who made some special contribution to the development of the church or the liberation of the "black man." But these token gestures show the pervasiveness of sexism in American culture. From the dawn of the slave trade until today, American society has been both racist and deeply sexist. The exploitation of black women has become a constant feature of American social and economic life, because they are assaulted simultaneously as workers, as blacks, and as women (triple oppression again, only now "worker" is the new designation for "slave"). This triple oppression continues to escape many black males entirely.[29]

To understand adequately the religious and social history of all African Americans in the United States, more work is required in documenting the particular struggles, concerns, ideals, and attitudes of black women. Black male historians, cultural critics, ethicists, liberation theologians, and biblical scholars must relearn their own history by grounding themselves and their methodologies in the wisdom and experience of their sisters.[30]

African American Men and Women under the Slave Regime

"During the entire slave period in the U.S. a brutal kind of equality was thrust upon both sexes. This process was dictated by the conditions of slave production within the overall process of capital accumulation in the South."[31] Black women working in the fields on cotton plantations were expected to pick just as much cotton as a man, bending their backs just like their sons, husbands, and fathers. In such a system the black man was not afforded even the appearance of a privileged situation with respect to the black woman. The authoritarian nature of slavery, with the white slaveowner exercising physical violence and intimidation to maintain social and political hegemony, allowed no notion of a black family provider or black head of household. The system of slavery depended upon the exploitation of the productive capacities of the entire enslaved population—men, women, and children. For this reason the black woman was completely integrated into the production force.[32]

To be sure, the special character of domestic labor during slavery involved work that was not exclusively female. Angela Davis elaborates:

> Slave men executed important domestic responsibilities and were not, therefore . . . the mere helpmates of their women. For while women cooked and sewed, for example, men did the gardening and hunting. (Yams, corn and other vegetables, as well as wild animals such as rabbits and opossums, were always a delicious addition to the monotonous daily rations.) This sexual division of domestic labor does not appear to have been hierarchical: men's tasks were certainly not superior to and were hardly inferior to the work performed by women. They were both equally necessary. Moreover, from all indications, the division of labor between the sexes was not always so rigorous, for men would sometimes work in the cabin and women might tend the garden and perhaps even join the hunt.[33]

It would seem then that what emerges from the their labor and domestic life in the slave quarters was a kind of *sexual equality*. The labor that slaves performed for their own sake and not for the benefit of their masters was also carried out on terms of equality. This is of particular note because within the confines of their family and community life, black people managed to accomplish a magnificent feat: "they transformed that negative equality which emanated from the equal oppression they suffered as slaves into a positive quality: the egalitarianism characterizing their social relations."[34] Since black women bore the weighty burden of equality in oppression, enjoyed equality with their men in their domestic environment, and also aggressively asserted their equality in challenging the inhuman institution of slavery, logic would dictate that this equality should extend to the religious realm. Early on it did, but this was later curtailed.

One of the greatest ironies of American slavery was that, in subjecting women to its ruthless exploitative system, a system that knew no gender distinctions, the groundwork was created not only for black women to assert their equality through their social relations but also to express it through acts of resistance. Slaveowners must have been aware of this, for it appears that they were attempting to sever the cord of equality through a special repression reserved for black women—rape. Raping black women was a violent ritual that paralleled the harsh political realities of slave agricultural production, not unlike plowing up fertile ground. Again, in Davis's analysis:

> In its political contours, the rape of the Black woman was not exclusively an attack upon her. Indirectly, its target was also the slave community as a whole. . . . In launching the sexual war on the woman, the master could not only assert his sovereignty over a critically important figure of the slave community, he would also be aiming a blow against the Black man. . . . Clearly the master hoped that once the Black man was struck by his manifest inability to rescue his woman from sexual assaults of the master, he would begin to experience deep-seated doubts about his ability to resist at all.[35]

Thus, the slavemaster and overseers made it clear that the slave woman and man could be equal in labor, but the slave woman had reserved for her an additional form of exploitation from which the black man could offer no protection (although some tried). Nevertheless, in the slave community there was laid the foundation for a system of relations that could be grounded in the promise of an egalitarian social and religious praxis. In this praxis there was an alternative paradigm to that of their oppressors.

Churches of Free Blacks, Post-Reconstruction, and Early-Twentieth-Century Political-Religious Activism

The black churches in free states in the North were involved in a variety of protest and reform activities, from the creation of economic enterprises and abolitionist activities to the building of a network of black schools. But black men ultimately dominated and led the churches, serving in the primary offices of the church—as pastors, evangelists, and deacons. On this account, the attainment of independence, leadership, and self-assertion is the attainment of "black manhood." William H. Becker, in his article "The Black Church: Manhood and Mission," argues that *manhood* is an important term in the independent black church tradition. He suggests that the concept and model of manhood was "one of the most important contributions, over the years, to the cause of black liberation. These models are delineated in the biographies, sermons, histories, and conference minutes of black churches, and are manifested in the lives and work of significant black churchmen."[36] Becker's article, which originally appeared in 1972, provides a very positive assessment of attaining black "manhood." To a certain extent, the independent and self-assertive *males* in the churches and on the churches' behalf accomplished much. Becker was correct that "the definition and assertion of black manhood has been a conscious motive and dominant theme throughout the history of the black church."[37] But the other half of the story goes untold again.

Already in 1816, Bishop B. W. Arnett could describe the organizing conference of the AME church as "the Convention of the Friends of Manhood Christianity."[38] Bishop Daniel Alexander Payne, one of the premier historical embodiments of black manhood, felt that the AME's separation from white control into an independent entity supplied the foundation for "our individuality and our heaven-created manhood."[39] Even in his seventies, when confronted with the prospect of riding in a segregated train, he chose to disembark, stating, "Before I'll dishonor my manhood by going into that car, stop your train and put me off."[40] The mission to redeem Africa was also imbued with manhood notions. S. F. Flegler, a pastor who led a group of thirty AME churchmen settlers to Liberia in 1878, delivered a statement in which he argued that "God Almighty never made a soul with more elements of manhood than mine; and I thank God there is sufficient African blood in me to thrill me with aspirations of manhood."[41] No one was more outspoken or noteworthy than the AME Bishop Henry McNeal Turner. He advocated not only mission to Africa but also mass migration to Africa, because he was convinced that black folks would never achieve full respect and rights in racist America. Turner therefore concluded (emphasis in the original): "*There is no manhood future in the United States for the Negro. He may eke out an existence for generations to come, but he can never be a man*—full, symmetrical and undwarfed."[42] While these examples come solely from the AME Church, I do not suggest that it cornered the market on such notions; black churchmen shared them across the board, even in the realm of black political activism.

Just as in the church, from the very beginning of black political activism in America, black men found it difficult to take seriously to any significant degree the oppression of black women. An essential aspect of their lack of concern stemmed from the development of patriarchal institutions within black civil society. In the social and economic sphere, black mutual aid societies, which were first started in Newport, Rhode Island, and in Philadelphia, provided their members with recreational facilities, provided families with modest economic protection in case of sickness or death, and created the foundations for black business development. On the whole, the major societies were founded, directed, and controlled by black men. Like the church, many black male activists identified the cause of black liberation with the ultimate attainment of "black manhood." This definition of freedom was a habituated response induced by white patriarchy, whether the black men of the period recognized this or not. Henry Highland Garnet's famous "Address to the Slaves of the United States," delivered at the 1843 Negro Convention, specifically called upon every black *man* to "resist aggression." He states further: "In every man's mind the good seeds of liberty are planted, and he who brings his fellow down so long, as to make him contented with a condition of slavery, commits the highest crime against God and man." Furthermore, Garnet reminds his audience of the transgressions and insults of whites upon black manhood:

> See your sons murdered, and your wives, mothers and sisters doomed to prostitution. . . . And worse than all, you tamely submit while your lords tear your wives from your embraces and defile them before your eyes. In the name of God, we ask, are you men? Where is the blood of your fathers? Has it all run out of your veins?[43]

Even the black newspapers established in the nineteenth century tended to print the antislavery speeches, manifestos, and essays written by black men. In addition, the black Convention Movement, a series of black political conferences begun in 1830 in Philadelphia, almost always involved only black men.[44] The radical newspaper editor T. Thomas Fortune in an 1887 polemic condemned whites as "the most consummate masters of hypocrisy, of roguery, of insolence, and of cowardice." He added that "many imagine that we are compelled to submit and have not the manhood necessary to resent such conduct. We shall labor as one man to wage relentless opposition to all men who would degrade our manhood."[45] The pan-African scholar and clergyman Alexander Crummell reminded blacks that the chief aim of civilization was the creation "of a true and lofty race of men. For *manhood* is the most majestic thing in God's creation."[46] Even Frederick Douglass, who was the leading male proponent of women's rights in the nineteenth century, fell victim to such notions, asserting in 1855 that the struggle for racial liberation meant that blacks "must develop their manhood, and not be too modest to attempt such development."[47]

To Douglass's credit, however, he was exceptional among all black male activists during his era in his open commitment to equality for women. He identified himself with militant white and black women in their struggle for suffrage and legal rights. In the first issue of the *North Star*, he drew notable political parallels between the battles against racism and sexism, declaring that "right is of no sex." He attended in 1848 the first national women's rights convention held at Seneca Falls, New York, and seconded the motion of Elizabeth Cady Stanton calling for women's voting rights. Douglass made a partial break with white feminists after the Civil War, when Susan B. Anthony, Elizabeth Cady Stanton, and others opposed the ratification of the Fifteenth Amendment unless it also mandated universal suffrage. Nevertheless, Douglass urged his supporters to endorse black male voting rights first. By 1869 the Equal Rights Association split, and many white feminists began to drift toward racist slogans to support their own cause.[48]

After Douglass's death, W. E. B. Du Bois arose to become the primary proponent of women's equality. Du Bois's commitment to women's rights began in 1887, when, as editor of the *Fisk Herald*, he stated: "the Age of Woman is surely dawning." In his essays in the *Crisis* and other periodicals, Du Bois emphasized that the struggle for black freedom must invariably include the demand for "the emancipation of women." In 1941 he pointed out with pride that many more black women were in the labor force than white women. In 1947 he urged black husbands to "share housework" and to shoulder the burdens of child-rearing equally. For half a century he reminded black men that "the hope of the Negro rests on its intelligent and incorruptible womanhood."[49] The shifting of sex roles and the creation of political, educational, economic, and especially religious opportunities for black women, however, disturbed many other black men.

Black Nationalists, the Civil Rights Movement, and Black Radicals

Marcus Garvey, the most successful black nationalist in reaching the masses, had a political approach toward black women's issues that was a bizarre mixture of romanticism, sexism, and race nationalism. In the 1923 edition of *The Philosophy and Opinions of Marcus Garvey*, he suggested that women were necessary yet conflicted beings: "She makes one happy, then miserable. You are to her kind, then unkind. Constant yet inconstant. Thus we have WOMAN. No real man can do without her." Like the black activists of the nineteenth century, Garvey identified black struggle with the attainment of manhood. He admonished his followers: "There is always a turning point in the destiny of every race, every nation, of all peoples and we have come now to the turning point of the Negro, where we have changed from the old cringing weakling, and transformed into full-grown men, demanding our portion as MEN."[50]

This concern and transformation into men made black men profoundly concerned with statistics that showed a declining number of children in black households. This caught the attention of Garvey. He warned his followers that "a decreasing birth rate and an increasing death rate . . . means the death of your race—the suicide of your race." In 1934, Garvey's Universal Negro Improvement Association issued a resolution condemning birth control for blacks. "Any attempt to interfere with the natural function of life is a rebellion against the conceived purpose of divinity in making man a part of his spiritual self," the sexist manifesto declared. "The theory of birth control . . . interfered with the course of nature and with the purpose of the God in whom we believe."[51]

Elijah Muhammad, the former Patriarch of the Nation of Islam, informed his followers that their women were unprepared for the "tricks the devils are using to instill the idea of a false birth control in their clinics and hospitals." According to the Nation (and many conservative black churches), God created women in order to serve their husbands and sons. This means for Elijah Muhammad, "The woman is man's field to produce his nation." Elijah's ministers frequently attacked black women and men who supported freedom of choice regarding birth control. Minister Louis Farrakhan wrote: "When the black woman kills her unborn child, she is murdering the advancement of her nation."[52]

It is no wonder that Malcolm X too fell prey to this patriarchal perspective. For many young blacks Malcolm X epitomized the best of "black manhood." Black actor Ossie Davis in his eulogy given at Malcolm's funeral declared: "He was our manhood, our own black shining Prince—who didn't hesitate to die, because he loved us so." Fortunately, Malcolm's views on black women changed considerably for the better over the course of his life. Like so many other male leaders, he also thought of politics as reserved for men. In the battle to eradicate racism, black women were important, but only a secondary factor. In his autobiography it is possible to discern the disdain he sometimes felt toward women for much of his early life. Malcolm admitted to Alex Haley, black novelist and journalist, that "you never can fully trust any woman."[53] Malcolm's view was a combination of patriarchal religious doctrine and ghettoized misogyny, which resulted in his earlier negative view of women. Malcolm gave a series of lectures in 1956 at the Philadelphia Temple in which he addressed women. On one of these occasions he remarked:

> How do you think this black man got in this state? By our women tricking him and tempting him, and the devil taught her how to do this. . . . The trickiest in existence is the black woman and the white

man. If you go to court with your wife, she will always win over you because the devil can use her to break down more of our black brothers.[54]

During this period in his life Malcolm viewed black women as the tool of white racist oppression and even compared her with the white man as the "trickiest in existence." Like most black male Christians, he derived his view in part from the biblical account of creation:

> Since the time of Adam and Eve in the garden, woman has led man into evil and the one she was created to serve became her slave. She rules him entirely with her sex appeal, her clothes are designed by man to accentuate those portions of her body related to sex, and when he fully dresses she undresses.[55]

Other notable black leaders started out with a similar sexist view.

Maulana Ron Karenga, West Coast cultural nationalist and founder of Kwanzaa, fell early on into the sexist definition of women's roles. He stated: "What makes a woman appealing is femininity, and she can't be feminine without being submissive." Imiri Baraka (formerly LeRoi Jones) stated likewise that black females had to inculcate "submitting to [their] natural roles" by assessing their attitudes toward their "man, house, and children." In her paper on the black family, Akiba ya Elimu suggested: "He [the black man] is the leader of the house/nation because his knowledge of the world is broader, his awareness is greater, his understanding is fuller and his application of this information is wiser" than that of the black woman.[56] Such a notion should not seem unusual for a woman who has internalized patriarchal rationalizations. In a similar manner, Kasisi Washao believed that the black family was "like an organ and the woman's function must be to inspire her man, to educate the children, and participate in social development. The man must provide security." Therefore, black women fortunate enough to have a man in their lives should "be humble and loving, appreciative, and resourceful, faithful, respectful and understanding . . . to provide continuous inspiration" for their husbands.[57]

Many male leaders of the Civil Rights Movement, while arguing for liberation from racism and classism, subtly reinforced patriarchal relations between men and women. This was the case for the most celebrated civil rights leader, Martin Luther King Jr. King made it clear that "women are as intelligent and capable as men," but he wanted his wife maker and mother for his children." His wife, Coretta Scott rated his view when she remarked, "He was very definite expect whoever he married to be at home waiting for him. . . to respect me as the head of the family.'"[58] King, like other b him, viewed the attainment of manhood as the goal of black liberation. He stated this in a *Face the Nation* interview:

> The Negro man in this country . . . has never been able to be a man. He has been robbed of his manhood because of the legacy of slavery and segregation and discrimination, and we have had in the Negro community a matriarchal family . . . in the midst of a patriarchal society . . . and I don't think any answer to that problem will emerge until we get the Negro man his manhood by giving him the kind of economic security capable of supporting a family.[59]

The underappreciation of women's gifts and contributions to the struggle for liberation—whether civil rights, black nationalism, or Black Power—again reflects the theme of black men attaining "manhood." This also suggests why there was a low visibility of black women in civil rights organizations and why many competent women in the movement were neglected and ostracized.

The Civil Rights Movement, however, began to lose momentum by 1964 when the desegregation of Southern civil society succeeded. During this time young militant black women and men began to reject integration. Black nationalism as a cultural and political expression was seized upon by a number of radical black youth. Across the country, hundreds of new political and educational institutions were developed within the theoretical framework of Black Power. Yet remarkably *few black activists elevated the question of sexism to primacy* within their practical political activities or their intellectual work. It is therefore not surprising that the actual practice of black militants did precious little to overturn the rampant sexism within black life. Black Power leaders showed little respect on the issue of gender.

For Stokely Carmichael, leader of the Student Non-violence Coordinating Committee (SNCC) in 1966, young black men had to assert themselves as males—politically and sexually. For the survival of the black man, black women would have to put away all forms of contraceptives—even the traditional and most unreliable device, the condom.

No single black activist, however, was more profoundly sexist than the celebrated ex-convict and writer of the Black Panther Party, Eldridge Cleaver. What is most important about Cleaver's writing is that black liberation is seen from beginning to end as an effort to assert one's manhood. He assured his hearers and followers: "We shall have our manhood. We shall have it or the earth will be leveled by our attempts to gain it."[60] This struggle for freedom apparently did not involve black women, since by their gender they already possessed what Cleaver dubbed "pussy power." According to Man-
g Marable, "From this standpoint, the white master had succeeded in

erecting a barrier between all Black men and women. Cleaver's conclusion was to mimic the worst features of white patriarchy."[61]

Nationalist, civil rights, or Black Power rhetoric and organizations dominated by black men have had little to say concretely about the exploitation of black women by their own institutions. In theory and practice the black protest movement was compromised and diminished by its inability to confront squarely the reality of sexism. The struggle for black liberation was the domain of black men. Such a masculine-centric view also influenced the development of a nascent black theology.

The Black Theology Movement

The achievement of "manhood" and the black freedom struggle were the impetus for the rise of the black theology movement. This movement developed in the mid-60s from a need for black people to think about themselves in a theologically mature manner and to provide a theological rationale that would, on the one hand, extrapolate from and assess the theological implications of Black Power and, on the other, vindicate the young civil rights workers laboring in the South. The pioneers of black theology convened under the leadership of Benjamin F. Payton, a Harvard-educated Baptist preacher and, at that time, executive director of the Commission of Religion and Race of the National Council of Churches of Christ. From this meeting was developed the National Committee of Negro Churchmen (NCNC), and a statement to that effect was formulated and published on July 31, 1966, in a full-page advertisement in the *New York Times*. The statement was influential, although the group was not aware that they were setting the stage for a new theological-political perspective called black theology.

The second signal event occurred three years later, after much tension between black and white churches over Black Power and "The Black Manifesto" controversy.[62] The statement on black theology by the National Committee of Black (formerly Negro) Churchmen (NCBC) expressed the development of a growing theological consensus among black church leaders and academics. James Cone, whose groundbreaking book *Black Theology and Black Power* had recently been published, was a key drafter of the statement.[63] The statement describing black theology and attacking white racism and oppression reads in part:

> Black Theology is a theology of black liberation. It seeks to plumb the black condition in light of God's revelation in Jesus Christ, so that the black community can see that the gospel is commensurate with the achievements of black humanity. Black Theology is a theology of "blackness." It is the affirmation of black humanity that emancipates

black people from white racism, thus providing authentic freedom for
both white and black people. It affirms the humanity of white people in
that it says No to the encroachment of white oppression.[64]

Much fruitful activity has developed from these initial theological forays into
exploring the black condition.

Dwight Hopkins has discerned four stages in the development of black
theology (he is himself a product of the fourth stage).[65] The first stage began
in 1966 with the statement on Black Power by the NCNC and culminated in
1969 with the publication of Cone's seminal work and the statement on black
theology by the NCBC. The second stage commenced with the formation of
the Society for the Study of Black Religion in 1970. In this stage black theology became an academic discipline, dealing in part with questions of liberation and reconciliation. The formation of the Black Theology Project
(1975), composed of church persons, community activists, and scholars with
connections with African Americans and the third world (that is, Africa,
Asia, the Caribbean, and Latin America), represents the third stage. The
broad range of participants during this stage represented black theology's
move toward liberation theologies in the third world and its relation to the
black church, feminism, and Marxism. The fourth stage, emerging in the
mid-eighties, emphasizes the exploration of theology from all aspects of black
life. That is, it represents a move to express a holistic approach to theology
that involves the analysis of race, class, gender, sexual orientation, and eco-
logical issues. In addition, the fourth stage seeks to deepen the ties between
the black church and the academy. It is at this stage also that black theology
began to respond to the challenge of black feminist and womanist scholars on
the issue of sexism (the first three stages did not recognize in any significant
way the latent sexism in the initial formulations of black theology).[66]

For example, there was sexism in the National Conference of Black
Churchmen "in their lack of public support for the ordination of women and
stubborn refusal to change the name of the organization to the more inclusive
title the National Conference of Black *Christians*. The fact that the NCBC,
despite the persistent objections of African-American women, did not modify its name until 1982 indicates how deeply sexism was entrenched in
nascent black theology." The notion that the attainment of black manhood
was more important than the liberation of black women was even quite
apparent in the early phases of black theology.[67] The reason for black male's
continuing posture on sexism is that racism is considered the greatest evil
that confronts the black liberation effort. "The underlying premise that governed their work was the naïve view that black liberation would be achieved
once segregation and institutional racism were eradicated from the church

and society." Like their forbears they failed to see that sexism is as serious a social and theological problem as racism. "Just as White theologians ignored slavery, segregation, and racism in their interpretation of the Christian gospel, Negro and black male theologians overlooked the gender oppression of black women in the formulation of their theological perspective."[68] The tradition of black manhood could reject the myth of white supremacy but have no problem tolerating white men's views of male superiority and female inferiority. As I have shown, the proponents could read the Bible as opposing white racism but accept its patriarchal bias. It is therefore startling that black women have nevertheless been faithfully dedicated to a church and a tradition that have historically demonstrated an unwillingness to view them as equal partners in the service of liberation. One reason is that black women love the church despite its limitations. Another reason (among many others) is that they were able to develop alternative ways to achieve their goals and resist total marginalization.

African American Women's Resistance Strategies

My review of black women's alternative strategies will center on two impor-tant women's movements: the first occurring in the nineteenth century and the second in the twentieth century. Both women's movements received impetus from the black liberation movements of each century. The first black liberation movement was to end slavery (a class issue), and the second was to end de facto segregation or Jim Crow (a race issue). In both cases, black women would gain insight and realize the shortcomings and sexism of the black liberation movements and also the shortcomings and racism of white-led women's movements. Over the long haul, they would develop institutions organized and run by themselves and a well-articulated theology to support their endeavors.

The Nineteenth-Century Women's Rights and Suffrage Movement:
The Rise of Black Women's Clubs and Conventions

The movement for women's rights emerged during the 1830s out of the anti-slavery movement. The antislavery movement allowed middle-class white women to "cut their teeth," as it were, and to explore activities that were not associated with their roles as wives and mothers.

> They learned how to challenge male supremacy within the anti-slavery movement. They discovered that sexism, which seemed unalterable inside their marriages, could be questioned and fought in the arena of political struggle. Yes, white women would be called upon to defend

fiercely their rights as *women* in order to fight for the emancipation of Black people.[69]

In the early days before the 1848 Seneca Falls Convention of women's rights, which is considered the "official" beginning of the movement, Sarah and Angelina Grimké were the most articulate voices to link the issues of slavery and the oppression of women. They also insisted that women could never get their freedom independently of black people, which exhibited the most promise for unity.[70] But this was not to be the case. Classism and racism thwarted the promise of women's and blacks' unity as the women's equality movement developed into the women's suffrage movement after the Civil War.

By 1869 the Fourteenth Amendment was already passed, granting the right of all males to vote, and the Fifteenth Amendment, which prohibited disfranchisement on the basis of race, color, or previous condition of servitude (but excluding gender), was on the verge of becoming law. Since black men—but not women, especially white women—would be given the right to vote, the race issue drove a wedge in the movement. The white middle-class women who led the movement would not unite around the notion of sisterhood with black women: it was "the Negro's hour," namely, that of black men. Their attack on black men became quite vicious, as the following statement by Elizabeth Cady Stanton makes unequivocally clear:

> "This is the Negro's hour." Are we sure that he, once entrenched in all his inalienable rights, may not be an added power to hold us at bay? Have not "black male citizens" been heard to say they doubted the wisdom of extending the right of suffrage to women? Why should the African prove more just and generous than his Saxon compeers? If the two millions of Southern black women are not to be secured the rights of person, property, wages and children, their emancipation is but another form of slavery. In fact, it is better to be the slave of an educated white man, than of a degraded, ignorant black one.[71]

Black women were not unaware of the implications of black men's getting the vote to the exclusion of women. Sojourner Truth articulated such at the 1867 Equal Rights Association (ERA) convention, where she opposed the Fourteenth Amendment because it denied black women the vote. She stated: "If colored men get their rights, and not colored women theirs, you see the colored men will be masters over the women, and it will be just as bad as it was before."[72] In the face of such outright racist rhetoric of their feminist white sisters, however, black women decided to forgo the sex question in order to unify with black men around the race question. Francis E. W. Harper, a noted poet and leading advocate of women's suffrage, symbolized this fact in a speech at the 1869 ERA convention in which "when it was a question of race, she let the lesser question of sex go."[73] While in reality the question of sex was no less important, her example demonstrates black women's willingness to forgo their own issue in order to support black men when racism reared its ugly head.

Although black women disagreed with the inherent racist attitudes of the women's suffrage movement, they did share some of its concerns about women's subordination and thought that their efforts and moral standing were essential for reform and progress of the race.[74] Some black men like Frederick Douglass and Charles Redmond, leaders in the black liberation movement, and church leaders like Henry Highland Garnett and Henry McNeal Turner supported the vote for women. Other black men offered the same kind of rhetoric that white racists proffered against blacks by invoking divine sanction for woman's lot. One church leader stated in the A.M.E. *Church Review* that "divine law makes no distinction between the sexes" but, in the realm of politics, "It may not be expedient to make them equal." Several Baptist clergymen waxed even more conservative, expressing their views at the turn of the century in a Virginia Baptist paper. They claimed to "prove through Bible authority that the only place for women in the church is that of singer and a prayer and that in teaching or preaching she is acting contrary to divine authority and that the exercise of the right of suffrage would be a deplorable climax to these transgressions."[75] As these examples indicate, the churches were not willing to recognize or support women's full participation in the church, and so it was no wonder that they did not support their social rights.

In the face of such attitudes, black women remained undaunted. Despite racism among white suffragists and sexism among some black church leaders, African American women by 1900 instituted suffrage clubs all over the country that included the National Association of Colored Women (NACW) and a special section of the NAACP.[76] As Giddings relates,

> By 1916 the women of the NACW could point to a long list of achievements. They had defended the race when no one else had. They had defended themselves when their men had not. The NACW had grown to fifty thousand members and it continued to sustain itself, without White largesse, as the first national Black organization (pre-dating the NAACP and the Urban League) to deal with the needs of the race.[77]

To be sure, the organization of the NACW, a watershed in the history of black women, resulted from the union of several black women's clubs (including the National Federation of Afro-American Women, headed by Mary Church Terrell) in 1896. The initiation of black women's clubs included such notable personalities as Harriet Tubman, Fannie Barrier Williams, Mary Church Terrell, and Ida B. Wells-Barnett, whose anti-lynching campaign helped to launch the modern Civil Rights Movement and brought the concerns of black women to the forefront of both black and women's rights.[78]

While the leaders and membership of social-political clubs included women with deep religious convictions, other black women established, headed, and participated in specifically religious organizations. In the 1880s black women under the direction of a white missionary, Johanna P. Moore, began to meet together to read the Bible in Memphis, Tennessee. On one chance occasion the white missionary invited Virginia Broughton, a graduate of Fisk University and schoolteacher in Memphis, to one of the meetings. This would be a fortuitous occasion, because the small "Bible Band" would become so popular among black women that they were encouraged to form themselves into a permanent mission station. The Bible Band was a black women's society organized for daily Bible study. The American Baptist Home Mission Society (ABHMS) granted their request for a permanent mission in 1887, and the Bible Band sought out Broughton's leadership skills. The Bible Bands increased in several locales, and many faced great pressure from male pastors to discontinue. Broughton remained steadfast and undaunted by such actions and became active in advocating for separate women's conventions.[79] The Bible Bands were just one example of the aspirations of black women to establish organizations that would bear the stamp of their own influence. This ambition would develop into several local and state women's conventions throughout the country, but especially in the South. After the three prominent black Baptist conventions merged to form the National Baptist Convention (NBC) in 1895, black Baptist women advocated for a separate national Women's Convention as an auxiliary.[80] This goal was achieved five years later. According to Higginbotham,

> The late date for women reflected not an afterthought but a hard-fought struggle for gender self-determination that began before 1895 and continued throughout the first two decades of the twentieth century. The black Baptist women's quest for national identity and voice draws attention to gender relations as relations of power in black communities, for their efforts, like earlier ones at the state level, incurred male resistance.[81]

In a similar fashion, Pentecostal women, especially women of COGIC, would also find alternative avenues of ministry in women-run and established denominational organizations (for example, the Women's Department of COGIC).[82]

It becomes apparent that the black women's club and convention movements share similar parallels. Both groups organized women to be a vital force for social change locally and nationally. Both groups addressed the same issues: race discrimination, violence, family and motherhood, equality of education, racial uplift, morality, labor concerns, self-help, suffrage, and gender biases, to name a few. While the two groups shared similar goals, there are also some significant differences. First, the two groups evolved from two different social contexts: the club movement tended to represent content middle-class black women, while the conventions represented a broader representation of black women. Second, the factors that sparked the club movement and awareness of the need for a national organization (resulting in the creation of the NACW) was more a response to the white racism of the women's suffrage groups than black men's sexism. The convention movement, on the other hand, sought to challenge the inequities and exclusions of women's work in the black community itself and foster women's self-determination.[83]

Thus in either case an emergent feminism had significant implications for black women and their work. It provided a rationale for the demand for greater participation of social, political, and religious matters. It also inspired women to establish and control their own organizations on the state and national levels. While black women did not demand or encourage a radical break with the church or other male-led institutions, they were able to find alternative avenues to accomplish their causes.

The Twentieth-Century Women's Liberation Movement:
The Rise of Womanist Theology

As far as most blacks were concerned, the emergence of the women's movement seemed untimely, intrusive, and irrelevant to the black freedom struggle. The roots of the modern women's movement are usually traced to the 1961 President's Commission on the Status of Women, chaired by Eleanor Roosevelt, and the 1964 Civil Rights Act, which provided a legal basis for women's rights.[84] White women had already been active in the Civil Rights Movement, participating in student sit-ins, voter registration, and freedom rides. Because of tensions created by whites, however, by 1964 SNCC moved to eliminate whites from the organization, especially white women who had begun to feel the feminist spirit. By this time white women had already begun to gravitate toward the budding women's movement and the predominantly white Students for a Democratic Society (SDS).[85] As Giddings notes, "White women developed their feminism in a Black organization and then turned the thrust of their activist energies elsewhere."[86] They would find out, however, that SDS men, when presented with "women's liberation," were no less sexist than the male members of SNCC. White feminist groups began to bud throughout the country, and in 1966 these groups merged with the National Organization for Women (NOW), which also sought to develop coalitions with prominent black women. And black women did participate in NOW, although their numbers were small.[87]

Although NOW accomplished some noteworthy goals in the late 60s, blacks did not take significant notice, because their accomplishments were overshadowed by urgent racial events—the death of Martin Luther King Jr., the riots that ensued, and the Black Power movement.[88] Black women by and large were also more involved and concerned about black unity and the black liberation struggle. By 1970 NOW was making a transformation that would further alienate black women; there was an influx of white women who were less concerned by larger political and economic issues and more concerned with the application of the meaning of feminism to their personal lives and relationships. This meant that the concerns of black women were neglected once again. Another factor that distracted black women from the women's movement was that the rise of the women's movement coincided with the frustrating demise of the black liberation movement.[89] However, as the women's movement in general gained momentum during the early 1970s, black intellectuals and activists, male and female, were forced to face up to the widespread sexist traditions within the black community.

The initial reaction of most blacks who responded to feminism was decidedly hostile. The women's movement was considered a "privileged white woman's movement."[90] Black women, according to some black men, should be more concerned about what happens to the race as a whole and not distracted by white "divide and conquer" tactics, because "we are all black." As mentioned above, the actual practice of the Civil Rights Movement—the black nationalism and Black Power movements in particular—was the perpetuation of patriarchal social and ideological structures. With the latter two movements, however, that patriarchy was carried out under the guise of "blackness." Cheryl Townsend Gilkes sheds important light on this issue when she states:

> One problem that developed in the late 1960s was the impact of a more exclusive political rhetoric within a growing black power movement, when the problem of "the Negro" became the problem of "the black man." The transition from "Negro" to "black" was a necessary phase in the public politics of race relations and in both black and white cultural consciousness and awareness, but an element of gender inclusiveness was lost in the process. Black women had always felt included in the term "Negro." Since one of the important themes of black preaching in all denominations was the problem of racial oppression, the rhetorical

switch from "Negro" to "black man" at precisely the moment that gender and women's rights became one of the most central issues of public politics may have been one of the most unfortunate contradictions of black liberation. . . . It is reasonable to argue that this shift invited a problematic departure from tradition that must be assessed in our reflections of the intersection of gender and race-ethnicity, particularly in the area of consciousness.[91]

The situation was not improved with the passage of affirmative action legislation. Many black males concluded that black women were about to seize the middle-income jobs that were just becoming available to them. This sexist notion was based upon the belief that black women would indeed be submissive, or less threatening to the white, male power apparatus than black males. "Contrary to the misgivings of male activists and theologians during the 1960s, black women's historic struggle for wholeness did not detract from the community's broader political struggle, rather, it enhanced it."[92] Thus, responding to this chasm between black liberation rhetoric and the harsh realities of black women's existence, progressive black female scholars, churchwomen, and activists fought back.[93] With the emergence of a more militant black feminism in the mid-seventies and womanism in the mid-eighties, the critique of sexism in the black community assumed more profound dimensions.

In the late 70s and early 80s African American women began to challenge the black church and black theologians and their interpretation of the Christian faith with its sole focus on racism to the exclusion of sexism. They also challenged white feminist scholars for not including a consistent and viable race component to their analyses of sexism. "While white feminist and black male theologians focus on sexism and racism respectively, womanist theologians highlight the inter-relatedness of race, sex, and class as multidimensional factors in the reality of black women's oppression."[94] This critique gave rise to what has been termed "womanism."

Womanism developed as a women's liberation struggle in the immediate wake of the Civil Rights and Black Power movements and in the context of the black liberation struggle and the white feminist (women's liberation) movement. Having been victimized and overlooked by both movements, black women sought to articulate a theology that would embody their historical and present experience and their aspirations for wholeness. *Womanist* is the designation many African American women have chosen for themselves. Womanist clergywomen and scholars, representing a broad range of disciplines (theology, ethics, social science, education, etc.), gained their initial impetus or inspiration from a dictionary-style definition of womanism that

Alice Walker provided in her book *In Search of Our Mothers' Gardens: Womanist Prose*. Walker states:

> Womanist. 1. From womanish. (Opp. of "girlish," i.e., frivolous, irresponsible, not serious.) A black feminist or feminist of color. From the black folk expression of mothers to their female children, "You acting womanish," i.e., like a woman. Usually referring to outrageous, audacious, courageous, or willful behavior. Wanting to know more and in greater depth than is considered "good" for one. Interested in grown-up doings. Acting grown up. Being grown up. Interchangeable with another black folk expression: "You trying to be grown." Responsible. In charge. Serious.
>
> 2. Also: A woman who loves other women, sexually and/or nonsexually. Appreciates and prefers women's culture, women's emotional flexibility (values tears as natural counterbalance of laughter), and women's strength. Sometimes loves individual men, sexually and/or nonsexually. Committed to the survival and wholeness of entire people, male and female. Not a separatist, except periodically, for health. Traditionally universalist, as in: "Mama, why we brown, pink, and yellow, and our cousins are white, beige, and black?" Ans.: "Well, you know the colored race is just like a flower garden, with every color flower represented." Traditionally capable, as in: "Mama, I'm walking to Canada and I'm taking you and a bunch of other slaves with me." Reply: "It wouldn't be the first time."
>
> 3. Loves music. Loves the moon. Loves the Spirit. Loves love and food and roundness. Loves struggle. Loves the Folk. Loves herself. *Regardless*.
>
> 4. Womanist is to feminist as purple is to lavender.[95]

Walker's definition of *womanist* touches upon four aspects: (1) it deals with African American language and folk traditions and so is grounded in black culture; (2) it highlights black women's experience—relationships and community life; (3) it explores black women's relationship to self, nature, and spirituality; and (4) it compares womanist experience to white feminism.[96] Walker's coinage of the term *womanist* inspired a generation of black women; many of them in various fields and disciplines have quoted, paraphrased, and alluded to this definition ever since. Not all black women, however, have readily embraced Walker's term and definition. bell hooks, for example, avers that some women use the term *womanist* to avoid asserting that they are feminists.[97] Cheryl Sanders was initially against Walker's definition because its advocacy of same-sex love (part 2 of her definition) did not represent traditional Christian ethics.[98] Nevertheless, the definition has gained ground. Although an African American woman did not use the term in a work before 1984 to describe a theological or ethical perspective, an article by Jacquelyn

Grant in 1979 titled "Black Theology and the Black Woman" challenged black theology's claim to be a liberation theology: it certainly could be such, but it neglected black women and their concerns. Grant also noted theological differences between black women and white feminist theology. In this way she set a place for womanist's seminal critiques of black theology and feminist theology. Katie G. Cannon's article "The Emergence of Black Feminist Consciousness," however, was the first written text to use the term *womanist*.[99] Her further work introduced womanism as an innovative and new category for all black women's religions. The term *womanist theology* was first used by Delores Williams in her article "Womanist Theology: Black Women's Voices."[100] She used Walker's definition to articulate a theoretical outline and sketch for black women's theology.[101]

Learning their lesson from the past shortcoming of the black liberation and feminist movements, womanists seek to do their work out of the multidimensional reality of black women that includes race, class, sex, and other forms of oppression and dehumanization. This is an important perspective because, as one womanist states: "the Black community is not free if any of its members are 'unfree' because of their color, gender, sexual preference or economic condition."[102] It is hopeful and commendable that many black theologians have responded positively to womanism. James Cone has asserted that "womanist theology is the most creative development to emerge out of the black theology movement."[103] There is much more work, however, to be done in black churches.

Conclusion

African American women have been kept out of the pulpit but not silenced, "hindered from helping"[104] but not deterred, marginalized in the freedom movements but never losing their self-respect and determination to achieve self-realization and social transformation. Part 3 explores how the Gal. 3:28 paradigm can be used to support current arguments for a more inclusive social vision of humanity and how it has already contributed historically to African American women's arguments for gender equality and their call to ministry.

❧ Part Three ❧

African American Women's Religious Experience and the Witness of Scripture

❧ 5 ❧
Vision, Envision, and Revision

Tell the world what the vision is. . . . God's provisions are for whomever God calls—male or female.[1]

The sisters love the Black Church too much to leave it in a patriarchal state, because there is a more excellent way.[2]

The black Christian tradition or the doctrine of "the equality of all people before God" served to challenge America to repent from its unjust and oppressive practices. It also equipped African Americans with a new social vision of humanity. But what neither black churches nor the tradition have ever done is to explore this very same principle in a self-critical analysis of the sexist practices of the black churches themselves. I hope to show how this principle through the paradigm of Gal. 3:28 can be used to establish an alternate model for black churches. As mentioned above, for blacks in general race and class issues are most important. Women of color have not opted to rigorously challenge the black church to consider its sins because the evil of racism has taken precedence over sexism. But if the black churches are to be faithful to their calling and their institutional principles, they must not wait for the eradication of racism before they do this critical self-evaluation. Oppression is oppression. But black men "are able to dismiss the sufferings of black women as unimportant because sexist socialization teaches them to see women as objects with no human value or worth."[3] This statement seems unduly harsh, and most men will argue that they see great value and worth in black women. But the question remains: are black women worth enough for black men to stand in solidarity with them around the issue of sexism, just as *they* have with us around racism?

Many black men express their greatest outrage and hostility toward white male power structures, but they are angry because they want access into that structure. "Their expressions of rage and anger are less a critique of the social order and more a reaction against the fact that they are not allowed full participation in the power game."[4] Black men must ask themselves difficult questions: can a society historically characterized by black enslavement, colonization, and imperialism provide the normative conception of women for the black church and society? "The important point is that in matters relative to the relationship between the sexes, black men have accepted without question patriarchal structures of the white society as normative for the Black community."[5] It is a contradiction for black men to protest against racism in the white church and society and then to fail to critique their relationship with black women and sexism in black churches. Exploring the Gal. 3:28 paradigm as a new liberative model for the black religious tradition might help to foster a move in this direction. This paradigm can be used to buttress African Americans' historical tri-dimensional struggle against oppression, something that the former historical paradigms have not been able to do.

Classic Biblical Models or Paradigms[6]

In Part 2 I argued that, despite its misuse to support racism and slavery, the Bible has traditionally been the most important source for the articulation of liberation by people of African descent in North America. Cain Felder suggests that the black church and others within black religious traditions give allegiance to biblical faith and witness, primarily because they see their own experiences depicted in the Bible.[7] African Americans were able to find within the Bible's theological language and the encoded experiences of its people analogous life situations and, more important, biblical models that echoed in many respects the intrinsic equality and humanity of all people before God. Scripture enabled African Americans to affirm a view of God that differed significantly from that of their oppressors. The intention of the slavemaster was to present to the slaves a conception of God that would make the slaves compliant, obedient, and docile. These desired qualities were supposed to make them better slaves and faithful servants of their masters. Many slaves rejected this view of God because it contradicted their African heritage and also because it contradicted the witness of the scriptures.[8]

Enslaved African American people found in the scriptures models of hope during specific historical moods and moments. That is, African Americans' religious and political uses of the Bible have corresponded to biblical formations of social history.[9] Several biblical models have informed African American experience, resulting in conceptual paradigms, such as exodus, wilderness and promised land, Ethiopia and Egypt, and captivity and exile/diaspora.[10]

The most important biblical model or paradigm of liberation in African American social and religious history is the exodus. The biblical account of the miraculous delivery of the children of Israel from slavery in Egypt under the leadership of Moses evoked similar hopes and dreams in the minds of the enslaved African American community. Outnumbered and closely controlled by the restrictive North American hegemonic slavocracy, African Americans found hope for liberation in a miraculous act of the divine for which the exodus motif served well. This motif configures the transfer of African American people from oppression to freedom under the leadership or inspiration of Moses-like figures.[11] In the Emancipation Proclamation African Americans realized that a decisive event had become a reality in their own historical experience. This presidential order, following the outbreak of the Civil War, confirmed to enslaved Africans in North America that the God who delivered the ancient Hebrew slaves from Egyptian bondage had responded to their oppression also. For this reason, they were convinced that the likelihood of continuing reenactments from biblical narrative could be expected. Theophus Smith notes:

> Henceforth many African American believers and converts would be convinced of the possibility that through prayer and expectation, the rough acts of obedience and righteousness, black folk could inherit divine promises of prosperity and freedom. Furthermore, an apparent precondition for such bestowals would appear to be their linkage to biblical models. That singular instance, the link between Lincoln's role in the emancipation and Moses' role in the Exodus, would distinguish itself as a kind of paradigm. In this manner a new development in the ancient tradition of biblical typology emerged in the collective psyche of a displaced people.[12]

However, less than ten years after the dream of freedom from slavery became a reality, it was soon dashed against the rocks of a failed Reconstruction effort and a new form of American aggression and oppression—Jim Crow. The biblical model most analogous to this historical mood and moment was the Hebrew experience of "wandering in the wilderness." While African Americans, like the ancient Hebrews, had been set free from slavery, they encountered debilitating setbacks and unrealized expectations. One ex-slave remarked during this trying period that black preachers encouraged their people by comparing their situation to that of the children of Israel wandering in the wilderness: "De preachers would exhort us dat us was de chillen o' Israel in de wilderness an' de Lord done sent us to take dis land o' milk and honey."[13]

W. E. B. Du Bois in the *Souls of Black Folk* also invoked the "forty years of wilderness" theme. In the African American experience the theme of "wilderness" can signify either the post-Reconstruction period of the late nineteenth century or the early colonial period.[14] Du Bois, like the preachers mentio by the ex-slave, applied the wilderness motif to the collapse of the r struction experiment and the failure to realize a democratic "prom in the South after the emancipation of the slaves in 1865.

> Years have passed away since then—ten, twenty, forty; fo
> national life, forty years of renewal and developmen

swarthy spectre sits in its accustomed seat at the Nation's feast. In vain
do we cry to this our vastest social problem. . . . The Nation has not yet
found peace from its sins; the freedman has not yet found in freedom his
promised land. Whatever good may have come in these years of change,
the shadow of deep disappointment rests upon the Negro people.[15]

Instead of reaching a biblical promised land, African Americans found their
fate to be conceived in the pattern of ancient Israel's wilderness experience.
Moreover, according to Smith, "true to the Bible's wilderness figure their
experience included the advent of new legal and juridical traditions. The new
laws were distinguished for their uniformly oppressive and toxic effects. This
situation fell far short of the dream of freedom long desired by black folk in
America since the colonial period."[16] Arguably, this period of "wandering"
remained applicable until the mid-twentieth century, ending with the rise of
the Civil Rights Movement.

With the emergence of the Civil Rights Movement of the 1950s and 1960s
and a renewed militancy, the exodus motif arose again. In this period the
wilderness figure gave way to the latter configuration in the exodus saga—
"possessing the promised land." African Americans felt that they were in a
position to move into the promised land filled with the "milk and honey" of
equal opportunity and social advancement. America as a "promised land" has
been a central idea for many ethnic and social groups throughout United
States history. It has especially been such for African Americans seeking reme-
dies from race and class oppression.[17] For many the first exodus experience liberated African Americans from a particular form of racial/class oppression,
namely, slavery. The new appropriation was to liberate the nation and African
Americans from racial and economic oppression (Jim Crow, that is, "separate
but equal" or, in reality, "separate but unequal," entailing second-class citi-
zenship). They wanted the nation to "judge not by the color of one's skin, but
by the content of one's character." This would make America an open and
democratic society for all of its citizens. If America could come to terms with
its racism, then America as the promised land of economic and social freedom, regardless of race or class, could be realized.

Finally, for our purposes (although more African American appropriations
of biblical paradigms could be advanced), in contemporary African American
religious thought the model of exile and diaspora has been evoked to express
the historical mood most analogous to the experience of biblical Israel. The
use of the term *African Diaspora* has become popular since the 1960s black
consciousness movement.[18] It was in the early 1970s, however, that C. Shelby
Rooks proposed that blacks should abandon the theme of the promised land,
along with that of the American dream, because the former had become tar-
⸺d by its crass reformulation into the latter. Rooks suggests that

the Biblical image which has been at the heart of the black [American's] faith in the eventual appropriation of the American myth must be replaced. . . . My own very untested suggestion about a possible new image is that of an African Diaspora based on the Biblical story of the Babylonian Exile and the Final Jewish Diaspora. It is to the end of the Biblical history of Israel that black America must look rather than to the beginning.[19]

Rooks's tentative suggestion in the 1970s to reconceive African American experience as analogous to the Babylonian captivity and the Jewish diaspora became increasingly applicable for many as the twentieth century ended.[20] Thus the paradigms of exile and diaspora have been seen as more appropriate paradigms for interpreting the contemporary aspects of the African American experience.

Critique of Classical Biblical Models in the African American Religious Tradition

The use of biblical models and paradigms reveals the importance of the Bible in the experiences and aspirations of African Americans in the past, present, and—undoubtedly—the future. But, as has been recognized more clearly in the last few decades, these classical biblical models have not been fully liberative paradigms. Recently there have been several critiques of some of the classical paradigms, especially the exodus motif. Delores Williams, for example, strongly suggests that we must question the assumption that African American theologians can without qualification continue to make paradigmatic use of the Hebrews' exodus and election experience as recorded in the Bible.[21] Indeed, she has uncovered some major fallacies in its usage that are difficult to ignore.

Williams advances several reasons for the inadequacies of the exodus paradigm for contemporary usage. First and foremost, the exodus paradigm can no longer serve as paradigmatic because it is not liberating for *all* the oppressed.[22] Black people historically and some black liberation theologians of late have identified so thoroughly with Israel's election and liberation that they have ignored "the figures in the Bible whose experience is analogous to that of black women."[23] Total identification with the Hebrews and not with the other people who were later victimized by the former slaves (like the Canaanites) privileges the children of Israel and overlooks the violence and subjugation that they later perpetrated on other peoples. In addition, it underscores the way in which black women (who are analogous to those victimized non-Hebrew slaves in the Bible) have been overlooked and made invisible. This means, moreover, that if the God of the Bible sanctioned th victimization, servitude, and annihilation of non-Hebrew peoples, then the God of the Bible is "partial and discriminatory."[24] If this obtains, then God is not against *all* oppression for *all* people: Israel alone is favored. "The point is that when non-Jewish people (like many African-American women who now claim themselves to be economically enslaved) read the entire Hebrew testament from the point of view of the non-Hebrew slave, there is no clear indication that God is against their perpetual enslavement."[25] It turns out that on a close reading of the Bible with this new perspective, God may not be on the side of all the oppressed but only the oppressed of the descendants of Israel. Williams further avers that if African Americans then identify with the non-Hebrew slave and not the Israelite, there is a nonliberating thread that runs through the Bible.[26]

Randall C. Bailey concurs to a certain extent with this assessment, suggesting further that the exodus/liberation narratives (particularly the "P" or Priestly source) are not concerned necessarily with liberation but with the competition between the religion of Israel and that of Egypt. This means that the exodus saga was not read as a narrative strictly about liberation from Egyptian slavery but as the conflict of competing religions.[27] "The leaving out of the liberation formula is not by chance. It is by design. The liberation is secondary."[28] Nevertheless, the liberation theme reasserts itself. As Bailey states:

> Unfortunately for P, this desire to supplant liberation thought with a call to piety did not win out in the tradition. The "signs and wonders" narrative was not allowed to stand alone. . . . In the final redaction of the Pentateuch, the "God of liberation" made more sense than the "God of Contest." As often happens, liberation wins out.[29]

While the liberation theme eventually carries the day, this conflict reveals that there were alternative readings of the exodus saga within the biblical tradition that were not concerned with social liberation. Moreover, the liberation narratives were originally concerned with class struggles and national struggles.[30]

It turns out that a close and critical reading of the exodus narratives by both Williams and Bailey exposes some hidden flaws in the paradigmatic use of this biblical model. It certainly has been useful in the struggle for freedom, but it can only be used cautiously now. This is not unusual with the appropriation of biblical paradigms: they are useful for certain social and historical ~~~ but new information and situations entail a reevaluation of their tion. The primary function of the exodus paradigm in African ligious history was that it could be invoked as a direct challenge s Clarice Martin clarifies:

> Whereas the legitimacy of the slave regulation in the *Haustafeln* [household codes] could be challenged rather handily based on explicit paradigms about liberation from slavery in such narratives as Exodus 14, biblical narrative does not contain an equally *explicit* and *consistent* paradigm about the liberation of women from patriarchy, androcentrism and misogyny.[31]

Although Martin does not analyze explicitly the exodus narrative but instead discusses the household codes of the New Testament and their injunctions to slaves, she clarifies cogently the dilemma of the classical biblical narratives. She perceives correctly that the appropriation of classical biblical paradigms in the African American experience (the exodus in particular) addresses only the liberation from class and/or race oppression. African Americans' religious and political discourse was and is dominated by these concerns. While these matters remain legitimate and necessary, they stop short of including a paradigm that would take seriously the concerns and sexist oppression of African American women.

In the preceding chapters I have shown that the struggle for voting rights for freedmen and for women's rights in the nineteenth century and the African American "male-led" Civil Rights Movement in the twentieth century downplayed the concerns of African American women. For blacks in general the race issue has been most important. Cheryl Townsend Gilkes states that

> black feminist theory has explicitly affirmed that "our situation as black people necessitates that we have solidarity around the fact of race." Black feminist church-women have not approached black religious institutions with the same level of indictment that white women have carried to theirs, in spite of the struggle over women in the pulpit.[32]

While Gilkes is basically correct, in the last two decades of the nineteenth century black Baptist women increasingly challenged such examples of gender inequality, working within the orthodoxy of the church to argue for their rights. In this way they held men accountable to the same text that authenticated their arguments for racial equality.[33] To be sure, an early voice of equality within the African American women's community, Anna Julia Cooper, did not give primacy to gender discrimination over and against race discrimination, since black women were oppressed both because of their race and because of their gender. In addition they had to contend with economic and educational discrimination—a third form of oppression.[34] Moreover, while womanist theologians of late have launched even more challenging critiques of sexism, black women have still been expected not to challenge African American churches and religious organizations to consider their own sexist practices because the evil of racism has had precedence over sexism.

The result is that sexist practices are perpetuated in these organizations. Black women are still expected to remain subordinate to black men and are discouraged from pursuing the preaching or pastoral ministries, both of which are prohibited to them through a misreading of Pauline injunctions. It is puzzling that the African American interpretive traditions, which found within the Bible models and paradigms of liberation from race and class oppression, were unwilling to explore the Bible to find equally liberating models to challenge the traditional roles and status of women. The unfortunate result is that the early African American interpretive traditions, while claiming to represent the universal concerns of black people, have been willing to accept uncritically paradigms of gender oppression based upon the same Bible that was used to argue for race and class liberation. It seems that "while the 'nonracist' principle called attention to a common tradition shared by black churches, it masked the sexism that black churches shared with the dominant white society."[35]

Galatians 3:28—A Model for the Black Churches' Quest for Liberation

What biblical model could (1) be inclusive of the multiple struggles of the African American experience, (2) fully embrace the concerns of African American women, and (3) counter (especially biblically derived) sexist ideologies? I propose that the biblical model that could adequately serve these purposes as we embark upon the twenty-first century is found in Gal. 3:28. A liberative biblical model based upon this passage is particularly in tune with the situation of African American women who have suffered triple oppression—that of race, class, and gender—in the church and in society. In the view of Anna Julia Cooper, black women represent the most oppressed group of women in America,[36] the only group in America that has historically experienced the full impact of this triple oppression. But black women did not use this as an excuse simply to claim a victim's status. Not only did they reenvision womanhood—indeed black womanhood—to mean something different from the dominant ideal in American culture, but they also advocated an ontological freedom and equality for *all* women. In addition, they reconceived the notion of *human being*: "humankind, male and female have been created ontologically free."[37] Christ was a prime example of the notion of *human being*; he exhibited the principles of freedom and equality in his life and work, for all are created in the image of God.[38] For this reason, the means of achieving social equality between the races and genders should be sought in Christian principles. Such ideals of universalism rooted in the Christian tradition were important early on for showing the common humanity shared by blacks and whites. While such notions remain appropriate, in recent thought among black women such notions are more nuanced.

Black feminists and womanist theologians have critiqued the rhetoric of "universalism" in both white and black theologians. According to Jacquelyn Grant,

> Blacks identify that universalism as white experience; and women identify it as male experience. The question then is, if universalism is the criterion for valid theology how is such a universalism achieved? This criterion must include not only Black women's activities in the larger society but also in the churches as well.[39]

I suggest that Gal. 3:28 is one means of meeting this challenge. Moreover, while Grant does not refer to Gal. 3:28 in her article "Womanist Jesus and Mutual Struggle for Liberation,"[40] it does provide a conceptual framework for her understanding of the mutual struggle of Jesus and African American women. For African American women Jesus was a central figure whom they experienced as (1) a co-sufferer, (2) an equalizer, (3) freedom, (4) a sustainer, and (5) a liberator.[41] Grant adds, moreover, an interesting twist to the Gal. 3:28 paradigm by showing how the three categories of race, class, and sex/gender have been used to oppress not only other human beings but even Jesus Christ. She argues that Jesus Christ has been imprisoned by patriarchy (the sin of sexism), white supremacy ideology (the sin of racism), and the privileged class (the sin of classism). This indicates that the Jesus of African American women has also suffered a *triple oppression*. "As such, Jesus has been used to keep women in their 'proper place': to keep Blacks meek, mild, and docile in the face of brutal forms of dehumanization; and to ensure the servility of servants."[42] Thus for many African American women any theory of liberation and equality has to deal with the total situation of oppression experienced by all black people. Hence womanists define liberation as the survival of the whole people—male and female, young and old, gay and straight.[43]

Although early African American interpretive tradition excluded an *explicit and consistent* critique of gender/sex oppression, the issue of sexism must still be examined in light of this interpretive tradition, which early on developed a hermeneutic of liberation. To achieve these goals new biblical models and paradigms should be considered that do not have the limitations of the previous classical biblical models and are sensitive to the issues of sex/gender oppression and the concerns of African American women. Galatians 3:28 has great potential as such a model, a theo-ethical paradigm compatible with African American aspirations for freedom and equality in the present and for the future. But these claims must be substantiated. Therefore, while I propose that Gal. 3:28 has the potential to meet the challenges of the historical quests for liberation for African Americans, it cannot be accepted uncritically. Thus, in what follows I evaluate its strengths and weaknesses as an effective model of liberation, especially for challenging sexism.

Galatians 3:28—A Potential Liberative Paradigm for African American Churches

Simply because the Gal. 3:28 paradigm was used in the early African American religious tradition does not mean that it can be indiscriminately applied to African Americans' contemporary situation without critical examination. The assessment of Gal. 3:28 as a liberative paradigm has not been fully excavated in contemporary African American scholarship. I therefore first address the various problems related to the appropriation of the paradigm: (1) the issue of authorial intent, that is, Paul's understanding and use of the saying, and (2) the gap between ancient and modern understandings of equality. Second, I address the issues particular to the African American situation: (1) universalism and universality as a mask for Eurocentrism, (2) fear of the loss of ethical/cultural identity (and the lack of an Afrocentric focus), (3) Gal. 3:28 as a potential tool of Eurocentric oppression, and (4) the fear of this paradigm being appropriated by gay and lesbian Christians.

Problems of General Interpretation and Appropriation[44]

The Issue of Authorial Intent. As noted above, Paul intended not to eliminate social roles and differences but to relativize them in relation to Christ. Baptism into Christ, therefore, means the creation of a new unity of humanity that includes all people indiscriminately, but that unity does not entail an elimination of social hierarchy or one's former status. When Paul addresses the baptismal confession in 1 Corinthians 7 and 12, there is no hint of equality, but there is unity. Furthermore, in the context of chapter 12 he not only excludes the final pair of opposites, male and female, but also uses the analogy of the body, in which some parts have lesser honor and other parts greater. In this same chapter on spiritual gifts, Paul provides an ordered list of "offices" in the assembly to emphasize difference within a hierarchical unity.[45] It appears then that for Paul and others in the ancient Mediterranean "unity . . . does not seem to deny hierarchy, even in the assembly. Indeed, appeal to interdependent hierarchy is the ubiquitous ancient Mediterranean and Medieval European way of conceiving any sort of social unity. Unity in antiquity almost never implied equality."[46]

The Divide between Ancient and Modern Understandings of Equality. Of the three texts that deal with unity using the baptismal confession (1 Cor. 7:14-24;

12:13; Gal. 3:28), only Gal. 3:28 is amenable to modern notions of egalitarianism.[47] However, even with Gal. 3:28 equality can be understood in terms of having (1) the same fundamental capacity as moral agents or (2) the same social and economic power, status, and economic benefits in an unchanging arrangement. While the first has been common throughout history and does not conflict with social hierarchy, the second has never been realized. Therefore, Paul may have held to some version of the first view, asserting that all people have the same moral capacity to approach God.[48]

Authorial intent does not always guide what an audience hears or reads. African Americans, appropriate to their situation, reshaped the oppressive Christianity they were given into a religion of hope and liberation. Even in the New Testament itself there is evidence of later Christian communities reshaping the image and legacy of Paul to meet new and challenging situations (hence the deutero-Pauline and Pastoral epistles). This process is unavoidable if the message is to remain meaningful. As to the second problem, African Americans did hold to the idea of equal moral agency. With respect to the second definition, they sought "equal opportunity" and "equal access" at least to pursue their human potential. They recognized that all people would not have the same economic and social power, but they were convinced that this should not hinder them from "the pursuit of happiness" as their abilities dictated (as Reverdy C. Ransom asserted; see chapter 3, pp. 94–95).

Problems Particular to African American Appropriation

On the one hand, when Paul's letters and legacy are rejected or viewed as useless for liberation (as was the case with some early African American interpreters of Paul), Gal. 3:28, while appearing to offer a liberative vision, seems to some too risky to embrace, because of the Pauline "baggage" that comes along with it. Thus the paradigm is rejected outright or neutralized because of the assessment of Paul's "conservatism" or "ambiguity." On the other hand, it has been rejected of late because there has been a shift in African Americans' historical-political self-understanding, the result of a revolution in scholarship in the 60s and 70s that emphasized the concerns of subjected peoples who were historically neglected and erased from historical, religious, and philosophical discourse.[49] In addition, the Civil Rights Movement, the aggressive ministry of Malcolm X, and the black student and black studies movements propelled the concerns of African Americans to the forefront of academic, religious, and political discourses. The emergence of black theology, resulting from this fertile climate, stimulated African Americans to reevaluate their history, religion, and self-identity. Some other later developments growing out of black theology that are pertinent to our topic are womanist theology and African American biblical hermeneutics. These have continued to benefit from this shift in consciousness. In short, then, a paradigm such as Gal. 3:28 can appear to be a negation of these gains. It has the potential to serve as a mask for Eurocentrism, aid in the loss of African and African American heritage, serve as a tool of Eurocentric oppression, and support gay and lesbian arguments for religious recognition and acceptance (for some, a negative function; see below).

Universalism and Universality: A Mask for Eurocentrism. In the early African American interpretive tradition, ideas of universalism rooted in the Christian tradition were important for showing the common humanity shared by blacks and whites. In recent thought among some African Americans such notions are rightly reexamined. Many identify such universalism as a cloak for advancing white experience. Molefi Asante has offered a critique of the Eurocentric ideology, contending that it masquerades as a universal view in the fields of intercultural communication, rhetoric, philosophy, linguistics, psychology, education, anthropology, history, and religion. He does not question the validity of the Eurocentric tradition within its context, but he simply argues that "such a view must not seek an ungrounded aggrandizement by claiming a universal hegemony."[50] His solution suggests a reversal, a counterperspective. He seeks to describe the possibilities of a world in which Africa, for example, is subject and not object.

Loss of Cultural and Ethnic Identity. Some African Americans fear that the phrase "no longer . . . for all of you are one," will lead to the loss of cultural and ethnic identity and uniqueness. In a nation where blacks (and other people of color) have had to contend with the loss of cultural heritage through the slave trade and racist notions of black inferiority, some feel that, having reclaimed a positive sense of "blackness" and a heritage as people of African descent, the use of such a paradigm will make them "invisible." African Americans should, therefore, seek paradigms that can reclaim a black/African heritage.[51] Already in the Bible there is evidence of black presence, but even here it has been made invisible in white biblical scholarship.[52] According to J. Deotis Roberts the African American community has taken a quarter century to focus on the search for its African heritage, and the quest for it is constant. The philosophy that supports this quest has been termed *Africentrism* (a slight change from the earlier term *Afrocentrism*), which is a historical and cultural perspective for people of African ancestry. It has gained popularity and respectability since it was developed by Molefi Asante and others.[53] Africentrism deconstructs much of Western classical history, reclaiming Egypt for Africa and challenging the hegemony of ancient Greece. For Asante, Africentricity is a dynamic intellectual theory, not a system of thought but a philo-

sophical and theoretical perspective. In the Africentric perspective the problem of location takes precedence over the topic under consideration. Africen-
trists contend that Africans and African Americans have been removed from
social, political, philosophical, and economic concerns in most discourse in
the West for more than five hundred years. Europe occupies all the intellectual and artistic seats in various areas of knowledge. An Africentric appraisal
of this situation notes that no room is left for other traditions.[54]

In this view, then, Gal. 3:28 may pose a confusion of the cause, since it
seems to point toward the dissolution of ethnic distinctions and their reinte-
gration under a new universalizing theme. This could serve to provide a chan-
nel for the reemergence of European cultural hegemony, potentially a tool of
oppression.

Galatians 3:28 as a Potential Tool of Eurocentric Oppression. This is exactly the
position of Nathaniel S. Murrell. He contends that the Rastas (Rastafarians)
approach the biblical text with a hermeneutics of suspicion, blackness, and an
"I-an-I" principle that allows them to deconstruct the Eurocentric hermeneutical tradition that ignores the plight of the poor who hear or read the Word.
The deconstruction does not proceed from the point of view of the powerful
class of society or race who determine the dominant political narrative on
human speech and reality—and, by extension, proper universal methods for
interpreting the Bible. It proceeds instead from the "situatedness" of the marginalized and oppressed people who desire to control their own reality, history, and personal destiny.[55] Therefore, Murrell contends that some texts in
the history of Christianity that were put to notorious use—to define, pro-
scribe, oppress, and exploit black people as "obedient slaves" or servants—are
not to be rationalized and explained away with "proper" hermeneutical and
exegetical tools but must be rejected de facto as corruptions of the Bible by
the white man to "down-press" the black man. Among several texts (Gal. 2:4;
4:8; Col. 3:11, 22; 4:1; Titus 2:9; and Philemon 16) appears Gal. 3:28.[56] For
him (and others), Galatians has moved from the potential to the actual realm
of oppression. Thus it would appear, as I have suggested above, that Paul's
ambiguity, the usefulness of his letters to oppressive regimes, the shift in
African Americans' sociopolitical consciousness, and the potential of Gal.
3:28 to suggest a universality that makes African Americans "invisible" have
in the final analysis rendered it ineffective as a paradigm of African American
liberation. I will argue below, however, that there is another way to view
these issues that provides a way out of these apparent problems.

Use of the Paradigm by Gay and Lesbian Christians. If the African American
churches and religious institutions have been sexist, they have been more

conservative on the issue of same-sex love. In almost all traditional black churches same-sex love is viewed as incompatible with Christian life and ethics. Therefore, any biblical appropriation that would lend itself to this cause is considered suspect and to be rejected. A statement by Irene Monroe in a sermon delivered on Gay Pride Day at Riverside Church in New York confirms this anxiety for some:

> I am reminded of Paul's letter to the Galatians (3:28) where he wrote, "there is neither Jew or Greek, neither male or female. . ."—and yes it also means neither straight nor gay—for "we are all one in Christ Jesus." Heretofore, the Jews had been known as the people of God and had been accepted into the family of God. Now all people had been accepted into the family of God and had been known as the people of God.[57]

Finding in Gal. 3:28 a universality that even supports same-sex love clarifies and confirms the fear for some that this paradigm supports a unity of humanity that is too universal.

Evaluating the Problems of African American Appropriation of Galatians 3:28. Considering the first concern, universalism and universality as a mask for Eurocentrism, I suggest that it would be improper to view the early black interpretive tradition's use of Gal. 3:28 as suggesting a universalism that would diminish the distinctive element of race, which is really a social, political, and ideological category, not a biological one. At any rate, African Americans in the early tradition were able to use the paradigm to argue for the equality and unity of humanity while at the same time establishing independent black churches and asserting their proud African heritage, and even to use it as a means to support protest and activism. In its political-religious usage the element "in Christ" has never limited it to the religious realm. So in view of the African American interpretive tradition, blacks used the paradigm to dismantle white supremacy and argue against a universalism that excluded them from the equation.

With respect to the second concern regarding the fear of the loss of cultural and ethical identity, within the interpretive tradition this paradigm was not used to argue that cultural and ethnic distinctiveness should be removed, but that such distinctiveness should not be used as a basis for the oppression of another human being. The interpretive tradition seemed to be aware of Victor Anderson's contemporary formulation of postmodern blackness. He states:

> Postmodern blackness recognizes the permanency of race as an effective category in identity formation. In addition, it recognizes that black identities are continually being reconstructed as African Americans

inhabit widely differentiated social spaces and communities of moral discourse. African American life and experience occurs in differentiated socio-economic spaces along divisions of education, income, and occupations. . . . In these multiple sites, African Americans are continually negotiating the various languages of race, class, gender, and sexuality.[58]

The paradigm was used to argue that African Americans were an equal partner and participant in the human family and as such should be given the rights, respect, and equal opportunity of every other human being to achieve their potential. But they did not want to cease being black or deny their heritage.

The third problem, which states that Gal. 3:28 is a passage that has been used as a tool of Eurocentric oppression, has not been corroborated in my research. On the contrary, my investigation has shown that this passage has been problematic for such an ideology because it would seem to argue the opposite point intended—all people are equal. So although Gal. 3:28 might have been used as a tool of oppression (in a few minor cases that I have not been able to find in the literature), African Americans found liberating potential in its broad social vision.

Finally, regarding gay and lesbian appropriation of Gal. 3:28, it is clear from our overview of the early Christian and African American interpretive traditions that it would be difficult to find support for such an interpretation. Nevertheless, particularly in the African American religious tradition, we have seen that the oppressors could not determine or control how this passage (or any other) was appropriated by blacks; nor can contemporary African American subscribers to this vision control or determine how other groups appropriate this egalitarian vision. On the whole, it still offers the greatest potential for challenging biblically supported sexist arguments.

The Potential of Galatians 3:28 for Challenging Sexism in African American Religious Institutions

Galatians 3:28 has the potential to serve as a liberating paradigm because it meets the criteria established above. I have suggested that in order for Gal. 3:28 to serve as an appropriate and effective paradigm it must (1) be inclusive of the multiple struggles of the African American experience, (2) fully embrace the concerns of African American women, and (3) counter sexist ideologies, especially biblically derived ones.

Interstructuring of Race, Class, and Sex

Galatians 3:28 is inclusive of the multiple struggles of the African American experience and can avoid some of the pitfalls of the earlier biblical models.

First, it is paradigmatic of the historical tri-dimensional struggles of African Americans. Since African Americans as a whole have struggled for freedom from all forms of oppression, Gal. 3:28 does not focus only on race and class but also sex/gender. Second, contemporary African American scholars have come to recognize the interesting interplay between these three categories in oppressing all black people. Rosemary Radford Ruether, a feminist theologian, coined the term *interstructuring* to describe the interrelated nature of race, class, and sex; she is one of the first white scholars to explore this phenomenon. She argues that while racism and sexism have been closely interrelated historically, they have not been exactly parallel. But they have been "interstructural elements of oppression within the overarching system of white male domination."[59] She asserts furthermore that "this interstructuring of oppression by sex, race, and also class, creates intermediate tensions and alienations—between white women and black women, between black men and white women, and even black men and black women. Each group tends to suppress the experience of its racial or sexual counterparts."[60] Those who have benefited most from this arrangement have been white men; those who have benefited least have been black women. But black people, especially black men, have not noticed or appreciated this phenomenon. In this vein, James Cone addresses some disturbing questions to black men about our lack of concern or interest in the topic of black male sexism. He asks:

> Why is it that many black men cannot see the analogy between racism and sexism, especially in view of the fact that so many black women in the church and in society have expressed clearly their experience of oppression? What is it that blinds black men to the truth regarding the suffering of their sisters? What is it that makes black church men insensitive to the pain of women ministers, and why do we laugh when they tell the story of their suffering that we have inflicted on them?[61]

Such questions must be at the root of any analysis of sexism addressed to black males, says Garth Baker-Fletcher. They are direct and specific.[62] Black men must realize that racism, sexism, and classism represent the corporate evils that are built into the very structure of the United States. There are striking similarities in their origins, ideologies, and practices. As a matter of fact, "race and sex are comparable to the extent that they form large permanent classes identifiable by indelible physical characteristics which fix one's status at birth."[63] Many others have begun to notice the connections between the interrelatedness of racism and sexism, just as all forms of oppression have a similar connection and function. Thus when black men discern these connections, they will be able to see the interstructuring of sex and race ideologies. In this way, Gal. 3:28 is compatible with the historical religious-political struggles against oppression: it can not only bring to light the connections among the three categories but also supply a theoretical and theological model for appraising them.

Inclusive of the Concerns of Black Women

Galatians 3:28 as a potentially liberative paradigm is compatible with black women's early and recent critiques of sexism in the African American religious tradition. The fruition of recent womanist theology, biblical interpretation, and ethics has supplied the tradition with a foundation for a vision of wholeness and has raised the consciousness of many regarding the concerns of black women and *all* who are oppressed. A paradigm based on Gal. 3:28 is not conceptually limited by biblical narrative traditions, nor is it in competition with the classical biblical paradigms or current paradigms and work that black women are doing; it is complementary. As Clarice Martin says, "A liberating anthropology is able to affirm that in Christ there is neither male nor female, but also, 'at the same time in Christ there is neither slave nor free, Jew nor Greek.'"[64] Since it is not limited to a narrative framework (or by Paul's use and understanding of it), it is open-ended and applicable to black women's stories, experiences, and traditions of struggle and survival. Not having a narrative framework, then, is one of its advantages. It can incorporate the stories of women (and indeed all blacks) who have had to contend with the tri-dimensional reality of race, class, and sex/gender.

A Counter to Biblically Derived Sexist Notions

Galatians 3:28 offers a challenge to arguments of natural or divinely ordained social orders. It was noted in Part 1 that Gal. 3:28 (compatible with Genesis 1) counters the order of the creation story in Genesis 2, in which woman derives from man. It also counters the subordinationist view of Genesis 3, which has been used to accuse woman for the fall of humanity for which she is "cursed" to bring forth children in pain and to submit to her husband (so 1 Tim. 2:11-15 and the household codes). This story was perfect for supporting patriarchy. In contradistinction, Gal. 3:28 envisions a new order of creation that challenges the pattern of the old. In the new creation, social roles are no longer vertical but horizontal. The activity of the Spirit in the Christian communities, empowering all indiscriminately (for the Spirit democratizes; Acts 2:17-21; cf. Joel 2:28-32), is evidence of this new order. Thus, since the household codes use the order of the "old" creation to understand social roles, they can be directly challenged by Gal. 3:28 as incompatible with the order of the "new creation" (sometimes called "the order of redemption").

The traditional stance on this issue is that God has ordained hierarchy in the church and in the family and that scripture teaches *functional differences*. In this perspective it is possible to talk about the equality of men and women before God and still maintain sexist and racist categories. These arguments follow a general pattern: "Men and women are equal before God by virtue of creation and redemption. Yet God assigned distinctive and complementary roles for men and women to full in their relation to each other. These roles are not nullified but clarified by Christ's redemption and should be reflected in the church."[65] As mentioned earlier (in chapter 2, above), whichever creation account informs one's perspective will also determine one's view of social ordering, as the following statements reveal:

> There *are* functional roles between men and women. Such differences do not imply superiority or inferiority but complementarity. Women are called to minister in the church in a variety of roles, but are not eligible to function as elders/pastors of the congregation. The reasons for their exclusion from such offices are not cultural and time-bound *but theological and timeless.*[66]
>
> The reason women are not allowed to teach or exercise authority over men is not because God is our Father or Christ is Son or because Jesus chose men for apostles or because women are inferior. Women cannot do these things because (1) the man was formed first and (2) the man was not deceived but the woman was. Whether or not these reasons seem fair or reasonable to us is irrelevant; they are God's reasons. . . . God has ascribed honor to the place of subordination.[67]

These types of arguments were enthusiastically used to justify the oppression of blacks during the antebellum period. African American churches must be wary of such notions, for the very same rationale was used to argue for the immutable, changeless, unalterable lot or "place" of blacks: *they are slaves by God's design!* Slaveholding ideology held that giving freedom to blacks would disrupt God's sacred order and the social order. Even after America emancipated the enslaved blacks from physical servitude, "well into the twentieth century similar ideologies were used to rationalize continual subordination of blacks and women—smaller brains, less intellectual capacity, weaker moral fiber, 'the woman's place,' 'the Negroes' place,' 'the contented woman,' 'the contented Negro,' and so on."[68] Arguments that center on the idea of a person's or group's "proper place" and contentment therein are based on ideas and notions of natural or divine order. Somehow women and blacks receive their position by nature or from God. *What the black churches must understand is that the idea of divine or natural order is very tenuous.* In any such system there are going to be those whose lot in life will be stamped with the divine seal of immutability, and an unchangeable social status. These persons have been allotted their place by design, and as such it should not be changed; if anyone should venture to do so, he or she will threaten the very peace and stability of that order. Such reasoning as this gives a static, eternal quality to social orders that are indeed only human constructs, which are constantly changing. Therefore, no system of human relations is eternal. Those that are oppressive and unjust must be challenged and changed. We can no longer blame God or nature to justify any oppressive human-created social order. We must be responsible as human beings for the systems we create—not only for their cause, but also for their solution. Galatians 3:28 challenges and offers an alternative view to such natural or God-ordained social orders. If there is such a thing, that order should validate and support freedom, equality, and equal opportunity for all of God's people!

A Counter to Biblically Argued "Curses"

In Gen. 3:16 women are "cursed" because they are blamed for having caused sin to enter into the world. Blacks, on the other hand, according to racist ideology have the "curse" of Ham (actually, the curse of Canaan, Ham's progeny) placed upon them because of Ham's sin against Noah, for which Noah cursed him (Gen. 9:25-27).

"Curse" of Woman	*"Curse" of Blacks*
To the woman he said, "I will greatly increase your pangs in childbearing; in pain you shall bring forth children, yet your desire shall be for your husband, and he shall rule over you."	"Cursed be Canaan; lowest of slaves shall he be to his brothers." He also said, "Blessed by the LORD my God be Shem; and let Canaan be his slave. May God make space for Japheth, and let him live in the tents of Shem; and let Canaan be his slave."

In both cases, in terms of the religious and ideological justifications of racial and sexist oppression, blacks and women are cursed from birth based upon the "original sin" of some ancestor of the same sex or race. In both cases the "curse" is continuous, affecting all those of the same sex or race who are born afterward. These curses are further used to justify the subordination and social status of women and blacks. In the case of woman, "your husband . . . shall rule over you"; in the case of blacks, "lowest of slaves shall he be to his brothers . . . let Canaan be his slave." The uniqueness of the African American female's situation is that she stands at the crossroads of two of the most well-developed ideologies in America, that regarding women and that regarding blacks.

Black women, in this racist and sexist view, have had to bear a particular bondage because, based on this notion, they have upon them both the "curse of woman" and the "curse of Ham." It was during the slavery era that these ideas were fashioned into a peculiarly American mythology. White males have been the primary beneficiaries of both sets of myths. These myths contain common elements that characterize blacks and women as infantile, irresponsible, submissive, and promiscuous. Both groups are consigned to roles that are subservient, have shared a relationship of powerlessness vis-à-vis white males, and have been treated as outsiders and inferiors.[69] The black woman's position in America's sex and race mythology has made it very difficult for her to escape the mythology. Black men could be rescued from the myth of the "Negro"—they could identify with things masculine, with things aggressive, and with things dominant. White women could defy the difficulty of the myth of "woman" by adopting the myth of "womanhood." This myth, which was developed in the late nineteenth century, allowed white women to be viewed as sober, virtuous, moral, and stable and thus escape the negative myths of woman that were attributed to black women—weak moral fiber, promiscuous, irrational, the epitome of motherhood with infinite sexual, life-giving, and nurturing qualities.[70] The seemingly impossible task confronts black women. According to Deborah Gray,

> If she is rescued from the myth of the Negro, the myth of woman traps her. If she escapes the myth of woman, the myth of the Negro still ensnares her. Since the myth of woman and the myth of the Negro are so similar, to extract her from one gives the appearance of freeing her from both. She thus gains none of the deference and approbation that accrue from being perceived as weak and submissive, and she gains none of the advantages that come with being a white male.[71]

Gray surmises further that, to be so "free," black women have at times appeared to be superwomen and have attracted the envy of black males and white females. Being thus exposed to their envy, black women have often become their victims.[72] But, as mentioned above and in the next chapter, black women did not relish the victim's status. They carved out a path through both problems, using Gal. 3:28, which envisioned a new order of humanity not based in "curses" but blessings (cf. Gal. 3:13-14; "Christ *redeemed us from the curse of the law,* having become a curse for us . . . that in Christ Jesus the blessing . . . might come"; RSV, emphasis added). But for the most part, while some blacks accepted a genealogy from Ham because it validated blacks as the descendants of the great empires of Africa (Gen. 10:6, "the descendants of Ham: Cush, Egypt, Put, and Canaan"), others rejected such a view of a "curse" on blacks (but not women, in some cases) because they saw it for what it was: a tool of racist oppression used to support an unjust social order. If this can be seen in the case of blacks, the same must be seen with respect to women: notions of a "curse" are used to justify their place subordinate to men.

As a result of this new perspective, the Gal. 3:28 paradigm can be used to affirm the tri-dimensional concerns of womanist scholars and black women in general. Such a paradigm could serve as a "wake-up call" to African Americans (especially male pastors, preachers, bishops, elders, and presidents of religious institutions) to consider liberation in holistic categories in both thought and practice. Emilie Townes's statement on a womanist ethics deserves serious consideration:

> Womanist ethics begins with the traditional role and place assigned Black women. An African-American woman contends with race, sex, class, and other sources of fragmentation. The challenge of a womanist social ethic is to create and articulate a positive moral standard, which critiques the arrogance and deadly elitism of dominance and is so bold as to name it as a systemic evil.[73]

Galatians 3:28 can assist black churches in thinking about such an ethic in a holistic manner.

Envisioning and Revisioning Human Relations: A Choice of Paradigms

At the end of chapter 2 I argued that the early church was confronted with two paradigms to guide its institutional and social vision. I also argued that these paradigms are embedded within the Bible and that certain passages support contrasting visions of human relations. African American churches confronted these same paradigms, rooted in either Gen. 1:27 or Genesis 2 and/or 3, in the past and continue to confront them today. Consider the following statements by an African American man and woman regarding women in ministry:

> [The man said:] I disagree [with] women in ministry. A man should be the head. . . . Jesus is coming back for a bride. The Church is the bride, so there is no place for women ministers. But if man does not do what he should, dominate the earth, I don't know about these women. I just don't believe in them.
>
> [The woman said:] I am definitely against female ministers in the pulpit. The Bible is our road map [read "paradigm"]. There is not one example, saying female preaching. . . . Women ministers use all kinds of examples to justify that they were called to the ministry. . . . It's very clear in Scripture that man was not made for woman, but woman for man. Just as Jesus is head of the Church, man is head of woman. No female should be in the pulpit. We can be ministers of a kind, as missionaries. Utilizing these gifts does not mean preaching from the pulpit—[I] hope they will stand on the Word and not allow women to be ordained or in the pulpit.[74]

The man's statement refers to 1 Cor. 11:2-16 to reject women's preachi[ng] ministry and also Gen. 1:26 regarding dominion but forgets that it re[fers] v. 27 that the "man" is created "male and female." Likewise, the statement recalls 1 Cor. 11:2-16 and its referral to the creation of Eve in Gen. 2:21-25 to argue against women preaching—at least from the pulpit. It is clear that the same oppressive paradigm that guided the early church still wields great influence in contemporary churches. The question is, which paradigm has been consistent with the black religious tradition and the black churches' endeavors for freedom and liberation for all people? It is the very paradigm based on Gal. 3:28 (and other passages in Acts), which is rooted in Gen. 1:27. Since this has been the case, African American churches have a critical choice to make if they want to remain faithful to their institutional origins and historical struggles for freedom and justice. Which paradigm will guide their institutional goals and vision for the future? A paradigm that has supported their oppression and included a constellation of arguments for black inferiority, justifications of slavery, subordination of women, violence, white supremacy, and segregation? Or will they choose a paradigm that has inspired visions of unity, human potential, protest, justice, liberation, equal opportunity, and wholeness? Recall our discussion of the early church and the development of "orthodoxy" built upon those passages of scripture that support a hierarchical model. It was and indeed is orthodoxy of this nature that has maintained and sustained oppressive political and social structures—slavery, colonialism, and Apartheid. African American churches must seriously consider the following statement by John W. Kinney, Professor of Theological Studies and Dean of the Samuel DeWitt Proctor School of Theology at Virginia Union University, Richmond, Virginia:

> I want to suggest to you that what we need in the new millennium is not a return to orthodoxy but a return to . . . counterworld imagination or . . . faithful disbelief. See, we have never been an orthodox people; we had to be unorthodox people; we had to be unorthodox to survive, because orthodoxy negated our being, and when you embrace orthodoxy, you're embracing the chains that enslaved you.
>
> We had to challenge orthodoxy to even claim our worth, our value, and our dignity. And the closer we get to orthodoxy, the more we move away from our great African heritage and the center of Christian truth, and we become like the enemy rather than a prophetic presence in the midst of the enemy. We're called to faithful disbelief. I refuse to believe _____ telling me. I refuse to preach and teach the distortions _____ esenting as God's truth.[75]

_____ arches were able to invoke this "counterworld imagina-
_____ isbelief" that Kinney urges and that is inspired by the
_____ and other like-visioned passages), and they were able to
_____ ge the skewed message given to them. They *envisioned* in
_____ pression a better day when slavery and oppression would

end. Slavery ended but oppression did not—neither racial nor sexist oppression. What must be done now is to engage in a *revision* of paradigms that do not include all of God's people and reject those that continue to support oppression. This can be done with some effort.

Thomas Kuhn introduced another useful term for understanding the purpose and function of paradigms: *paradigm shift*. He argued that every scientific revolution and breakthrough involved a break with the tradition, with old ways of thinking, with old paradigms. Paradigms in general serve as a guide for how humans view society, the church, politics, their attitudes and behaviors. Thus black churches need a paradigm shift in order to fulfill their potential and historical posture as not only nonracist, nonclassist institutions but also nonsexist institutions. Galatians 3:28 can aid in such a shift.

Conclusion

The use of Gal. 3:28 as a liberative paradigm is not without its problems, but it can include within its orbit a vision of equality regardless of race, class, and sex/gender. With a touch of irony, Nelle Morton asks us to consider "what might happen with women in the holy places: behind the pulpit, proclaiming the word, breaking the bread, consecrating the elements, baptizing, burying, and marrying."[76] I think black churches might experience the powerful rush and outpouring of the Holy Spirit, as did the early church, which democratized social relationships and passed judgment on the social order of patriarchy. Both daughters and sons of the church, prophesying, bore witness to a new social order in which "there is no longer Jew or Greek, there is no longer slave or free, there is no longer male and female; for all of you are one in Christ Jesus" (Gal. 3:28). This radical challenge to the social order of patriarchy contradicts the "divinely ordained" position of women below men. Such a paradigm is needed especially in African American churches and religious institutions where sexism continues. If things continue like "business as usual," we must take note of Francis Wood's warning:

> As long as men continue to define themselves by using the masters' tools
> of dominance and subordination, whether by commission or omission,
> as their measure of manhood, there will be no justice in the church.
> Until there is a new understanding and regard for the full personhood of
> all women with their gifts and talents in the church, we will not bear the
> yoke of Jesus. Instead, we will continue to bear the yoke of preserving
> patriarchal privilege.[77]

Already, however, within the black religious tradition lie seeds of hope. African American women have led the way in the process.

6

Women, Word, and Witness

Remember the "surprise at sunrise" on Easter Morning when Christ was not in the tomb, confined, but risen for *all* of us. Christ rose that we [women] too could be set free and use our treasures and gifts for his glory.[1]

New Faith is the key that unlocks all . . . that God is saying to us. Yes, God speaks to [and through] women powerfully and profoundly.[2]

Women in the African American Christian tradition did not wait for ecclesiastical approval or denominational ordination to fulfill their callings as preachers and ministers of the gospel. Although support and approval from the institutional churches and denominations would have been readily received, these women had only their relationship with and faith in God, combined with support from close friends and those who were transformed by their ministries to sustain their conviction. In this chapter I will discuss the basis upon which historical and contemporary African American women have argued for their equality in the churches and how they have justified their calling to the preaching and pastoral ministries. The ministry, death, and resurrection of Jesus, the descent of the Spirit at Pentecost (in Acts 2 and the other important passages in Acts), and Gal. 3:28 are significant sources for these endeavors.

African American Women in Ministry in Mainline Denominations

The current situation of black women among the largest African American denominations reflects an ambiguous polity and policy toward them. Statistics are inadequate to capture the contours of women active in ministry in the various denominations who function with or without official denominational approval.[3] Looking at ordination traditions and attitudes among the mainstream denominations might prove more productive.

The National Baptist Convention, U.S.A., Inc. (NBC) is the largest black Baptist denomination, and it still does not recognize the ordination of women at the level of national policy. The NBC chooses to leave the issue of women's ordination to the local church and its associations. However, despite delegates' efforts to encourage the acceptance of women's ordination on the national level, it has been rejected. "Contrary to the Baptist legacy of congregational autonomy and freedom of conscience, local and regional Baptist associations will go to great lengths to restrain churches and pastors from ordaining women."[4] The NBC has yet to recognize and appreciate the egalitarian principles of its black Christian tradition. The Progressive National Baptist Convention (PNBC), the third largest black Baptist denomination, however, practices an open policy toward ministry at the local and national levels. According to its current president, Dr. C. Mackey Daniels, "the PNBC strongly advocates the fulfillment of Baptist democratic principles and tenets and faithfully practices freedom of opportunity and equal access to office for clergy or lay, male or female, thereby assuring the broadest possible participation of all its members."[5] Although the NBC and PNBC differ in their official policy toward women clergy, both denominations contain member churches pastored by women. While we might hope that the NBC and other historic black Baptist denominations will follow PNBC's lead and make women's ordination a matter of national policy, there are no immediate signs that this will happen soon.

The black Methodist denominations, AME, AME Zion, and CME, all ordain women. The AME Zion was the leader among black churches in ordaining women and granting laity rights to women. They were the first black or non-black denomination to ordain women and recognize complete gender equality as early as 1900.[6] The CME and AME followed this policy in 1948. However, they elected no women bishops until the year 2000, when the Rev. Dr. Vashti Murphy McKenzie was elected a bishop of the AME Church. The other two have yet to follow in this progressive action.

The largest of the Pentecostal denominations, Church of God in Christ (COGIC), does not officially ordain women, while some other Pentecostal denominations do. The Pentecostal denominations that ordain women have pastors, elders, and presiding bishops who are women. COGIC deserves special mention, because, like the other Pentecostal denominations, it recognizes as the foundation of its religious vision Acts 2, which recounts the democratizing descent of the Holy Spirit at Pentecost. But the modern Pentecostal tradition has recognized this event primarily for its validation of speaking in tongues, not its race, class, and sex barrier–breaking implications (see chapter 1). Several scholars have recognized that socially the modern COGIC movement was initially "a response to racism and exclusion in American culture."[7] Two pioneering women, Lucy Farrow and Neely Terry, were among the ministers at the Azusa Street Revival in Los Angeles between 1906 and 1909 (commonly recognized as the roots of the American Pentecostal movement), and many other COGIC women have taught, founded churches, raised money, and served as "evangelists." Nevertheless, a grand opportunity to challenge sexism was again put on the back burner in deference to concerns regarding racism. Like other black denominations, "Pentecostals rely on an interpretation of Paul that keeps governance in the hands of males."[8] COGIC women have been taught that "to be submissive was the glorious role of sanctified women in the church. A true sign of submission to God was submission to those who had rule over you, such as your husband and minister."[9] It is no surprise then that positions as pastors, bishops, general overseers, and in some cases general church administrators continue to elude Pentecostal women.[10] The General Board, however, does sanction women taking over churches when a pastor dies or one is not available—until a man is appointed.[11]

Given the present situation among the mainline black denominations, Gilkes has remarked insightfully that "the picture for women in the ordained ministry *within the historically African-American denominations* is not good. . . . The full empowerment of the church to speak to the needs of all African-American people cannot be accomplished without the full empowerment of women at every level."[12] African American women have voiced such concerns to black churches for quite some time using principles of biblical equality, urging them to actualize fully Gal. 3:28.

Appropriating Galatians 3:28 in Its Complete Form

African American male church leaders have often recognized the importance of black women's active support in the local churches and in denominational structures, as well as their efforts toward racial self-help and self-reliance. Nevertheless, many traditionally have not recognized their leadership potential or their confessed callings to pulpit and pastoral ministry. "Thus tainted by the values of the larger American society, the black church sought to provide men with full manhood rights, while offering women a separate and unequal status."[13] As I have shown, African American men and women from slavery to freedom rejected scriptural texts that in any way supported human bondage and race prejudice. In their quest for freedom and equality, while many African American men have quoted from Galatians the words "There is no longer Jew or Greek, . . . slave or free," African American women have called attention to the implications of Gal. 3:28 in its more complete form: "There is no longer Jew or Greek, . . . slave or free, . . . male and female; for all of you are one in Christ Jesus."[14] They have appealed to Gal. 3:28 and other passages that support the principles of equality to address not only issues of race and class but also issues of gender and sex. African American women have agreed fully that the principle of the equality of all people before God should entail the eradication of racism and classism. Why should this principle not extend to sexism? They certainly believed it did and in accordance with the African American interpretive tradition used Gal. 3:28 and the salient passages from Gen. 1:27 (*imago Dei*), Acts 2, and others to support their convictions.

Historic African American Women Preachers

In his classic work *Black Preaching*, Henry Mitchell skillfully traces the history of the "Black Fathers and Sons" of preaching, but mentions nothing of the "Black Mothers and Daughters" of preaching.[15] The problem is not that the source material is unavailable. There are rich sources of information for the lives and ministries of these valiant women in their memoirs, letters, and autobiographical narratives. However, Mitchell's book, written in the 1970s, reflected a general attitude of many black males, neglecting women's roles and contributions. To be sure, Mitchell's subsequent work, like that of many other black male scholars, has attempted to correct these earlier errors. There remains to be written a comprehensive history and analysis of black women preachers. The scope of this book does not allow me to discuss in detail Nancy Prince, Elizabeth Keckley, Silvia Dubois, Suzie King Taylor, Amanda Berry Smith, and Rebecca Cox Jackson, all of whom exercised their gifts of ministry against the odds. I can only point to a few noteworthy examples of early black women preachers.

Toward the end of the eighteenth and early nineteenth centuries, the black fathers of preaching saw no contradiction between the attitude of white Christians toward blacks and their own attitude toward black women. The interaction between Jarena Lee and Rev. Richard Allen, founder and first bishop of the African Methodist Episcopal Church, is a classic example of this historical dilemma. Jarena Lee was born free in Cape May, New Jersey, on February 11, 1783, and was the second black woman of historical record known to preach. She recounts that her call came after a period of sanctification:

> Between four and five years after my sanctification, on a certain time, an impressive silence fell upon me, and I stood as if some one was about to speak to me, yet I had no such thought in my heart. But to my utter surprise there seemed to sound a voice which I thought I distinctly heard, and most certainly understood, which said to me, "Go preach the Gospel!" I immediately replied aloud, "No one will believe me." Again I listened, and again the same voice seemed to say, "Preach the Gospel; I will put words in your mouth, and will turn your enemies to become your friends."[16]

After some initial doubts, she became convinced that she had been called by God to preach and committed herself to the ministry, though it put her at odds with men both in and out of the church.[17] Nevertheless, she went to Rev. Allen to tell him that she felt it was her God-given duty to preach the gospel: "I now told him, that the Lord had *revealed* it to me, that I must preach the gospel."[18] After listening intently he replied that "our discipline knew nothing at all about it—that it did not call for women preaching."[19] Lee left this meeting disheartened, and she did not practice her ministry for eight years. After this time, however, her faith was renewed, and she pronounced this warning to the church, both black and white: "O how careful we ought to be, lest through our bylaws of church government and discipline, we bring into disrepute even the word of life. . . . Why should it be thought impossible, heterodox, or improper, for a woman to preach? Seeing that the Savior died for the woman as well as the man."[20] Jarena Lee understood that the resurrection of Jesus radically changed the social and religious status of women. She understood the institutional biases of the church and warned against bylaws taking precedence over Christ's law of love and liberty for all people. Because of Christ's liberating resurrection, she never bothered to address the prohibitions in 1 Corinthians or 1 Timothy: "If a man may preach, because the Savior died for him," she remarked, "why not the woman? Seeing he died for her also. Is he not a whole Savior, instead of a half one?"[21] The she addressed how Mary was the first to proclaim (that is, the first preacher) of the resurrection despite disputes over the fact that she did not *expound upon a biblical text*:

> Did not Mary first preach the risen Savior, and is not the doctrine of the resurrection the very climax of Christianity? . . . Then did not Mary, a woman, preach the gospel? For she preached the resurrection of the crucified Son of God. But some will say, that Mary did not expound the Scripture, therefore, she did not preach, in the proper sense of the term. To this I reply, it may be that the term preach, in those primitive times, did not mean exactly what it is now made to mean; perhaps it was a great deal more simple then, than it is now—if it were not, the unlearned fishermen could not have preached the gospel at all, as they had no learning.[22]

Although Rev. Allen did acknowledge her call and gifts of ministry some years later, he did not give her official ordination to preach, but only a verbal acknowledgment for her to hold prayer meetings and exhortations. Despite the lack of official ecclesiastical sanction, what Lee did was to preach the Word, and she had a large following of people. One might even say that she served in a pastoral role. At any rate, her strongest argument for her calling to preach was her practice of ministry. Even though she was denied ordination, her gifts could not be denied.

Another freeborn African American women, Zilpha Elaw, was born and grew up near Philadelphia around 1790. According to her own account, she was converted at an early age and became filled with the Holy Ghost. In 1821, Elaw attended her second camp meeting, which attracted an estimated seven thousand people, including many blacks. It was there that she received her call and the injunction that "thou must preach the gospel; and thou must travel far and wide." After a rather lively sermon, the people were crying and praising God, and she heard a voice tell her to go outside of the tent and the voice spoke to her. She stood at the door of the tent and began to exhort the people. Then she experienced her call in a vision and in a similar manner to Lee's:

> After I had finished my exhortation, I sat down and closed my eyes; and there appeared a light shining round about me as well as within me, above the brightness of the sun; and out of that light the same identical voice which had spoken to me on the bed of sickness many months before, spoke again to me on the camp ground, and said, "Now thou knowest the will of God concerning thee; thou must preach the gospel; and thou must travel far and wide." This is my commission for the work of the ministry, which I received, not from mortal man, but from the voice of an invisible and heavenly personage sent from God.[23]

Having been divinely commissioned to preach, Elaw put aside all concerns for family and friends in order to be obedient to her commissioning. Persecuted and ridiculed, in 1827 she decided to pursue an itinerant ministry. For thirteen years she preached throughout the Northeast and also to black congregations in small Southern towns. In June 1840, Elaw sailed for England, where she remained for six years, publishing her memoirs in London in 1846. Nothing is known of Elaw after this publication, and it is possible that she died in England.[24]

In the 1830s, having been influenced by the growing abolitionist movement, black women began to refute biblical arguments demanding their silence as public speakers. "In 1832 women didn't speak in public, especially on serious issues like civil rights and, most especially, feminism."[25] Yet it was the year 1832 when Maria Stewart started her one-year public speaking career in Boston; she was "the first American-born woman to stand at the lecture platform and speak on political-religious issues."[26] Maria Stewart took up a life of public political-religious oratory and activism at a time when it was deemed highly inappropriate for a woman to do so. Giddings asserts that, "the moral urgency of their being black and female . . . suffused black women

with a tenacious feminism, . . . which was articulated before . . . whites . . . providing the first rationale for American women's political activism." Giddings
argues that black women "bypassed the barrier of religious thought that cir-
cumscribed even radical white activists until the late 1830s. . . . Black women
had been able to justify their activism even earlier."[27] Stewart defended her
right to speak publicly on political and religious issues by appealing to biblical precedent and by defining herself as a passive instrument in God's
hands.[28] "Methinks I heard a spiritual interrogation—'Who shall go forward,
and take off the reproach that is cast upon the people of color? Shall it be a
woman?' And my heart made its reply—'If it is thy will, be it even so, Lord
Jesus!'" She also recounts a "call" experience not to the preaching ministry as
such, but to take up the lectern for the cause of black freedom and women's
rights. She compares her situation to Paul's: "And truly, I can say with St.
Paul that at my conversion I came to the people in the fullness of the gospel
of grace [Rom. 15:29]."[29] She remarks furthermore,

> I felt I had a great work to perform; and was in haste to make a profes-
> sion of my faith in Christ, that I might be about my father's business
> [Luke 2:49]. Soon after I made this profession, The Spirit of God came
> before me, and I spake before many. . . . A something said within my
> breast, "Press forward, I will be with thee." And my heart made this
> reply, Lord, if thou wilt be with me, then I will speak for thee as long as
> I live. And thus far I have every reason to believe that it is the divine
> influence of the Holy Spirit operating upon my heart that could possibly
> induce me to make the feeble and unworthy efforts that I have.[30]

Thus like her preaching sisters before her Stewart had a spiritual experience
in which the Spirit commissioned her to speak.

Stewart's farewell speech to her Boston friends on September 21, 1833,
"contains a discussion of the right of women to aspire to the highest positions
of responsibility and authority in both religious and public spheres."[31] To do
this, she had to deal with arguments that stemmed from the Pauline passages;
she rejected their use in justifying slavery and sexism. "Stewart in her
speeches did what biblical critics before had done: give priority to the statements and actions of Jesus so that they became arguments for the limited
nature of Pauline injunctions."[32] She asks:

> What if I am a woman; is not the God of ancient times the God of these
> modern days? Did he not raise up Deborah, to be a mother, and a judge
> in Israel [Judges 4:4]? Did not queen Esther save the lives of the Jews?
> And Mary Magdalene first declare the resurrection of Christ from the
> dead? . . . St. Paul declared that it was a shame for a woman to speak in
> public, yet our great High Priest and Advocate did not condemn the

woman for a far more notorious offense than this; neither will he con-
demn this worthless worm. . . . Did St. Paul but know of our wrongs and
deprivations, I presume he would make no objections to our pleading in
public for our rights. Again; holy women ministered unto Christ and
the apostles; and women of refinement in all ages, more or less, have had
a voice in moral, religious and political subjects. Again; why the
Almighty hath imparted unto me the power of speaking thus, I cannot
tell.[33]

Stewart then provides a historical overview of women throughout the ages
who performed great deeds and broke social norms. This tradition has not
been abrogated but God still moves women through the Spirit: "Why cannot
a religious spirit animate us now? Why cannot we become divines and scholars? Although learning is somewhat requisite, yet recollect that those great
apostles, Peter and James, were ignorant and unlearned."[34] Near her closing
she asks a question of her African American audience:

What if such women as are here described should rise among our sable
race? And it is not impossible. *For it is not the color of the skin that makes
the man or woman, but the principle formed in the soul.* Brilliant wit will
shine, come from whence it will; and genius and talent will not hide the
brightness of its luster.[35]

This statement is important because it contains a formulation that portends
those of Du Bois and King. Du Bois stated: "Through all the sorrow of the
Sorrow Songs there breathes a hope . . . that sometime, somewhere, men will
judge men by their souls not by their skins." In a similar fashion is King's
famous dictum: "Do not judge a man by the color of his skin but by the content of his character." Such formulations were developed to address racism.
Stewart's statement was designed to address sexism: "For it is not the color of
the skin that makes a man or a woman, but the principle formed in the soul."

Another religious activist and preacher, Sojourner Truth, was probably
second only to Frederick Douglass as the outstanding orator of black liberation during the mid-nineteenth century. Born as "Isabella" in Ulster County,
New York, in 1797, she was one of twelve slave children who were sold away
from their parents. In 1843 she began to speak out on her personal ordeal as
a slave at abolitionist gatherings and assumed the name Sojourner Truth.[36]
Angela Davis describes the Akron, Ohio, women's meeting of 1851 in which
"Sojourner Truth single-handedly rescued the . . . meeting from the disruptive jeers of hostile men. Of all the women attending the gathering, she alone
was able to answer aggressively the male supremacist arguments of the bois-
terous provocateurs."[37] The white male leader of the jeers argued that it was
incredible for women to desire the vote because they could not even walk over

a puddle or get into a carriage without the help of a man. Sojourner Truth then gave her impromptu speech "Ain't I a woman?" She stated that she herself had never been helped over mud puddles or into carriages. "And ain't I a woman?" Then she instructed him: "Look at me! Look at my arm," rolling up her sleeve to reveal the "tremendous muscular power" of her arm.[38]

> I have ploughed, and planted, and gathered into barns and no man could head me! And ain't I a woman? I could work as much and eat as much as a man—when I could get it—and bear the lash as well! And ain't I a woman? I have borne thirteen children and seen them most all sold off to slavery, and when I cried out with my mother's grief, none but Jesus heard me! And ain't I a woman?[39]

The only black woman attending the Akron convention, Truth accomplished what her white sisters were incapable of doing, because, according to the chairperson, "there were very few women in those days who dared to 'speak in meeting.'"[40] Her speech dealt a crushing blow to the "weaker sex" argument, and she also refuted the thesis that the Bible and Christian tradition supported male dominance. She remarked, "That little man in black there, he says women can't have as much rights as men, because Christ wasn't a woman. Where did Christ come from? From God and a woman! Man had nothing to do with him."[41] With quick wit and insight born of experience, Truth again countered sexist arguments against women's right to speak publicly and to plead for equality. Truth's quick wit and insight can be seen in her spin on Eve's sin. While Eve has been blamed for the cause of sin entering the world resulting in the fall of humankind, this was hardly an argument against women's capabilities. On the contrary, it supported women's capabilities: "If the first woman God ever made was strong enough to turn the world upside down all alone, these women together ought to be able to get it right side up again! And now they are asking to do it, the men better let them."[42] The general principle that governed Truth's arguments is the biblical notion of equality, which is "read" through her experience as a black woman in a racist and sexist society. Such a view allowed her to reimagine biblical narratives to glean liberative re-readings.

Julia A. J. Foote, a member of the AME Zion Church and preacher of the nineteenth century with Holiness influences, was born in Schenectady, New York, in 1823. Foote was among the pioneering black women preachers who began their ministries before the Civil War. Ignoring the gender conventions of her day and insisting on her right to preach placed her in conflict with her family, friends, and black ministers who were against women preaching. In 1895 Foote was the first woman to be ordained a deacon and in 1899 was the second woman to be ordained an elder in the AME Zion Church. Foote practiced her ministry until around 1900. "For more than fifty years, she served as an itinerant evangelist and a Methodist holiness preacher, traveling and lecturing widely at camp meetings, revivals, and churches in California, the Midwest, the Northeast, and Canada."[43] In her spiritual autobiography, *A Brand Plucked from the Fire* (1879), Foote, like Lee and Elaw before her, describes her call to the ministry in terms of the Spirit's prompting and the reproach that followed:

> Though I did not wish to pain any one, neither could I please any one only as I was led by the Holy Spirit. I saw, as never before, that the best men were liable to err, and that the only safe way was to fall on Christ, even though censure and reproach fell upon me for obeying his voice. Man's opinion weighed nothing with me, for my commission was from heaven, and my reward was with the Most High.

In pursuing her ministry against the grain of social convention, Foote argues that her call came from God; therefore, what "man" had to say was irrelevant, because she answered to a higher calling. Foote furthermore presents a strong argument for supporting women preachers from the Joel prophecy (Acts 2) and Gal. 3:28. In her use of the baptismal confession, the phrase "male and female" was *the* essential element of the saying:

> I could not believe that it was a short-lived impulse or spasmodic influence that impelled me to preach. I read that on the day of Pentecost was the Scripture fulfilled as found in Joel ii. 28, 29; and it certainly will not be denied that women as well as men were at that time filled with the Holy Ghost, because it is expressly stated that women were among those who continued in prayer and supplication, waiting for the fulfillment of the promise. Women and men are classed together, and if the power to preach the Gospel is short-lived and spasmodic in the case of women, it must be equally so in that of men; and if women have lost the gift of prophecy, so have men.
>
> We are sometimes told that if a woman pretends to a Divine call, and thereon grounds the right to plead the cause of a crucified Redeemer in public, she will be believed when she shows credentials from heaven; that is, when she works a miracle. If it be necessary to prove one's right to preach the Gospel, I ask of my brethren to show me their credentials, or I can not believe in the propriety of their ministry.
>
> *But the Bible puts an end to this strife when it says: "There is neither male nor female in Christ Jesus"* [Gal. 3:28]. Philip had four daughters that prophesied, or preached. Paul called Priscilla, as well as Aquila, his "helper," or, as in the Greek, his "fellow-laborer." Rom. xv. 3; 2 Cor. viii. 23; Phil. ii. 5; 1 Thess. iii. 2. The same word, which, in our common translation, is now rendered a "servant of the church" in speaking of

Phoebe (Rom. xix. 1.), is rendered "minister" when applied to Tychicus. Eph. vi. 21. When Paul said, "Help those women who labor with me in the Gospel," he certainly meant that they did more than to pour out tea.[44]

After using Joel's prophecy and Gal. 3:28 to support her argument for women's ministry, Foote lists New Testament women who practiced ministry with the Holy Spirit's sanction. However, for Foote the "no longer male and female" category of Gal. 3:28 entailed an end to the debate over women preachers. She recognized that if the black Christian religious tradition agreed that concrete implications should be expected from the first two elements of Gal. 3:28 (related to race and class), the same principle applied equally to the third element without further qualification. She emphatically states, "the Bible puts an end to this strife." In her argument the call of men and women to ministry is subject of the commissioning of the Holy Spirit without distinction. Thus she advocated a challenge to the polity and propriety of black churches, and even more she issued a bold challenge to her African American sisters to pursue their calling without fear of what others might say and do or how they might use Paul to silence them:

> Sisters, shall not you and I unite with the heavenly host in the grand chorus? If so, you will not let what man may say or do, keep you from doing the will of the Lord or using the gifts you have for the good of others. How much easier to bear the reproach of men than to live at a distance from God. Be not kept in bondage by those who say, "We suffer not a woman to teach," thus quoting Paul's words [1 Cor. 14:34], but not rightly applying them.[45]

The manner in which Paul's words are "rightly applied" for Foote is to read his injunctions as time-bound or limited to the cultural-historical situation of the local church in which they were given. This is so because Joel's prophecy, Gal. 3:28, and the example of women in ministry in the New Testament supply the bases for a correct view of the situation. This was true also for the black Baptist leader Virginia Broughton.

Gilkes maintains that it was in the Afro-Baptist tradition that arguments surrounding women's roles proved most troublesome. Between 1880 and 1900 an intensive struggle surrounding women's roles was based on concerns about leadership and conformity to patriarchal principles. This situation gave rise to the institutional basis for black feminism and the establishment of organizational autonomy among women. "Despite the overwhelming sexism among black Baptist men, even the content of their arguments against women's ordination has been shaped by the tradition of biblical debate established by women theologians of the ANBC [NBC]."[46] A leading figure in this debate, Virginia Broughton, an educated black Baptist churchwoman of the late nineteenth century, appropriated biblical themes to inform her understanding of women of her own time. In her book *Women's Work, as Gleaned from the Women of the Bible* (1904), she "summed up the ideas that had marked her public lectures, correspondence, and house-to-house visitations since the 1880s, and she sought to inspire the church women of her day 'to assume their several callings.'"[47]

Broughton argued that woman's relationship with Jesus provided a model that supported an alternate view of women's duties outside the home because she understood woman's primary obligation to be to God rather than to husband. This notion was realized in Broughton's own life in which she had to pronounce her allegiance to God above marriage and family. Unconverted when she began her mission work, Broughton's husband demanded that she end her career because it took her away for several days at a time from home and family. According to Higginbotham,

> When he asked, "When is this business going to stop?" Broughton replied with what she termed a divinely inspired answer. "I don't know," she hurled at him, "I belong to God first, and you next; so you two must settle it." . . . Her husband eventually came around to her way of thinking, "after a desperate struggle with the world, the flesh, and the devil." Broughton was able to convince her husband that she was called by God for missionary work and that "to hinder her would mean death to him."[48]

Broughton not only was able to challenge her husband's demands to cease her missionary work but also as creatively circumvented Paul's injunction to silence women in church. Broughton maintained that a woman's commitment to God surpassed her traditional roles and responsibilities. Paul himself maintained that humankind was both carnal and spiritual. But Broughton insisted: "Woman according to the flesh is made for the glory of man; but when recreated in Christ or born of the Spirit, she is recreated for such spiritual service as God may appoint through the examples given in his Word." Joel's prophecy that both "sons and daughters would prophesy" confirmed this.[49] Furthermore, in her defense of women's work in the church, she could point to examples of women of the Bible to support her claim. She described the biblical judge Deborah as a woman with a task that was independent of the will or control of her husband. She also employed Gal. 3:28 to support women's roles within and without the church. For Broughton God alone uses whom God pleases without distinction, so long as they have a willing heart. Along these lines she asserted:

> [Deborah's] work was distinct from her husband who, it seems, took no part whatever in the work of God while Deborah was inspired by the

Eternal expressly to do His will and to testify to her countrymen that He recognizes in His followers neither male nor female, heeding neither the "weakness" of one, nor the strength of the other, but strictly calling those who are perfect at heart and willing to do his bidding.[50]

Surprisingly, Broughton did not condone women preachers. According to Evelyn Brooks Higginbotham, "despite the broad number of roles that Broughton believed the Bible authorized and her rather unusual autonomy within her own household, she explicitly warned women against the danger of aspiring to roles that had no female precedents in the Bible. She denied that women should have access to the clergy or perform the clergy's role of establishing new churches, baptizing converts, and administering the Eucharist."[51] It is clear that for Foote the "no longer male and female" element of the baptismal saying settled the problem related to women in the preaching ministry. For Broughton, on the other hand, the saying could open the doors of opportunity for women to use their gifts in various ways in the church as long as it did not counter the traditional understanding of the biblical injunctions related to women's roles. In their separate ways, they recognized the implications that could be drawn from Gal. 3:28 to empower women for ministry. While "no longer male and female" meant for Broughton widening the opportunity for women to serve in the church within traditional parameters, for Foote, in particular, it represented a new pattern of relationships that rested on equality between men and women in preaching, ministry, and service within the church.

The same reality is expressed by Florence Spearing Randolph (see chapter 3). Like Julia Foote before her, she was a member of the AME Zion Church, the first black denomination to grant women suffrage (1876) and full clergy rights (1894). Randolph was among a small group of women in the late nineteenth century who functioned as evangelists, received license to preach, and were ordained as deacons and elders in the AME Zion Church. In the same way as her sisters before her, in her pursuit of a preaching career she defied gender conventions and went against the wishes of her husband, family, and friends. She excelled above her peers by receiving appointments to pastor a number of churches. Ultimately, her crowning achievement was serving as pastor of Wallace Chapel AME Zion Church in Summit, New Jersey (1925–1946). Beginning her ministry in the late 1880s, she was profoundly influenced by the Holiness teachings and example of Julia Foote.[52] In her sermon "Antipathy to Women Preachers," Randolph begins by referring to the women in Jesus' ministry who remained faithful throughout his career and were witnesses to his crucifixion and resurrection. Because of their unwavering faith these women were granted the privilege of being the first preachers of the resurrection: "You have been faithful, you persevered for the truth and hence you are honored by God and are first commissioned." She goes on to say:

> But notwithstanding the fact that the first gospel message was delivered to the women, there always has been and still is great antipathy to women preachers. But God, with whom there is neither Jew nor Greek, bond nor free, male nor female, in His wonderful plan of salvation has called and chosen men and women according to His divine will as laborers together with Him for the salvation of the world.[53]

Randolph cites all three pairs of the saying to stress not only the call of women to ministry but also the mutual work of ministry that men and women are to share together in God's plan of salvation. Galatians 3:28, used in its fullest form by African American women, reflects their concerns to push its meaning to include not only issues of sex/gender discrimination but also the collaboration of men and women in the plan of salvation without distinctions based on sex.

Rosa A. Horn was born on December 2, 1880, in Sumter, South Carolina. Initially joining the Methodist Church as an adult, she later joined the Fire Baptized Pentecostal Church and a short time later became an evangelist and was ordained into the Pentecostal ministry. After her marriage to William Horn, she and her husband finally settled in Brooklyn, New York, in 1926; in the same year she established the Pentecostal Faith Church in Harlem. The church grew and by 1934 was located in five cities. Known as Mother Horn by her followers, she was an extremely effective speaker and possessed great charisma. Horn was educated and cultured unlike some of the other Pentecostal, Holiness, and Spiritualist preachers. In 1933 she began a thirty-three-year radio ministry. She died on May 11, 1976.[54]

Bishop Horn, like the women before her, had to justify her calling despite her personal charisma and educational background. Along these lines she preached "Was a Woman Called to Preach? Yes!" on a black radio station in New York City during the late 1930s. The sermon seeks biblical authority for women's preaching by referring to Joel's "last days" prophecy in which sons and daughters prophesy.

> Note that when God said your sons and your daughters shall prophesy (preach)[,] that meant man and woman. You can't hinder the woman any-how, for the prophecy of Jeremiah 31:22, 606 B.C., is now being fulfilled which saith, "For the Lord hath created a new thing in the earth, A woman shall encompass a man." That's the Word! Are they not doing it? They are filling the pulpits and not only filling the pulpits, but

bringing in precious sheaves for the Master, for He is coming soon. . . . Did not the Lord say that He would pour out His spirit upon all flesh in the last days? Yes, the last days, saith God, the last days. When you see the women preaching in the pulpit, preaching in the house, preaching in the streets, preaching everywhere, these are some of the signs of the last days. . . . To whom did Jesus give the first message? Did He not say to the Marys at the tomb, "Go and tell Peter and my disciples to meet me in Galilee?" Instead of obeying the Word of God given to them by the women, those disciples were standing around talking. . . . Surely the Lord has called the women, under the Law and under Grace and he uses them whenever he needs them.[55]

For Horn, scripture confirmed the contemporary activity of women in ministry; she also referred to a vast array of biblical women to support her argument that God uses women to proclaim the gospel. She argued that biblical women not only were equal to men in leading godly lives but often excelled men in doing God's work.[56]

Quinceila Whitlow, another woman preacher and evangelist of note during her day, was born in Mercer, Tennessee. Before entering the ministry, she spent several years in the nursing profession after graduating from the Chicago School of Nursing. Although little else is known about her life or her career as an evangelist, in 1940 the editor of the CME *Christian Index* described her as "an Evangelist of high standing," whose "lectures are splendid and far-reaching. Those who hear her can never forget."[57] It is fortunate, however, that at least one of her sermons in which she cites Gal. 3:28 is left to posterity. In this sermon, "The Woman in the Ministry of Jesus Christ," Whitlow affirms women's right to preach the gospel and in the process applauds women's changing status in the church. Her sermon also "reflects the rhetoric of campaigns to recruit women into the workplace during World War II, declaring that there is a 'growing spirit of equality' in the country as 'new fields of labor' open to women."

> The position which woman occupies today under the elevating influence of Christianity and the growing spirit of equality is a matter of rejoicing among the best and most thoughtful minds in all classes. The new fields of labor that are opening to her, the widening spheres of influence which she is entering and filling with highest credit to herself and with greatest benefit to mankind. This cannot but awaken gratitude and hope in the heart of womanhood.[58]

Therefore, just as in the world of labor, the church needs to recognize the talents and gifts of women and develop a more open policy of leadership toward them. As evidenced in the following quotation, she echoes the arguments of many black female preachers before her. In her argument she confirms "that

gender is irrelevant when it comes to doing God's work; conversion and sanctification, not gender, truly qualify someone for the ministry."[59] Whitlow asserts:

> We need in our churches today eager and alert women, talented and
> accomplished women, skilled and artistic women, but far more than that
> we need Christian women, who with trusting faith and undaunted hope,
> will behold the Saviour despised and rejected of men, a man of sorrow
> and acquainted with grief. . . . No one has done so much for womanhood
> as Jesus. When His words proclaimed that in Him there is, "neither
> male nor female["] but He is the Saviour of all that blessed truth that
> became the Christian constitution for womanhood.
>
> Can you not see why womanhood has found a powerful appeal in the
> Gospel of Jesus Christ[?] May God save the woman of the Gospel from
> the brazen rejection of the narrow-minded critic. . . . Let the woman
> stand fast in her calling. We cannot sit idly by while modern denial con-
> tinues to rain blasphemous blows upon our Saviour. We must plead His
> cause and stand up for His truth. We must be prepared to stand alone to
> uphold the glorious truth of the Gospel. . . . I am praying to God that
> the ministers of our churches will help to stamp out this false doctrine
> that is being practiced in our churches today.[60]

In Whitlow's sermon, she attributes the baptismal saying directly to Jesus,
because for her and several other African American women Jesus is the ultimate source of liberation for women. For Whitlow, the gospel of Jesus Christ
contained the essence of what came to fruition in Paul's (and the early Christian missionary movement's) declaration of human unity and equality. This
connection is what makes it possible for her to proclaim that "womanhood
has found a powerful appeal in the Gospel of Jesus Christ." While Whitlow's
use of the term *womanhood* is understandable in view of the time in which she
writes, contemporary womanists and feminists no longer resort to such a term
as *womanhood* because of its essentialist connotations. They recognize instead
that all women are different because of a combination of variables—race,
class, geography, and sexual status.[61] Nevertheless, Whitlow sought to
encourage those who were opposed to women preachers to help stem the tide
of "antipathy" and end the "false doctrine" that women cannot practice ministry in the church. Again, like several women before her, Gal. 3:28 served as
the crux of her argument.

These examples highlight the importance of the idea of the "equality of all
people before God," supported by black women's interpretive traditions of
Gal. 3:28 (especially "no longer male and female"), Acts 2, and examples of
women in both the Old and the New Testaments. Black women have used
these biblical arguments to call the church to live out the full implications of
Gal. 3:28.

Contemporary African American Women Preachers

Moving from the historical situation to the contemporary, we find that the more things change the more they remain the same. Although several denominations have theoretically acknowledged the right of women to preach and to be ordained, many women are still put in a position in which they have to argue and justify their ministries. Today a number of contemporary women practice ministry, but I will be able to present only a representative sampling.

Pauli Murray was born in Baltimore on November 20, 1910. She was an educator, attorney, and Episcopal priest, and she described herself as an "unabashed feminist" and forthright advocate of women's rights. In her struggle for women's rights, she wrote the amendment that provided for inclusion of women in Title VII of the Civil Rights Act of 1964, prohibiting discrimination in employment. She also wrote the brief for *White v. Crook*, which dismantled state laws that denied women the right to serve on juries, and she was a leader in the struggle to have women admitted to law schools. She was also a cofounder of the National Organization for Women (NOW). She wrote several books and two autobiographies. Murray was ordained an Episcopal priest on January 8, 1977, at the age of sixty-seven, becoming the first black female and the second African American ordained to the priesthood in the Protestant Episcopal Church. She died of cancer on July 8, 1985.[62]

Murray's many sermons and writings reflect her struggles against racism and sexism. On the latter issue, she preached the sermon "Male and Female He Created Them" on May 21, 1978. She notes a commonly overlooked fact that *man*, as used in Genesis, actually means "humanity." God created "humanity" male and female. This interpretive oversight is used to validate the oppression of women in churches and society. Murray contends instead that because all humanity is created male and female, sexism is in direct opposition to God's plan for creation.[63] She asserts:

> In the very beginning of Holy Scripture is expressed the most liberating idea known to humanity—Man is made in the image of God, and Man here means male *and* female. *They*, not *he*, are to have dominion over the earth. This theme is repeated in Gen. 5: "When God created man, he made him in the likeness of God. Male and female he created them, and he blessed them and named them Man when they were created."
>
> Despite the clarity of this language that male and female both share the reflection of their Creator at the creaturely level and both share equally in the dominion over the earth, what has in fact happened is that sexism—the dominance of a patriarchal male-oriented society—is the oldest and most stubborn form of human oppression and has served as a model for other forms of human exploitation and alienation.[64]

The Rev. Dr. Prathia Hall, distinguished American Baptist pastor, preacher, educator, lecturer, and pioneering woman in ministry, held Master of Divinity and doctoral degrees from Princeton Theological Seminary. As a student in the 60s Dr. Hall was a leader in SNCC in Alabama and Georgia. She later became Associate Dean of Spiritual and Community Life, Director of the Harriet L. Miller Women's Center, and Dean of African American Ministries at United Theological Seminary in Dayton, Ohio. Dr. Hall also pastored the Mount Sharon Baptist Church in Philadelphia for nearly a quarter century and was recently an associate professor at Boston University School of Theology, holding the Martin Luther King Jr. Chair in Social Ethics. Dr. Hall specialized in womanist theology, ethics, and African American church history. She died on August 12, 2002, following a long illness.[65] It is not surprising that, despite a list of distinguished credentials and experience, she, like Murray and others before them, had to address sexism in the church. In her sermon "Beyond Eden" she reexamines Genesis 2 and 3 to locate the patriarchal basis of sexism in black churches and the black community.[66]

> African American churches have in large measure adopted the patriarchal attitudes of white Christians regarding women. . . . To the extent that black churches have accepted the patriarchal doctrines and practices of white churches, we are today faced with a black religious dilemma that has critical implications for our struggle for liberation. The issue is larger than women in the church. Indeed, the issue relates to our survival as a total people.[67]

Recognizing that the roots of such sexism are based in the biblical text, she shows how both women and men possess the image of God, as expressed in Gen. 1:27 and 5:1. Given this oft-overlooked fact, she argues that there is really no basis for women's subordination or inferiority to men: "What I am trying to tell you sisters and brothers, is that there is no biblical grounding for separation and alienation among you. There is no biblical grounding for believing that somehow some of you are better than others. . . . God has created you in equality and harmony and dignity."[68]

Ella Pearson Mitchell, educator, preacher, and much-sought-after conference speaker, has held a number of pastoral, teaching, and administrative positions in her long and illustrious career. She and her husband, the Rev. Dr. Henry Mitchell, have been in ministry for approximately sixty years. In the introduction of her first volume of sermons by black women ministers, *Those Preaching Women*, she recounts not only her own difficulties as a woman in ministry but also argues the right of all women to minister, with church sanction. Mitchell justifies the equal right of women to preach and pastor based on Acts 2:17-18 (cf. Joel 2:28-29). For her, the descent of the Spirit opened the way for a new social and religious order: "Your sons and *your daughters shall prophesy*" (emphasis in the original). She argues that "the foundational proclamation from the text is that God pours out his Spirit indiscriminately."[69] Since this is the case, *flesh* can and must mean both female and male *flesh*, with no distinction implied. "God's blessings would be on *all* flesh, regardless of nationality, race, age, sex, or social rank."[70]

Mitchell then recounts the gallant acts of biblical women such as Deborah, Hilkiah, and Huldah—women who held high positions in ancient Israel as judges, priests, and prophets. For her, these are "blinding shafts of light indicating that God [was] breaking through those cultural biases and progressively revealing [God's self] in even higher dimensions in regard to women—just as God has done in regard to minorities."[71] Much of her argument up to this point is in accord with the traditional types of arguments and justifications presented by most historical black women preachers. In this respect, we see that the equality of all people before God is the main theme, whether implicit or explicit. Mitchell then makes *the* important hermeneutical move of comparing the biblical statement to blacks' experience of oppression in America. She also makes the connection between sexism and racism: "Now those who want women to be subordinate and who wish to quote Paul, let me warn you that if you take Paul's statements [about women] . . . , you must do the same thing for slaves. And in that case, you would have to be a slave and find yourself a master."[72] This is an important point in regard to black churches and their practice of sexism because the interconnections between racism and sexism are difficult to deny. Mitchell exhorts the church to seek the examples in the scripture where God keeps trying to break through oppressive social structures. One of the most radical breakthroughs, Mitchell suggests, is Gal. 3:28.

Cynthia L. Hale, Pastor of Ray of Hope Christian Church, Disciples of Christ, in Atlanta, Georgia, in her sermon "Women Transformed by Christ . . . Filled with Power" (Luke 8:1-3) touches upon the relationship between Jesus and women. It is Jesus who transforms women's situation and supplies them with the power to overcome oppression and to come to a self-realization of their own power and gifts.

> In the presence of Jesus, women are transformed and filled with power. This power enables women to break from the societal norms and expectations that prohibit them from living up to their highest potential. This power helps rid women of negative perceptions and images that cause them to feel inadequate and inferior. This power allows women to recognize within themselves feminine worth and value without having

to take on the image of men or have men validate their existence. . . .
Jesus, then, was about the task of infusing women with the spiritual
strength and confidence of believing in themselves as equal children
under God.[73]

Jacquelyn Grant, Professor of Systematic Theology at Interdenominational Theological Center in Atlanta, communicates womanist themes and
principles in her sermon, "Faithful Resistance Risking It All: From Expedi-
ence to Radical Obedience" (Esth. 4:13-16). She compares the situation of
African American women with that of Esther, who also had to deal with the
interconnected issues of race and class.

> The connectedness of life at various levels is demonstrated in this story.
> Here we see the interlinkages of racism and sexism. Esther could escape
> the harsh realities of anti-Semitism only for a season, as Mordecai said.
> And even though she was a queen, she was still a woman, and in jeop-
> ardy on occasion. She and her predecessor, Vashti, were under absolute
> male domination.

Grant then goes on to express the themes of interconnectedness on a global
level, arguing that all oppression—race, class, and sex—is related:

> African-American womanist scholars have begun to emphasize this type
> of interconnectedness. Perceiving the interstructuring of racism, clas-
> sism, and sexism, they have insisted that the "we-ness" informs the "I-
> ness," even though the "I-ness" is our concrete starting place for all
> theological analysis. Our one concrete starting place locates us in the
> whole of reality. From there we recognize that the struggle for liberation
> is a global struggle. The oppression of blacks in the United States is not
> unrelated to the oppression of blacks in South Africa and the oppression
> of the indigenous peoples of Latin America or Australia.[74]

Leontine T. Kelly is a bishop in the United Methodist Church. In her sermon "A Call to Witness" (Isa. 43:1-10), she relates the story of an encounter
she had with an African American man.

> I remember the man who stopped me on my way to my church one Sun-
> day morning. He asked me, "Are you the woman who is the pastor of the
> church up on the corner?" I said, "Yes!" He said, "You are doing a great
> job." I said, "Thank you, you've made my day." I started away. He said,
> "Wait a minute. Come back here. There's only one thing wrong with
> that. You don't have any business doing it." He began to quote my
> brother Paul, from Corinthians. Then I said, "Sir, there are two hundred
> fifty children over at that church right now and I don't have time to
> stand here and defend my ministry to you. Besides, Paul didn't call me,
> Jesus called me."

This experience caused Kelly to reflect upon Paul's significance in spreading the gospel and making it accessible to the Gentile world:

> It took a Paul, however, to interpret the grace of God to include the Gentile world. Paul understood that the purpose for his salvation was not just to accept the Word in the sight of God, but it was to push back the perimeters of Judaism to understand the clear words of Jesus, "You shall be my witnesses."

These witnesses, Kelly relates, are called and empowered by God through the Holy Spirit. Paul recognized this, and so did Joel centuries before Paul:

> In the letter to the Romans, Paul reminds us that we are not called to conform to this world but to become transformers by the power of God's Spirit. Even Joel understood that new visions would be needed and it would take the Spirit upon all flesh: ". . . and your sons and your daughters shall prophesy, your old men shall dream dreams, your young men shall see visions: And also upon the servants and upon the handmaids . . . will I pour out my spirit" (Joel 2:28-29, KJV).[75]

Kelly, despite both the stranger's comments that Sunday morning and Paul's comments in his letter to the Corinthians, found a basis in Jesus and the Joel prophecy for supporting her ministry.

Summary

This overview of historical and contemporary African American women shows that the idea of the "equality of all people before God" is still a driving force for supporting an inclusive vision of human relations. In terms of justifying their call to ministry, women can find both a friend and a foe in Paul. Like Paul, women have had to argue for and support their call to ministry based upon a vision or experience without "official recognition" by institutions (cf. Galatians 1–2). In addition, Paul's apostolic status was continuously questioned and challenged (cf. 2 Corinthians 3–7; 10–13). Thus it turns out that, "ironically, the individual criticized for leaving us with the most difficult passage regarding women in ministry, Paul, is the one New Testament minister who spent his life defending his existence as a minister. Women can receive direction and instruction from him."[76] As we have seen, African American women have had their problems with Paul, but they have also found inspiration in him. Paul, read in light of his pastoral struggles and efforts to build the church, offers a more fruitful approach to his letters.

Contemporary African American Male Preachers:
Supporting the Sisters

African American preaching women have undoubtedly always had male supporters. In their spiritual narratives and biographies black women tell stories
of preaching, praying, and conversions that occurred within their ministries
that included both males and females. Some African American men, like
Frederick Douglass, Bishop Henry MacNeal Turner, the Reverend J. Francis
Robinson, and W. E. B. Du Bois, have been more vocal and outspoken in the
support of their sisters' struggles for equality. Such individuals recognized
the interconnectedness of oppression, realizing that they could not be totally
free until all black people were free. Several contemporary African American
male pastors and other religious leaders recognize this fact and have become
more vocal in their support of black women preachers.

Already in the 1950s, Bishop Ozro T. Jones of COGIC recognized the
importance of Gal. 3:28 and its potential to abolish race, class, and gender discrimination. Jones suggested that the "proper place of women in the church is
an age-old debate and from all appearances, it seems that it perhaps will be an
eternal one—at least for most mortals." He also realized that this has occurred
because "too often humanity has looked to the misty heights of theory rather
than the lowly foothills of practice and necessary human service."[77] For this
reason, in opposition to COGIC church polity, Bishop Jones, one of the General Board members, has ordained women in his Pennsylvania jurisdiction for
some time.[78] Bishop Jones believed that a positive assessment of Christian
women's work could be made because Christianity had addressed the status of
women more profoundly than other religions by insisting that Christ died for
all people indiscriminately. As mentioned above, this is an important argument in Galatians 3 in that, since Christ died for all people (3:1), all humanity has equal access to grace and the Spirit. Moreover, such an idea recognized
the humanity and intrinsic value of each person. Hence Jones could write:

> But lest we forget, this has been possible because Christianity has
> defined women to be persons. In so doing, Christianity has insisted that
> women are not commodities or an inferior breed, or something like "fac-
> tory rejects" of the human race, conceptions which held (and hold) sway
> wherever humanity has lived in the era of B.C. (before Christ). FOR
> PERSONS FOR WHOM CHRIST DIED any incidental physical con-
> dition is no longer a barrier to freedom, or dignity, or value as a person
> whether that physical condition be social distinction, be race ("Jew or
> Greek"), class ("bond or free"), or sex ("male or female"). They all share
> one spiritual destiny and nature and value in Christ. They all are "fellow
> heirs" of the promise in Christ.[79]

"Although the statement," Gilkes informs us, "contains problematic assumptions about the history of religions and cultural universals, it prefigures by nearly two decades some of the major (and no less problematic) arguments of contemporary Christian feminists."[80] Indeed, Jones has even prefigured the basic presupposition of this book's argument! As noted earlier, this theme is supported by a number of scriptural motifs, not the least of which is the idea that Christ died for all humankind. Jones's argument is in continuity with the African American religious tradition's stress on the "equality of all people before God." African American male preachers have also begun to draw upon this important theme in order to garner support for their sisters in ministry.

Ella P. Mitchell recently collected and edited the sermons of several preaching women and men in her book *Women: To Preach or Not to Preach?* This includes sermons of several male and female preachers who answer the question in the affirmative. In their sermons several themes of the African American religious tradition are employed to address this issue. John W. Kinney, Dean and Professor of Theology, School of Theology, Virginia Union University, and Pastor of the Ebenezer Baptist Church in Beaver Dam, Virginia, preached "Surprise! Surprise! Surprise!" (Luke 24:1-12, 21-24) for the ordination of Margaret Nelson at Greater Corinth Baptist Church in San Antonio, Texas.[81] In this sermon he deals with features of the black male sexism that continues to prevail in some black churches:

> I had the experience once of sharing in a conversation with a group of persons that included a woman who was preparing for ministry. One of the men there said, "Listen, sister, do you believe in the Bible?" She said, "Why, of course I do!" He said, "Well, we can stop this conversation right now." "Why?" she said. He responded, "The Bible says that women should be silent; we should not suffer a woman to teach or let her usurp authority over the man (1 Timothy 2:12)—You believe it; I believe it; the Bible said it. That settles it. Let's quit talking about this and move on."
>
> Now she was a very gifted woman, so she got into exegesis and analysis of Scripture texts. She said, "Now wait a minute! You pulled out your text; let me pull out mine. Let's deal with the whole Word!" Then he said, "No! No! No! What does the Bible say? The Bible says, 'Be silent.'" She said, "The Bible didn't say that; Paul said that." They went round and round. Finally I just raised a question. "Do you feel that you are treating this woman the way that Jesus would treat her?" And he said, "I'm not talking about Jesus; what does the Bible say?"

The unnamed woman in this scenario, like many black women before her, had to challenge biblically derived sexist notions and also to clarify who called her: it was not Paul but Jesus. I'm sure that the black male in the story would have a completely different interpretation of the exhortation "slaves be submissive to your masters." Kinney then addresses the basis of the misguided and misinformed attitudes that support such ideas—Gen. 3:16.

> Where did we get this idea that the man is over the woman? When we turn to Genesis 3:16, it says that because of the woman's sin the man shall "rule over" her. Now we've got to make up our minds in the church. Are we going to preach what God intended, "that the two shall be one," or are we going to preach what sin caused, as if Christ had never had anything to do with the sins of all of us? Are you going to preach God or are you going to preach sin? Read it! The reality is that we are so comfortable with our traditions, so comfortable with the ego investments we have in keeping things as they are, we don't run to Jesus: we run to each other.[82]

In Kinney's other writings he addresses this same passage and suggests that if Gen. 3:16 is the basis of human relationships, what we have is a model of relationships based upon "the curse." But in Christ the curse of the law has been removed: Gal. 3:13, "Christ redeemed us from *the curse of the law* by becoming a curse for us—for it is written, 'Cursed is everyone who hangs on a tree.' "[83] For this reason, human relationships should be based upon what has been accomplished in Christ as expressed in Gal. 3:28. This idea is the model that guides W. Franklyn Richardson's vision.

Richardson is Senior Pastor of Grace Baptist Church in Mt. Vernon, New York, and General Secretary of the National Baptist Convention, USA. Like Kinney's, his message "Faith that Denies the Context" (Isa. 40:4) was preached at the installation service for a female colleague, in this case the late Dr. Prathia Hall, at United Theological Seminary in Dayton, Ohio. He kept this commitment, he relates, even though he was invited by the World Council of Churches to be in Zimbabwe to meet with Nelson Mandela. That he would forgo this once-in-a-lifetime opportunity to meet with the legendary South African freedom fighter to preach at the installation of a woman preacher astounded and irritated some of his African American male colleagues. Slowly but surely he felt that providence was at work:

> At first I was not sure why the Lord led me to do that, but I went on. Later, I got a call from a newspaper reporter, and he said to me that some of my brothers and colleagues were upset that I was preaching in a service where a woman was being installed. Then I knew why God wanted me to be there, because beyond specific locations and personalities, the same thing that was going on in South Africa was going on there that night in Dayton.[84]

Richardson realized that the racist and oppressive attitudes that supported Apartheid in South Africa guided the sexist and oppressive attitudes of black churchmen in America. This small but important analogy can help black males recognize the interconnectedness of all oppression, just as black women of the past as well as present womanist scholars and pastors have been trying to impress upon us for some time. For Richardson this entails a broadening of black churches' vision that can indeed recognize the interrelatedness of life:

> The problem we have in the churches is that so many of us have no sense of vision. The function of this vision of faith is to instruct our actions until we arrive at our destinations. . . . But then, when we do have vision, it is often parochial. It's *my* family, *my* church, *my* people, *my* denomination, *my* sex. It's always selfish and narrow. But it seems to me that God has an interrelated world, a global family and we know all that. The truth of the matter is that everything today is tied together. . . . I'm excited about the *isness* of God—about what God is doing right now in this time, in this location. I'm excited about God's isness in the ordination of women, which represents a movement of history that has great potential.[85]

J. Alfred Smith Sr., Senior Pastor of the Allen Temple Baptist Church in Oakland, California, is the former president of the Progressive National Baptist Convention, and Visiting Professor of Homiletics at several San Francisco Bay Area seminaries. He preached "Surprise: Guess Who's Coming to the Pulpit" (Luke 24:10) as a trope of the 60s movie dealing with racism, *Guess Who's Coming to Dinner*, which starred Sidney Poitier. The connection between racism and sexism is hinted at already in the title. He exhorts male leaders and laypersons to give preaching women the hearing they deserve:

> Give to our sisters the courteous hearing that our sisters give to us. Women of the cloth must tell their story. No male orator can tell it with the flavor of feminine insight. Let them alone to tell us how Jesus brought them through the long agony of lonely nights and the aching anxiety of endless days. Let them tell how the risen Christ forged their suffering into alloys of pure gold. Let them tell how Jesus helped them assume so-called masculine responsibilities while maintaining feminine sensibilities. Let them tell how they wept at blood-soaked Calvaries and marched through the interim of waiting upon the Lord.[86]

Jeremiah A. Wright Jr., Senior Pastor of Trinity United Church of Christ in Chicago, preached a sermon titled "Surprise Party!" (Mark 16:9-11; Luke 24:8-11, 22a). In this sermon Wright recounts the situation regarding the return of the female disciples of Jesus from the empty tomb who, when they told the male disciples of Jesus' resurrection, were not believed. Wright draws parallels to today, when women preachers declare their messages and are not believed by some male listeners or members of the preaching guild. Wright asserts:

> Both Mark and Luke describe a situation that has not changed much in almost two thousand years. God surprises the church by what God shows to a woman! Jesus reveals himself as the *Risen* Lord to a woman! He tells her, corroborates John, to go tell the *men* what God has done, what God is doing, what the Lord has said to her, and how the Lord has commissioned her. And when she obeys the Lord, the church doesn't believe her! (Luke says the church doesn't believe *them*—none of the women!) Both Mark and Luke describe a situation that has not changed much in almost two thousand years. . . . God still surprises the church as it approaches the twenty-first century. God still surprises the church by what God shows to *women*. . . . The church did not and still does not want to hear the message that the Lord gives women because the church has a problem with women! But let us please be clear that that is *our* problem. That is *not* God's problem! So let's stop trying to put God's stamp of approval on the mess we are making of God's ministry! The women couldn't get a hearing because they were women![87]

Gardner C. Taylor, one of the "deans" of black preachers, is Pastor Emeritus of the Concord Baptist Church in Brooklyn, former President of the Progressive National Baptist Convention, and was Visiting Professor of Homiletics at various seminaries and theological schools. His sermon "Three Women and God" (based on the book of Ruth) compares racism with sexism and declares that both distort the vision of the kingdom of God. Speaking of slavery and the legacy of Jim Crow, Taylor says: "How sad that we who are the heirs of that tradition should come now to a place where we do not know what is the next step we ought to take." He infers that the black church should have learned its lesson regarding sexism from the mistakes of the nation regarding racism:

> As the nation has chosen to turn away from its democratic vision by its choice of racism and sexism, so have we in our churches chosen to distort the vision of the kingdom of God by limiting the full exercise of the gifts of women. We have excluded women from the pulpit and other areas of church leadership and dared to claim that this is God's will. We are guilty of an unholy liaison between sexism and the privilege of power. This is not of God. There is in Christ neither Jew nor Greek, neither bond nor free, neither male nor female.[88]

In the final analysis, Taylor argues that the aspect of the kingdom of God that supports this egalitarian vision is Gal. 3:28.

The late Samuel H. Proctor in his sermon "The Four Daughters of Philip, the Deacon" (Acts 21:8b-9) addresses the issue of sexism and women's call to ministry from a very different angle. He looks at family life and what parents must do to shape the character of their children. The evangelist Philip and his wife offered to the church four daughters who were prophets. How did they do this? Proctor perceives in this narrative an important element that is normally overlooked.

> In order for Philip and his wife to give to the young church four daughters speaking for the Lord, they had to guarantee to each one that she was God's precious person, and patiently guide each one into the deep, safe channels of the finest human development. If we are to save our nation, the human race, the family of God, we will have to find out how Philip and his wife did it for their four daughters.[89]

James A. Forbes Jr., Senior Pastor of the Riverside Church in New York City and former Engle Professor of Preaching, Union Theological Seminary, New York City, declares in his sermon "Ministry on the Eve of a New Millennium" (Revelation 20) that the new millennium poses several challenges for ministers and the church. However, in the final analysis the vision the church needs is an inclusive vision, and it is God who will equip ministers to meet that challenge. Thus Forbes encourages ministers to "tell the world what the vision is. . . . God's provisions are for whomever God calls—male or female."[90] One could argue that Gal. 3:28 supports this vision.

G. Daniel Jones is Senior Pastor of Grace Baptist Church in Germantown, Pennsylvania. He is also the 1984 American Baptist Ministers Council sermon award recipient for E.R.A. (Equal Rights Amendment) advocacy. His sermon "E.R.A." (Luke 10:38-42) quotes Gal. 3:28 as a substantial component of his call to equality.

> There is equality in Christ. "There is neither Jew nor Greek, there is neither slave nor free, there is neither male nor female" (Galatians 3:28). There is wholeness in Christ. There is completeness in him.
>
> This equality in Christ means mutual respect, mutual partnership, and equal opportunity. It means that one sex has no superiority over the other. It means promoting human kindness and human interests by eradicating any form of oppression, slavery, or suppression. It means that sexual hierarchy or pecking order for advancement is a no-no. It is a no-no in the kingdom of God. It means that a change is taking place; a change must take place, for Christ's sake and for the sake of righteousness. It means that Jesus is change. He is the necessary change. He is the light. He is hope in a world of social darkness.

> He calls us, male and female. He calls us from all walks of life. He
> calls us to awaken from centuries of spiritual slumber. He calls us to risk.
> He calls us to launch into the deep.[91]

Jones's challenge ends where we began. Bishop O. T. Jones saw in Gal. 3:28
the basis for a new vision of human relationships in the church and in society.
While male ministers could use a variety of texts and techniques to commu-
nicate the egalitarian themes of the Bible, none is clearer than Gal. 3:28 for
opposing the triple threat to human freedom and equality, namely, oppression based on race, class, and sex.

Conclusion

It comes as no surprise to say that Gal. 3:28 is the ideological and theological foundation upon which the black Christian tradition is built. Several
African American female and male preachers utilized this principle of "the
equality of all people before God" to justify the equal rights of women to
preach and to pastor (although few women specifically addressed pastoring in
their arguments, the same principle would apply). Just as the black churches
found hope, dignity, and inspiration to form independent congregations in
the midst of harsh criticism by whites, so too have black women found in this
principle a means by which to criticize bias and sexism in the black church.

Conclusion:
"We've Come This Far by Faith"

We've come this far by faith, leaning on the Lord, trusting in his Holy Word, He's never failed us yet. Oh, oh, oh, oh, oh, oh, oh, can't turn around, we've come this far by faith.

This book *will certainly not* bring an end to the centuries-old debate about women in the ministry. Nevertheless, I have attempted to show that there can be found within the New Testament, early Christian history, and the African American Christian tradition the seeds for hope and change. Therefore, in spite of criticisms that may be advanced about the particulars of my exegesis of some very problematic biblical texts or my interpretation of the historical and theological issues, I am convinced that the thesis of this book with respect to black women and all women in the ministry is founded upon a secure exegetical, historical, and theological basis.

Black churches (and black male leaders) must be willing not only to admit the inequity of the current situation with respect to women but also to act in concert with women to change church polity and policy and to challenge the sexist attitudes of church and society. Black churches have no trouble doing this with racism, but when it comes to sexism against black women in the black church, much remains to be done. Both racism and sexism must be seen as oppressive systems. Sexism, however, has a reality and significance peculiar to itself for black women, because it is a "form of oppression suffered by black women at the hands of black men."[1] Peter Paris characterizes the situation in following manner:

> Though the doctrine of human equality under God implies that none—including blacks—are justified in their attempts to subordinate the humanity of others, its application to blacks is often obscured by the prevalence of white racism in all walks of life. Thus, although blacks are guilty of oppressing other blacks . . . , the churches generally give their attention to the fact that all blacks are oppressed by the greater force of white racism, which is considered the greater evil and possibly the source of all sin.[2]

But, as James Cone informs us, the reality is that black churches are some of the most sexist institutions in the black community, and black ministers often appeal to the Bible to justify the subordinate role defined for women. I have tried to explicate James Cone's statement that "while many black males, both ministers and lay, have little difficulty rejecting Paul's command to slaves to be obedient to their masters as justification of black slavery, they seem incapable of taking a similar stance in relation to Paul's comments [or the misrepresentation of Paul's comments] about women."[3] Bettye Collier-Thomas suggests that given the percentage of black women in African American churches, they themselves might effectively be able to eliminate sexism and gender discrimination in the church. The African American religious tradition provides evidence that black Christian women have consistently raised their voices in print, in the pulpit, and in the pew against these forms of discrimination. But it seems that, for the most part, many black women have agreed with the tradition that racism has posed a greater threat than sexism. For this reason, many have chosen to devote their energies almost exclusively to eradicating racism. Nevertheless, African American women continue to be divided over which is of greater importance—racism or sexism.[4] If "equality of all people before God" is to be actualized in terms of sexism—just as it has for racism and classism—what is the role of black churches in this struggle?

Since black churches have a long history of struggle against racism and classism, they should be in the vanguard of the struggle against sexism—for it too is oppression on the same level as racism. If this is done, black churches can fulfill the complete vision of Gal. 3:28, a vision that has influenced their own development, contributed to their understanding of "the equality of all people before God," and inspired their religious-political rhetoric of "freedom and justice for all, regardless of race, creed, or color." If the black church and black people are going to create new roles for ministry, it must be realized that the present status of women in the ministry is unacceptable. If the gospel of equality is about eliminating the subordinate and oppressive status of persons based on physical characteristics, then gender as a justification for oppression is a physical characteristic and must be ended as a means of measuring one's social and ecclesiastical opportunities and potential. Since the gospel for the black church has historically been about liberation and has the potential to offer the possibility for creating new formations of human relations, we must take this opportunity to do so now, not in the future eschaton. Social roles are not *eternal*; they are human formations and as such can be changed by humans.

The black church must share in the struggle for the equality of women in the ministry of the Word. If women are oppressed and the black church is against oppression, its message must include the struggle of black women to gain access to all forms of ministry in the church. If this is not done, "the church cannot possibly be a visible manifestation that the gospel is a reality, for the gospel cannot be real in that context. One can see the contradictions between the churches' language or proclamation of liberation and its action by looking both at the status of black women in the church as laity and black women in the ordained ministry of the church."[5] The call for such action to end sexism in black churches is nothing new in the African American religious tradition, although the challenge was issued only after slavery's end. In 1899 the Reverend J. Francis Robinson issued such a clarion call to the churches on behalf of women.

> The slaves have been emancipated; now let us emancipate women! The unconditional and universal and immediate emancipation of womanhood is the demand of the age in which we live; it is the demand of the spirit of our institutions; it is the demand of the teachings of Christianity; it is her right, and, in the name of God, let us start a wave of influence in this country that shall be felt in every State, every county, every community, every home and every heart.[6]

But even if the black churches do not join en masse in the struggle, black women must continue the work to which they have been called. Many have preached and validated their calling to the ministry regardless of the criticisms and obstacles advanced against them, just as the black church justified its calling as a separate entity, which challenged America's practices and ideology concerning their existence. Black churches based their conviction on the black Christian tradition; so also have many black women preachers, ministers, and pastors.

The final assessment of the roles and challenges of African American women in black churches cannot be written by black men, no matter how sympathetic we might be to the struggle against racism and sexism. Women have been the foundation of black churches, culture, and society, yet their contributions have been generally ignored or relegated historically to second-class status. The effects of black sexism in the black churches in America will end only when black men begin to seriously challenge and uproot the patriarchal assumptions and institutions that still dominate black religious, civil, and political society.[7] Despite hardships, black women in the churches have performed the tasks of ministry against the established social norms and roles society has forced upon them as women. They believed that it was more important to obey God than to obey man (Acts 4:19). Moreover, black women did not and cannot wait for attitudes to change; they must continue their heritage of faith and courage and fulfill their calling to ministry.

There is hope on the horizon. The Rev. Dr. Vashti McKenzie was elected bishop in 2000 in the AME Church, and the Rev. Dr. Suzan Johnson Cook

(Baptist) was elected President of the Hampton University Ministers' Conference in 2002. These are major steps in the right direction. We can only hope that this is the beginning of significant changes in black churches.

Finally, I invite both black women and black men to consider a potent challenge by Theresa Hoover to black women to continue in and advance further their powerful heritage:

> With such a heritage of strength and faith, black women in the churches today must continue strong in character and in faith. They must reach other sisters and brothers with a sense of the commonality of their struggles on behalf of black people, and ultimately all humanity. They must continue to work within the "walls" of the church, challenging theological pace-setters and church bureaucrats; they also must continue to push outward the church "walls" so it may truly serve the black community. They must be ever aware of their infinite worth, their Godliness in the midst of creatureliness, and their having been freed from the triple barriers of *sex*, *race*, and *church* into a community of believers.[8]

This book offers a modest contribution to Hoover's challenge to African American churches. It is my hope that it may also serve as a source of encouragement to women and men in African American churches who are convinced that "an end to this strife" is on the horizon.

Notes

Introduction

1. James H. Cone and Gayraud S. Wilmore, eds., *Black Theology: A Documentary History*, 2 vols., 2nd ed. (Maryknoll, N.Y.: Orbis, 1993).

2. Delores S. Williams, *Sisters in the Wilderness: The Challenge of Womanist God-Talk* (Maryknoll, N.Y.: Orbis, 1993).

3. Cain H. Felder, *Troubling Biblical Waters: Race, Class, and Family* (Maryknoll, N.Y.: Orbis, 1989).

4. Arthur D. Griffin, *By Your Traditions: A Theological Perspective on Women in the Gospel Ministry* (Chicago: Black Light Fellowship, 1989).

5. See, for example, Clarice J. Martin, *Tongues of Fire: Power for the Church Today* (Louisville, Ky.: Presbyterian Church [U.S.A.], 1990); idem, "The *Haustafeln* (Household Codes) in African American Biblical Interpretation: 'Free Slaves' and 'Submissive Wives,'" in Cain Felder, ed., *Stony the Road We Trod: African American Biblical Interpretation* (Minneapolis: Fortress Press, 1990), 206–31; and idem, "Womanist Interpretations of the New Testament: The Quest for Holistic and Inclusive Translation and Interpretation," in *Black Theology,* 2:225–44.

6. Cheryl Townsend Gilkes, *If It Wasn't for the Women: Black Women's Experience and Womanist Culture in Church and Community* (Maryknoll, N.Y.: Orbis, 2001).

7. C. Eric Lincoln and Lawrence Mamiya, *The Black Church in the African American Experience* (Durham, N.C.: Duke University Press, 1990).

8. Ella Pearson Mitchell, ed., *Those Preaching Women*, vol. 1: *Sermons by Black Women Preachers*, vol. 2: *More Sermons by Black Women Preachers* (Valley Forge, Pa.: Judson, 1985, 1988).

9. Ella Pearson Mitchell, ed., *Women to Preach or Not to Preach? 21 Outstanding Preachers Say Yes* (Valley Forge, Pa.: Judson, 1991).

10. Bettye Collier-Thomas, ed., *Daughters of Thunder: Black Women Preachers and Their Sermons 1850–1979* (San Francisco: Jossey-Bass, 1998).

11. Sheron C. Patterson, *New Faith: A Black Woman's Guide to Reformation, Re-creation, Rediscovery, Renaissance, Resurrection, and Revival* (Minneapolis: Fortress Press, 2000).

12. Evelyn Brooks Higginbotham, *Righteous Discontent: The Women's Movement in the Black Baptist Church* (Cambridge: Harvard University Press, 1993); Paula Giddings, *When and Where I Enter: The Impact of Black Women on Race and Sex in America* (New York: Bantam, 1984).

13. Angela Y. Davis, *Women, Race, and Class* (New York: Vintage, 1983).

14. This definition is loosely based on the concept discussed in Stephen Breck Reid, *Experience and Tradition: A Primer in Black Biblical Hermeneutics* (Nashville: Abingdon, 1990).

15. Wilmore, *Black Theology*, 1:3.

16. Ibid., 1:217–18.

17. Peter J. Paris, *The Social Teaching of the Black Churches* (Philadelphia: Fortress Press, 1985).

1. Jesus, Paul, and a New Paradigm

1. Richard A. Horsley and Neil Asher Silberman, *The Message and the Kingdom: How Jesus and Paul Ignited a Revolution and Transformed the Ancient World* (Minneapolis: Fortress Press, 2002).

2. Horsley and Silberman, *Message*, 231.

3. See Bart Ehrman, *The New Testament: A Historical Introduction* (Oxford: Oxford University Press, 2000).

4. Horsley and Silberman, *Message*, 232.

5. I am following the lead of Elisabeth Schüssler Fiorenza, *In Memory of Her: A Feminist Theological Reconstruction of Christian Origins* (New York: Crossroad, 1983), 205–41.

6. Schüssler Fiorenza, *In Memory*, 103; Horsley and Silberman, *Message*, 204.

7. Ross S. Kraemer, *Her Share of the Blessings: Women's Religions among Pagans, Jews, and Christians in the Greco-Roman World* (New York: Oxford University Press, 1992), 138.

8. Horsley and Silberman, *Message*, 58–59.

9. Ibid., 5–6.

10. Schüssler Fiorenza, *In Memory*, 118–30.

11. Ibid., 122 and 130.

12. Horsley and Silberman, *Message*, 56.

13. Ibid., 129–30.

14. Schüssler Fiorenza, *In Memory*, 137–38.

15. Ibid., 138–39.

16. Ibid., 140–54.

17. Ibid., 141.

18. Ibid., 142.

19. Dieter Georgi, *The Opponents of Paul in Second Corinthians: A Study of Religious Propaganda in Late Antiquity* (Philadelphia: Fortress Press, 1986).

20. Kraemer, *Her Share*, 138.

21. Schüssler Fiorenza, *In Memory*, 142, 46.

22. Schüssler Fiorenza, *In Memory*, 147–48.

23. Some scholars note that Luke's short story pits Mary against Martha. In this text Jesus affirms Mary's sitting at his feet and chides Martha who is busy doing "women's work." "They thus reread the story as permitting women to step out of the gender roles assigned to them, but at the cost of denigrating women who engage in the work of sustaining life" (Mary D'Angelo, "Reconstructing 'Real' Women from Gospel Literature," in Ross Shepard Kraemer and Mary Rose D'Angelo, eds., *Women and Christian Origins* [New York: Oxford University Press, 1999], 105–28; 107).

Other feminist scholars have detected in the Greek terms for "serving" or "ministry" a more subtle argument for denying women from serving at the community ritual table—Martha's role in the story (that is, the Lord's Supper or Communion)—but allowing them to sit silently as disciples. See Elisabeth Schüssler Fiorenza, *In Memory*, 165–66. See also her article, "A Feminist Critical Interpretation: Martha and Mary, Lk 10:38-42," *Religion and Intellectual Life* 3/2 (Winter 1986): 21–36.

24. Ben Witherington III, *Women in the Ministry of Jesus: A Study of Jesus' Attitudes to Women and Their Roles as Reflected in His Earthly Life,* Society for New Testament Studies 51 (Cambridge: Cambridge University Press, 1984), 101.

25. Ibid.

26. Kraemer, *Her Share*, 141.

27. Horsley and Silberman, *Message*, 54.

28. Ibid., 7.

29. Jerome Murphy-O'Connor, *Paul: A Critical Life* (Oxford: Oxford University Press, 1997), v.

30. See Demetrius K. Williams, "Paul's Anti-Imperial Discourse of the Cross: The Cross and Power in 1 Corinthians 1–4," in *Society of Biblical Literature Seminar Papers 2000* (Atlanta: SBL Press, 2000), 796–823.

31. Horsley and Silberman, *Message*, 10.

32. Williams, "Paul's Anti-Imperial Discourse of the Cross."

33. Dennis R. MacDonald, *There Is No Male and Female: The Fate of a Dominical Saying in Paul and Gnosticism* (Philadelphia: Fortress Press, 1987), 14.

34. Hans Dieter Betz, *Galatians: A Commentary on Paul's Letter to the Churches in Galatia,* Hermeneia (Philadelphia: Fortress Press, 1979), 189–90; Richard A. Horsley, "Paul and Slavery: A Critical Alternative to Recent Readings," in Allen D. Callahan et al., eds., *Slavery in Text and Interpretation* (Semeia 83/84; Atlanta: Society of Biblical Literature, 1988), 153–200.

35. Daniel Boyarin: *A Radical Jew: Paul and the Politics of Identity* (Berkeley: University of California Press, 1994), 181.

36. Ibid., 193.

37. Frank J. Matera, *Galatians*, ed. Daniel J. Harrington, Sacra Pagina 9 (Collegeville, Minn.: Liturgical, 1992), 147.

38. Robin Scroggs, "Paul and the Eschatological Woman," *JAAR* 40/3 (1972): 283–303; 293.

39. Betz, *Galatians*, 195; Scroggs, "Paul," 292; Schüssler Fiorenza, *In Memory*, 208–9.

40. Scroggs, "Paul," 283.

41. MacDonald, *No Male and Female*, 15.

42. S. Scott Bartchy, *ΜΑΛΛΟΝ ΧΡΗΣΑΙ: First-Century Slavery and the Interpretation of First Corinthians 7:21,* SBLDS 11 (Missoula, Mont.: Scholars Press, 1973), 174.

43. MacDonald, *No Male and Female*, 16; emphasis in the original.

44. Elizabeth Schüssler Fiorenza, "Rhetorical Situation and Historical Reconstruction in 1 Corinthians," *NTS* 33 (1987): 386–403; 397.

45. Schüssler Fiorenza, *In Memory*, 180–85.

46. Cf. Rom. 1:16; 2:9f.; 3:9; also 1 Cor. 1:24; 10:32; Acts 14:1; 18:4; 19:10; 20:21. Paul undoubtedly knew of this formula (Rom. 1:14). In Col. 3:11 both are combined, expanded, and rearranged: "There cannot be Greek or Jew, circumcised and uncircumcised, barbarian, Scythian, slave, free man, but Christ is all and all."

47. Betz, *Galatians*, 191.

48. Ibid.

49. Acts presents Peter as the first to carry the gospel to Gentiles, but he was inconsistent with his interaction among them because of the social pressure applied by more conservative members of the Jewish church (Acts 11:1-18; 15:6-11; cf. Gal. 2:11-21).

50. *The New Oxford Annotated Bible with the Apocrypha: Revised Standard Version*, exp. ed. (New York: Oxford University Press, 1965, 1977). From the introduction to Galatians.

51. Schüssler Fiorenza, *In Memory*, 210.

52. Betz, *Galatians*, 192–93.

53. Ibid., 195.

54. "The ancient church did not lavish much attention on this letter because it was taken up with questions about life in this world and the gospel is not concerned with trivia." Edward Lohse, *Colossians and Philemon: A Commentary on the Epistles to Colossians and to Philemon*, Hermeneia (Philadelphia: Fortress Press, 1971), 187.

55. See Allen D. Callahan, *The Embassy of Onesimus: The Letter of Paul to Philemon* (Valley Forge, Pa.: Trinity Press International, 1997). This commentary advances the thesis begun in his "Paul's Epistle to Philemon: Toward an Alternative Argumentum," *Harvard Theological Review* 86/4 (1993): 357–76. See pp. 44–54 of *Embassy of Onesimus* for a discussion of the blood relationship between Philemon and Onesimus.

56. Lohse, *Colossians and Philemon*, 190, notes that Apphia may be Philemon's wife. Since her name follows immediately after Philemon's, one can assume that she is his wife. The lady of the house had to deal closely with the slaves. Therefore, she also had to give her opinion when the question of taking back a runaway slave was raised.

57. Ibid., 187.

58. Norman R. Petersen, *Rediscovering Paul: Philemon and the Sociology of Paul's Narrative World* (Philadelphia: Fortress Press, 1983), 290.

59. Ibid., 289.

60. Lloyd A. Lewis, "An African American Appraisal of the Philemon-Paul-Onesimus Triangle," in Cain H. Felder, ed., *Stony the Road We Trod: African American Biblical Interpretation* (Minneapolis: Fortress Press, 1991), 232–46.

61. W. G. Rollins, "Slavery in the NT," in *The Interpreter's Dictionary of the Bible: An Illustrated Encyclopedia*, Supplementary Volume, ed. Keith Crim (Nashville: Abingdon, 1976), 831.

62. Bartchy, *ΜΑΛΛΟΝ ΧΡΗΣΑΙ*, 129.

63. Ibid., 133.

64. Paul had already told the Corinthians in 1:26 that not many among them were wise (*sophoi*) according to human standards (*kata sarka*), not many were powerful (*dynatoi*), nor were many of them of noble birth, or well-born (*eugeneis*).

65. Bartchy, *ΜΑΛΛΟΝ ΧΡΗΣΑΙ*, 151.

66. See ibid., 155–59, for an explanation of this verse in terms of *mallon chresai*. Bartchy argues that on this phrase hinges the key to understanding 7:21-22. He translates the phrase to put Paul in a favorable light. From what follows it seems that Paul considered the freedom of the slave secondary to his or her "calling to Christ," which does not necessarily imply social freedom from human oppression.

67. This verse develops the theme of emancipation: "you have been bought with money." This could be explained in light of the sacral emancipation of slaves as practiced in Delphi: the slave is liberated by being symbolically sold to Apollo. This could be what Paul was referring to, for he tells them not to become slaves of men. See Hans Conzelmann, *1 Corinthians: A Commentary on the First Epistle to the Corinthians*, Hermeneia (Philadelphia: Fortress Press, 1975), 128, and Bartchy, *ΜΑΛΛΟΝ ΧΡΗΣΑΙ*, 121–26.

68. Schüssler Fiorenza, *In Memory,* 218–19.

69. Betz, *Galatians*, 200.

70. Schüssler Fiorenza, *In Memory*, 225.

71. Ibid.

72. Ibid., 227.

73. Ibid., 230.

74. Antoinette Clark Wire, *The Corinthian Women Prophets: A Reconstruction through Paul's Rhetoric* (Minneapolis: Fortress Press, 1990).

75. See Conzelmann, *1 Corinthians*, 245, and Schüssler Fiorenza, *In Memory*, 230–31.

76. Robert W. Allison, "Let Women Be Silent in the Church (1 Cor. 14:33b-36): What Did Paul Say, and What Did It Mean?" *JSNT* 32 (1988): 27–60.

77. Betz, *Galatians*, 196, and Schüssler Fiorenza, *In Memory*, 205–6.

78. Cf. *Gospel of Thomas* 22; *Gospel of the Egyptians* 2; *Gospel of Philip* 78; see also Betz, *Galatians*, 196 nn. 118–20.

79. Wayne Meeks, "The Image of the Androgyne: Some Uses of a Symbol in Earliest Christianity," *History of Religions* 13 (1974): 165–208.

80. Boyarin, *Paul*, 189.

81. MacDonald, *No Male and Female*, 16, 25.

82. Meeks, "Image," 207.

83. Matera, *Galatians*, 146.

84. James D. G. Dunn, *The Epistle to the Galatians* (Peabody, Mass.: Hendrickson, 1993), 207.

85. MacDonald, *No Male and Female*, 130.

86. Meeks, "Image," 208.

87. Scroggs, "Paul," 283 n. 1; original emphasis.

88. Stanley K. Stowers, "Paul and Slavery: A Response," *Semeia* 83/84 (1998): 295–311; 304.

89. Schüssler Fiorenza, *In Memory*, 218.

90. MacDonald, *No Male and Female*, 116.

91. Scroggs, "Paul," 291.

92. See Ignatius's letter to Polycarp 4:3ff. He tells Polycarp, bishop of Smyrna, not to buy the freedom of slaves from the church's treasury. Again we can see the ambiguous response on the part of church leaders to this serious issue for the church.

2. Scripture, Subjugation, and Silence

1. Catherine and Richard Kroeger, "Strange Tongues, or Plain Talk?" *Daughters of Sarah* 12/4 (1986): 10.

2. See Robin Scroggs, "Paul and the Eschatalogical Woman," *JAAR* 40 (1970): 283–303.

3. S. C. Barton, "Paul's Sense of Place: An Anthropological Approach to Community Formation in Corinth," *NTS* 32.2 (1986): 225–46.

4. Ibid., 323.

5. Elisabeth Schüssler Fiorenza, *In Memory of Her: A Feminist Theological Reconstruction of Christian Origins* (New York: Crossroad, 1983), 211.

6. Ibid., 214.

7. Ibid. Cf. Craig S. Keener, *Paul, Women and Wives: Marriage and Women's Ministry in the Letters of Paul* (Peabody, Mass.: Hendrickson, 1992), 73–88, in which he suggests that it refers to all uneducated women.

8. Ibid.

9. Hans Conzelmann, *1 Corinthians: A Commentary on the First Epistle to the Corinthians*, Hermeneia (Philadelphia: Fortress Press, 1975), 245.

10. Ibid., 245.

11. William O. Walker Jr., "The 'Theology of Woman's Place' and the 'Paulinist' Tradition," *Semeia* 28 (1983): 101–12.

12. Robert W. Allison, "Let Women Be Silent in the Churches (1 Cor. 14:33b-36): What Did Paul Really Say, and What Did It Mean?" *JSNT* 32 (1988): 27–60.

13. Ibid., 29.

14. Ibid.

15. Ibid., 30.

16. Ibid., 36.

17. Ibid., 47.

18. Ibid.

19. Ibid., 46.

20. Ibid., 48.

21. Ibid.

22. Ibid., 49.

23. Issues summarized here are more fully discussed by Dennis Duling and Norman Perrin, *The New Testament: An Introduction*, 2nd ed. (New York: Harcourt Brace Jovanovich, 1982, 1974), 262–82.

24. Ibid., 279.

25. Ibid., 262.

26. Walker, "Theology of Women's Place," 101.

27. Ibid., 104.

28. Allison, "Let Women Be Silent," 52.

29. Ross S. Kraemer, *Her Share of the Blessings: Women's Religions among Pagans, Jews, and Christians in the Greco-Roman World* (New York: Oxford University Press, 1992), 146.

30. Antoinette Clark Wire, *The Corinthian Women Prophets: A Reconstruction through Paul's Rhetoric* (Minneapolis: Fortress Press, 1990), 119, 123; see the entire section 116–34.

31. Margaret M. MacDonald, "Rereading Paul: Early Interpreters of Paul on Women and Gender," in Ross Shepard Kraemer and Mary Rose D'Angelo, eds., *Women and Christian Origins* (New York: Oxford University Press, 1999), 236–53; 246; also Keener, *Paul, Women and Wives*, 47.

32. Keener, *Paul, Women and Wives*, 101.

33. Kraemer, *Her Share*, 150–51.

34. Keener, *Paul, Women and Wives*, 118.

35. Schüssler Fiorenza, *In Memory*, 245.

36. David. L. Balch, *Let Wives Be Submissive: The Domestic Code in 1 Peter* (Chico, Calif.: Scholars Press, 1981), 33–38.

37. Quoted in Schüssler Fiorenza, *In Memory*, 255.

38. Ibid., 256.

39. Ibid., 256.

40. Ibid., 257.

41. Ibid.

42. Frank Stagg, "The Gospel, *Haustafeln*, and Women: Mark 1:1; Colossians 3:18-4:1," *Faith and Mission* 2/2 (1985): 60.

43. Schüssler Fiorenza, *In Memory*, 252.

44. Ibid., 253–54.

45. Ibid., 269.

46. Clarice J. Martin, "The *Haustafeln* in African American Biblical Interpretation: 'Free Slaves' and 'Submissive Wives,'" in Cain Felder, ed., *Stony the Road We Trod: African American Biblical Interpretation* (Minneapolis: Fortress Press, 1990), 210–13.

47. William Herzog, "The 'Household Duties Passages': Apostolic Traditions and Contemporary Concerns," *Foundations* 24 (1981): 204–15.

48. Balch, "Let Wives Be Silent," 81; Martin, "The *Haustafeln*," 210–11.

49. Schüssler Fiorenza, *In Memory*, 245–51.

50. Dennis Ronald MacDonald, *The Legend and the Apostle: The Battle for Paul in Story and Canon* (Philadelphia: Westminster, 1983).

51. Quoted in Dennis Ronald MacDonald, *There Is No Male and Female: The Fate of a Dominical Saying in Paul and Gnosticism* (Philadelphia: Fortress Press, 1987), 106 n. 1.

52. Kraemer, *Her Share*, 154.

53. Thomas Kuhn, *The Structure of Scientific Revolutions*, 3rd ed. (Chicago: University of Chicago Press, 1996), 150.

54. Elaine Pagels, *The Gnostic Gospels* (New York: Random House, 1979), 72–73.

55. Ibid., 81–82.

56. Ibid., 82.

57. Ibid., 82–83.

58. Tertullian, *On the Veiling of Virgins*, 9.

59. Ibid., 79.

60. Ibid., 76.

61. Kraemer, *Her Share*, 157.

62. William L. Andrews, ed., *Sisters of the Spirit: Three Black Women's Autobiographies of the Nineteenth Century* (Bloomington: Indiana University Press, 1986), 36.

63. Scroggs, "Paul and the Eschatalogical Woman," 292.

64. Ibid., 293.

65. Ibid., 302–3.

3. Proclamation, Protest, and a New Principle

1. Joseph R. Washington, *Black Religion: The Negro and Christianity in the United States* (Boston: Beacon, 1964), 33.

2. Willard M. Swartley, *Slavery, Sabbath, War, and Women: Case Issues in Biblical Interpretation* (Scottdale, Pa.: Herald, 1983).

3. See Helmut Koester, *Introduction to the New Testament* (Berlin: de Gruyter, 1980, 1982, paperback 1987), 2:261–308, and Norman Perrin and Dennis Duling, *The New Testament: An Introduction,* 3rd ed. (New York: Harcourt Brace Jovanovich, 1982, 1974), 371–93.

4. See M. I. Finley, *Slavery in Classical Antiquity* (New York: Barnes and Noble/Herffer, 1960, 1964), also his *Economy and Society in Ancient Greece* (New York: Viking, 1952, 1982); and S. Scott Bartchy, *ΜΑΛΛΟΝ ΧΡΗΣΑΙ: First-Century Slavery and the Interpretation of I Corinthians 7:21* (Missoula: University of Montana Press, 1973) as representative of scholarly agreement on this point.

5. See James O. Buswell, *Slavery, Segregation and Scripture* (Grand Rapids: Eerdmans, 1964), 5.

6. Kelly Miller, *Race Adjustment: Essays on the Negro in America* (New York: Neale, 1908), 115; cf. Buswell, *Slavery*, 11.

7. The proslavery argument was based significantly upon the Bible. Cf. Buswell, *Slavery*, 9–11.

8. Ibid., 12.

9. Trevor Bowen, *Divine White Right: A Study of Race Segregation and Interracial Cooperation in Religious Organizations and Institutions in the United States* (New York: Harper & Brothers, 1934), 107; Buswell, *Slavery*, 13.

10. Buswell, *Slavery*, 13–14.

11. Ibid., 14–15.

12. Ibid., 15.

13. Ibid., 15.

14. Ibid., 16.

15. Ibid., 17.

16. Ibid., 17–18.

17. Ibid., 59–60.

18. Clarice J. Martin, "The *Haustafeln* in African American Biblical Interpretation: 'Free Slaves' and 'Submissive Wives,'" in Cain Hope Felder, ed., *Stony the Road We Trod: African American Biblical Interpretation* (Minneapolis: Fortress Press, 1990), 215, quoting A. Leon Higginbotham Jr., *In the Matter of Color: The Colonial Period*, Race and the American Legal Process vol. 1 (New York: Oxford University Press, 1978), 37.

19. Albert J. Raboteau, *Slave Religion: The "Invisible Institution" in the Antebellum South* (New York: Oxford University Press, 1978), 102, 116.

20. Buswell, *Slavery*, 27.

21. Raboteau, *Slave Religion*, 128.

22. Ibid., 132.

23. Gayraud S. Wilmore, *Black Religion and Black Radicalism: An Interpretation of the Religious History of Afro-American People*, 3rd ed. (Maryknoll, N.Y.: Orbis, 1998), 28.

24. Raboteau, *Slave Religion*, 148.

25. Ibid., 148.

26. Wilmore, *Black Religion*, 4.

27. Ibid., 46.

28. Buswell, *Slavery*, 34.

29. Wilmore, *Black Religion*, 27–28.

30. Raboteau, *Slave Religion*, 238.

31. Wilmore, *Black Religion*, 24.

32. Buswell, *Slavery*, 30–31.

33. Ibid., 34.

34. Raboteau, *Slave Religion*, 241.

35. Cited in Milton Sernett, *Afro-American Religious History: A Documentary Witness* (Durham, N.C.: Duke University Press, 1985), 191.

36. Ibid., 192–24.

37. Ibid., 102.

38. Ibid., 106.

39. James H. Cone, *The Spirituals and the Blues* (Maryknoll, N.Y.: Orbis, 1972), 43–52.

40. Cone, *Spirituals*, 47, 49, 52.

41. Clarice J. Martin, "'Somebody Done Hoodoo'd the Hoodoo Man': Language, Power, Resistance, and the Effective History of Pauline Texts in American Slavery," *Semeia* 83/84 (1998): 203–33, 213.

42. Neil Elliot, *Liberating Paul: The Justice of God and the Politics of the Apostle* (Maryknoll, N.Y.: Orbis, 1994), 9.

43. Brian K. Blount, *Then the Whisper Put on Flesh: New Testament Ethics in an African American Context* (Nashville: Abingdon, 2001), 119.

44. Amos Jones Jr., *Paul's Message of Freedom: What Does It Mean to the Black Church?* (Valley Forge, Pa.: Judson, 1984), 37.

45. Blount, *Whisper*, 120–21.

46. Abraham Smith, "Putting 'Paul' Back Together Again: William Wells Brown's *Clotel* and Black Abolitionist Approaches to Paul," in Allen D. Callahan et

al., eds., *Slavery in Text and Interpretation*(Semeia 83/84; Atlanta: Society of Biblical Literature, 1998), 251–62.

47. Peter J. Paris, *The Social Teaching of the Black Churches* (Philadelphia: Fortress Press, 1985), xiv.

48. Vincent L. Wimbush, "The Bible and African Americans: An Outline of an Interpretative History," in Felder, *Stony the Road*, 81–97; 90.

49. Vincent L. Wimbush, "Reading Texts through Worlds, Worlds through Texts" *Semeia* (1993): 129–39, 132.

50. The Holy Spirit's descent at Pentecost and the prophecy of Joel, "Your sons and daughters shall prophesy" (Acts 2); "God is no respecter of persons" (Acts 10:34-36, KJV); "[God] hath made of one blood all nations of men for to dwell on all the face of the earth" (Acts 17:26, KJV).

51. Wimbush, "The Bible and African Americans," 90.

52. Paris, *Social Teaching*, 11. Paris states further: "Their raison d'être is inextricably tied to the function of opposing the beliefs and practices of racism by proclaiming the biblical view of humanity as they have appropriated it, that is, the equality of all persons under God. Thus their moral aim is theologically grounded. The doctrine of human equality under God is, for them, the final authority for all matters pertaining to faith, thought, and practice. In short, its function in the black experience is categorical, that is, it is unconditional, absolute, and universally applicable" (14).

53. Ibid., 11.

54. Ibid., 12.

55. Ibid., 10–13.

56. Wilmore, *Black Religion*, 37.

57. Cf. Elisabeth Schüssler Fiorenza, *Bread Not Stone: The Challenge of Feminist Biblical Interpretation* (Boston: Beacon, 1984), 15–18. Schüssler Fiorenza herself has been influenced by and engages with the history of African American hermeneutics. This is expressed clearly in her edited volume, *Searching the Scriptures: A Feminist Critical Introduction*, vol. 1 (New York: Crossroad/Herder & Herder, 1977), which is dedicated to the memory of Anna Julia Cooper, the nineteenth-century black feminist/womanist of great learning and of committed advocacy for women's rights and equality. In this volume Schüssler Fiorenza informs her readers that "singling out *The Woman's Bible* as *the* milestone in the history of women's biblical interpretation not only risks overlooking the contributions of women of color to biblical hermeneutics. It also continues white feminist gender discourse inscribed in *The Woman's Bible* that does not recognize the constitutive kyriarchal *differences* among and within women. In so doing, it is not only in danger of perpetuating a feminist historical discourse that celebrates the work of those nineteenth-century feminists with 'fair skin' and forgets or represses feminist achievements of women from the 'Dark Continent' but also in danger of perpetuating the cultural myth of 'true womanhood.' . . . As long as feminist interpretation focuses on the universalizing of gender discourse, its vision remains one-sided and partial" (12).

58. Wilmore, *Black Religion*, 78; Paris, *Social Teaching*, 10.

59. Joseph R. Johnson, "Jesus the Liberator," in James H. Cone and Gayraud S. Wilmore, eds., *Black Theology: A Documentary History*, 2 vols., 2nd ed. (Maryknoll, N.Y.: Orbis, 1993) 1:207.

60. Ibid., 211.

61. Allen Dwight Callahan, "'Brother Saul': An Ambivalent Witness to Freedom," *Semeia* 83/84 (1998): 235–50; Abraham Smith, "Putting 'Paul' Back Together Again: William Wells Brown's *Clotel* and Black Abolitionists' Approaches to Paul," *Semeia* 83/84 (1998): 251–62; Martin, "The Haustafeln"; Cain Hope Felder, *Troubling Biblical Waters: Race, Class, and Family* (Maryknoll, N.Y.: Orbis, 1989).

62. Albert B. Cleage, *The Black Messiah* (New York: Sheed and Ward, 1968); James H. Cone, *God of the Oppressed* (New York: Seabury, 1975); Howard Thurman, *Jesus and the Disinherited* (Richmond, Ind.: Friends United Press, 1981); Delores S. Williams, *Sisters in the Wilderness: The Challenge of Womanist God-Talk* (Maryknoll, N.Y.: Orbis, 1993).

63. Williams, *Sisters in the Wilderness*, 146–47.

64. Felder, *Troubling*, 147.

65. Callahan, "Brother Saul," 249.

66. See Demetrius K. Williams, "African American Churches and Galatians 3:28: A Brief Assessment of the Appropriation of an Egalitarian Paradigm," in Shelly Matthews, Cynthia Briggs Kittredge, and Melanie Johnson-DeBaufre, eds., *Walk in the Ways of Wisdom: Essays in Honor of Elisabeth Schüssler Fiorenza* (Harrisburg, Pa.: Trinity Press International, 2003) for some initial thinking along this line.

67. See, for example, Latta R. Thomas, *Biblical Faith and the Black American* (Valley Forge, Pa.: Judson, 1976); Jones, *Paul's Message of Freedom*; Felder, *Troubling*; Wimbush, "The Bible and African Americans."

68. Vincent Wimbush, who has been one of the trailblazers in the emerging field of African American biblical hermeneutics, mentions the significance of Gal. 3:28 for African Americans in two important works: "The Bible and African Americans," 90, and "Reading Texts through Worlds," 62. He also expounds briefly upon the African American historical context and the hermeneutical framework in which the passage's import emerged. But he does not provide an analysis of the function of Gal. 3:28 within African Americans' religious-political rhetoric from actual sermons, speeches, or narratives. He does provide, however, samples of speeches and statements employing seminal quotes and allusions from Acts ("Reading Texts through Worlds," 132–36), which were used in conjunction with Gal. 3:28 to support the overall principle of human unity and equality. These observations, to be sure, do not diminish Wimbush's contributions in this area but allow room for the lacuna to be filled, if even in a cursory fashion.

69. Raboteau, *Slave Religion*, 305.

70. In the deutero-Pauline tradition of Col. 3:13, however, the freedom of women and slaves is curtailed by the household codes (Col. 3:18-4:1). But the author of Colossians does expand upon the ethnic categories and in this way emphasizes particularly the "neither Jew nor Greek" pair. Perhaps this author recognized Paul's own unequivocal commitment to this category in particular.

71. In Anthony B. Pinn, ed., *Making the Gospel Plain: The Writings of Bishop Reverdy C. Ransom* (Harrisburg, Pa.: Trinity Press International, 1999), 170–76.

72. Ibid., 173–74.

73. Ibid., 176.

74. Quoted in Paris, *Social Teaching*, 51.

75. Vincent L. Wimbush, "Biblical Study as Liberation: Toward an Afro-Christian Hermeneutic," 142, in Gayraud S. Wilmore, *Afro-American Religious Studies: An Interdisciplinary Anthology* (Durham, N.C.: Duke University Press, 1989), 140–54.

76. Howard Thurman, *The Creative Encounter* (New York: Harper & Row, 1954), 152.

77. Abraham Smith ("Putting 'Paul' Back Together Again," 255) inadvertently identifies the passage as Gal. 3:27; Pennington is probably referring to Col. 3:11, as the following discussion will suggest.

78. C. Peter Ripley, ed., *The Black Abolitionist Papers*, vol. 1, *The British Isles, 1830–1865* (Chapel Hill: University of North Carolina Press, 1985), 129.

79. Pennington was not scheduled to offer a speech, but after being well-received and greeted by a hearty applause from the audience, he offered a resolution that took the form of a speech. "Pennington's remarks typified the tendency of black abolitionists to turn public discussions on any issue into a forum for considering slavery" (editor's comments, *Black Abolitionist Papers,* 129).

80. "Speech by J. W. C. Pennington, Delivered at Exeter Hall, London, England, 21 June 1843," in *Black Abolitionist Papers*, 129–33, 132.

81. Smith, "Putting 'Paul' Back Together Again," 255. While Smith states that Pennington exploits Gal. 3:28, Pennington is most likely alluding to Col. 3:11. Pennington's quote of Col. 3:11 works better than the archetypal paradigm of Gal. 3:28, it would appear, because in the context of Col. 3:11 the deutero-Pauline author encourages his readers to put to death the practice of various sins and selfish behaviors (3:5-8) that are a part of the "old humanity" and to become participants in the "renewal" through Christ: "seeing that you have stripped off the old self with its practices and have clothed yourselves with the new self, which is being renewed in knowledge according to the image of its creator. In that renewal there is no longer Greek and Jew, circumcised and uncircumcised, barbarian, Scythian, slave and free; but Christ is all and in all!" (Col. 3:9-11). The context of this passage, referring to human sinfulness and the need for renewal, fit Pennington's rhetorical purposes in his speech quite well.

82. William L. Andrews, ed., *Sisters of the Spirit: Three Black Women's Autobiographies of the Nineteenth Century* (Bloomington: Indiana University Press, 1986), 85–86.

83. Bettye Collier-Thomas, *Daughters of Thunder: Black Women Preachers and Their Sermons, 1850–1979* (San Francisco: Jossey-Bass, 1998), 48–51.

84. Ibid., 129.

85. Ibid., 129.

86. Wimbush, "Reading Texts through Worlds," 135.

87. Callahan, "Brother Saul," 244.

88. Gerda Lerner, *Black Women in White America: A Documentary History* (New York: Vintage, 1973), 136.

89. Lerner, *Black Women*, 39.

90. Raboteau, *Slave Religion*, 294.

91. Ibid.

92. Ibid.

93. Ibid., 295.

94. Cf. Cornel West, *Prophesy Deliverance: An Afro-American Revolutionary Christianity* (Philadelphia: Westminster, 1982), 39–41.

95. Cited in Pinn, *Making the Gospel Plain*, 166–70.

96. Ibid., 166.

97. Ibid., 167.

98. Ibid., 167.

99. Wimbush, "Reading Worlds through Texts," 137.

100. Wilmore, *Black Religion*, 78.

101. Ibid., 74.

102. Ibid.

103. Ibid., 78.

104. Ibid.

105. Ibid.

106. Wilmore, *Black Religion*, 57.

107. Aldon D. Morris, *The Origins of the Civil Rights Movement: Black Communities Organizing for Change* (New York: Free Press, 1984), 14.

4. Pulpit, Power, and Prohibitions

1. Lucy Parsons, 1905; quoted in Manning Marable, *How Capitalism Underdeveloped Black America: Problems in Race, Political Economy, and Society* (Boston: South End, 1983), 69.

2. Cheryl Townsend Gilkes, *If It Wasn't for the Women: Black Women's Experience and Womanist Culture in Church and Community* (Maryknoll, N.Y.: Orbis, 2001), 129.

3. Charles H. Pleas, *Fifty Years Achievement (History): Church of God in Christ* (Memphis: Church of God in Christ Publishing House, n.d. [circa 1957]), 35; quoted in Gilkes, *If It Wasn't*, 123.

4. bell hooks, *Ain't I a Woman: Black Women and Feminism* (Boston: Beacon, 1981), 88.

5. Ibid., 99.

6. Theresa Hoover, "Black Women and the Churches: Triple Jeopardy," in James H. Cone and Gayraud S. Wilmore, eds., *Black Theology: A Documentary History*, 2 vols., 2nd ed. (Maryknoll, N.Y.: Orbis, 1993), 1:380.

7. Jacquelyn Grant, "Black Theology and the Black Woman," in *Black Theology*, 1:423.

8. Ibid.

9. Gilkes, *If It Wasn't*, 209.

10. E. Franklin Frazier, *The Negro Church in America*, and C. Eric Lincoln, *The Black Church since Frazier* [2 works in 1 vol.] (New York: Schocken, 1974), 116.

11. Frazier, *Negro Church*, 48.

12. Ibid.

13. Lincoln, *Black Church since Frazier*, 116.

14. Frazier, *Negro Church*, 48. For the assertion of "manhood" and male leadership in historiography on slavery and plantation relations between black males and females in response to Stanley M. Elkins, *Slavery: A Problem in American Institutional and Intellectual Life*, 3rd ed. (Chicago: University of Chicago Press, 1976), see Deborah White Gray, *Ar'n't I a Woman? Female Slaves in the Plantation South* (New York: Norton, 1985), 17–23.

15. Quoted in Delores C. Carpenter, "Black Women in Religious Institutions: A Historical Summary from Slavery to the 1960s," *Journal of Religious Thought* 46/2 (1989–90): 7–27; 20, 21.

16. Frazier, *Negro Church*, and Lincoln, *Black Church*, 33.

17. Angela Y. Davis, *Women, Race, and Class* (New York: Vintage, 1983), 88.

18. Jacquelyn Grant, "Black Theology and the Black Woman" in *Black Theology*, 1:323–38; here esp. 325–26.

19. Ibid., 326.

20. Frazier, *Negro Church*, and Lincoln, *Black Church*, 36.

21. Ibid., 39.

22. Rosemary Radford Ruether, *New Woman, New Earth: Sexist Ideologies and Human Liberation* (New York: Crossroad, 1975), 127.

23. Frazier, *Negro Church*, and Lincoln, *Black Church*, 39–40.

24. Ibid., 40.

25. Ibid., 48–49.

26. Henry H. Mitchell, *Black Preaching* (Philadelphia: Lippincott, 1970).

27. Theresa Hoover, "Black Women and the Churches," 293–303; 294.

28. In this section I have benefited greatly from chapter 3, "Grounding with My Sisters: Patriarchy and the Exploitation of Black Women," in Marable, *Capitalism*, 69–103. Those who read Marable's chapter will recognize that I have borrowed plentifully from his excellent overview.

29. An observation by Deborah White Gray (*Ar'n't I a Woman?*) is quite telling on this point: "For antebellum black women, however, sexism was but one of three constraints. Most were slaves, and as such were denied the 'privilege,' enjoyed by white feminists, of theorizing about bondage, for they were literally owned by someone else. They were slaves because they were black, and even more than sex, color was the absolute determinant of class in antebellum America. To be of color was a mark of degradation, so much so that in most Southern states one's dark complexion was *prima facie* evidence that one was a slave. Black in a white society, slave in a free society, woman in a society ruled by men, female slaves had the least formal power and were perhaps the most vulnerable group of antebellum Americans. Certainly Sarah and Angelina Grimké thought so. For these two abolitionist and feminist leaders no other group of people were so degraded and brutalized. The whip on the slave woman's shrinking flesh became for them a symbol of male inhumanity and more than enough reason for American women to unite. Few, they thought, could fail to

believe that the slave woman's lot was the most intolerable, the most sorrowful, and the most pitiable of all" (pp. 17–18).

30. Marable, *Capitalism*, 69.

31. Ibid., 70.

32. Angela Davis, "Reflections on the Black Woman's Role in the Community of Slaves," *Black Scholar* 3 (December 1971): 7; cf. Marable, *Capitalism*, 70–71.

33. Davis, "Reflections," 17–18.

34. Davis, *Women*, 18.

35. Davis, "Reflections," 13; cf. Marable, *Capitalism*, 74.

36. William H. Becker, "The Black Church: Manhood and Mission," in Timothy E. Fulop and Albert J. Raboteau, eds., *African American Religion: Interpretive Essays in History and Culture* (New York: Routledge, 1997), 179–99; 180; references are from this edition; a reprint of *JAAR* 40 (1972): 316–33.

37. Ibid., 180.

38. Ibid.

39. Ibid., 183.

40. Ibid.

41. Ibid., 189.

42. Ibid., 190.

43. Cf. Marable, *Capitalism*, 76–77.

44. Marable, *Capitalism*, 76. The black newspapers mentioned above included John Russwurm's *Freedom's Journal* (1827), Martin Delany's *Mystery* (1843), Frederick Douglass's *North Star* (1848) and the *Anglo-African* of New York City (1859).

45. Quoted in John Bracey, August Meier, and Elliott Rudwick, eds., *Black Nationalism in America* (New York: Bobbs-Merrill, 1970), 215–16.

46. Meier et al., *Black Nationalism*, 140–41. My emphasis.

47. Ibid., 62; cf. Marable, *Capitalism*, 77.

48. Marable, *Capitalism*, 77.

49. Ibid., 80.

50. Ibid.

51. Ibid., 82–83.

52. Ibid., 84.

53. Ibid., 90–91.

54. James H. Cone, *Martin and Malcolm and America: A Dream or a Nightmare?* (Maryknoll, N.Y.: Orbis, 1991), 275.

55. Cone, *Martin and Malcolm*, 276.

56. Marable, *Capitalism*, 97.

57. Ibid., 98–99.

58. Cone, *Martin and Malcolm*, 274.

59. Ibid., 277.

60. Eldridge Cleaver, *Soul on Ice* (New York: Delta, 1968), 61, cited in Marable, *Capitalism*, 93.

61. Marable, *Capitalism*, 93.

62. Gayraud S. Wilmore, *Black Religion and Black Radicalism: An Interpretation of the Religious History of African Americans*, 3rd ed. (Maryknoll, N.Y.: Orbis, 1998), 233–44; Cone and Wilmore, *Black Theology*, 1:16; James Foreman, "The Black Manifesto," in *Black Theology*, 1:27–39.

63. Wilmore, *Black Theology*, 1:15–17; see Wilmore, *Black Religion*, 222–52, for fuller account.

64. Cone, "Black Theology: Statement by the National Committee of Black Churchmen, June 13, 1969," in *Black Theology*, 1:38.

65. Dwight N. Hopkins, *Introducing Black Theology of Liberation* (Maryknoll, N.Y.: Orbis, 1999), 7–12.

66. James Cone discusses his enlightenment on the interrelatedness of sexism and racism in *Black Theology*, 1:279–81.

67. Mark Chapman, *Christianity on Trial: African American Religious Thought before and after Black Power* (Maryknoll, N.Y.: Orbis, 1996), 147.

68. Both of the preceding quotes can be found in Chapman, *Christianity on Trial*, 136.

69. Davis, *Women*, 30, 39.

70. Ibid., 40, 44, 45.

71. Ibid., 70.

72. Ibid., 83.

73. Ibid., 84.

74. Paula Giddings, *When and Where I Enter: The Impact of Black Women on Race and Sex in America* (New York: Bantam, 1984), 81.

75. Ibid., 120.

76. Ibid., 129.

77. Ibid., 135.

78. Ibid., 93, 95.

79. Evelyn Brooks Higginbotham, *Righteous Discontent: The Women's Movement in the Black Baptist Church* (Cambridge: Harvard University Press, 1993), 69–73.

80. Ibid., 58, 64; The three conventions that merged into the NBC in 1895 are the National Baptist Educational Convention (NBEC), the National Foreign Mission Convention (NFMC), and the American National Baptist Convention (ANBC) (65).

81. Ibid., 151.

82. See Gilkes, "The Role of Women in the Sanctified Church," in *If It Wasn't*, 76–91; and H. Carlyle Church Jr., "The Accommodation and Liberation of Women in the Church of God in Christ," *Journal of Religious Thought* 52.2/53.1 (1997): 77–90; 80–87.

83. Higginbotham, *Righteous Discontent*, 150–51.

84. Giddings, *When and Where*, 299.

85. Ibid., 301–3.

86. Ibid., 303.

87. Among the prominent black women were Ailene Hernandez, former ILGWU (International Ladies' Garment Workers Union) organizer and Equal Employment

Opportunity Commission (EEOC) commissioner; Pauli Murray, an Episcopal priest and lawyer; Fannie Lou Hamer; Representative Shirley Chisholm (Dem., New York); Addie L. Wyatt, international vice president of the Amalgamated Meat Cutters Union; and Anna Arnold Hedgeman, former executive director of the National Council for a Permanent Fair Employment Practices Committee and assistant to the administrator of the Federal Security Agency (ibid., 301–2).

88. Ibid., 304.

89. Ibid., 306, 308.

90. In one widely read 1971 essay published in *Ebony* magazine, Helen King denounced "women's lib" as a white petty bourgeois fad that had little or nothing to do with the interests of black women. In *The Black Scholar*, Elizabeth Rood charged that white feminists had opportunistically usurped issues such as affirmative action from blacks. "It can be argued that women's liberation not only attached itself to the black movement," Rood explained, "but did so with only marginal concern for black women and black liberation, and functional concern for the rights of white women" (Marable, *Capitalism*, 95).

91. Gilkes, *If It Wasn't*, 139.

92. Mark Chapman, *Christianity on Trial*, 154.

93. Marable, *Capitalism*, 101–2.

94. Chapman, *Christianity on Trial*, 149.

95. Alice Walker, *In Search of Our Mother's Gardens: Womanist Prose* (New York: Harcourt Brace Jovanovich, 1983), xi–xii.

96. Hopkins, *Introducing Black Theology*, 130.

97. bell hooks, *Talking Back: Thinking Feminist, Thinking Black* (Boston: South End, 1989).

98. Cheryl J. Sanders, "Christian Ethics and Theology in Womanist Perspective," in *Black Theology*, 2:336–44. Renee Hill ("Who Are We for Each Other? Sexism, Sexuality and Womanist Theology," in *Black Theology*, 2:345–51) has critiqued womanist theology because of its neglect of gay and lesbian concerns.

99. Katie G. Cannon, "The Emergence of Black Feminist Consciousness," in Letty M. Russell, ed., *Feminist Interpretation of the Bible* (Louisville: Westminster, 1985).

100. Delores S. Williams, "Womanist Theology: Black Women's Voices," in *Black Theology*, vol. 2.

101. Hopkins, *Introducing Black Theology*, 132.

102. Kelly Brown Douglass, "Womanist Theology: What Is Its Relationship to Black Theology?" in *Black Theology*, 2:290–99; 295.

103. Cone, *Black Theology*, 2:257.

104. According to Higginbotham (*Righteous Discontent*, 150), Nannie Helen Burroughs's speech "How the Sisters Are Hindered from Helping," given at the National Baptist Convention in the fall of 1900, marked not only the beginning of her career but also the beginning of the Women's Convention, Auxiliary to the National Baptist Convention. She was only twenty-one years old when she delivered this speech.

5. Vision, Envision, and Revision

1. James Forbes Jr., "Ministry on the Eve of a New Millennium," in Ella Pearson Mitchell, ed., *Women to Preach or Not to Preach? 21 Outstanding Preachers Say Yes* (Valley Forge, Pa.: Judson, 1991), 123.

2. Sheron C. Patterson, *New Faith: A Black Woman's Guide to Reformation, Recreation, Rediscovery, Renaissance, Resurrection, and Revival* (Minneapolis: Fortress Press, 2000), 152.

3. bell hooks, *Ain't I a Woman: Black Women and Feminism* (Boston: Beacon, 1981), 88.

4. Ibid., 99.

5. Jacquelyn Grant, "Black Theology and the Black Woman, " in James H. Cone and Gayraud S. Wilmore, eds., *Black Theology: A Documentary History*, 2 vols., 2nd ed. (Maryknoll, N.Y.: Orbis, 1993), 1:326.

6. Cf. Demetrius K. Williams, "The Bible and Models of Liberation in the African American Experience," in Randall C. Bailey, ed., *Yet with a Steady Beat: Contemporary U.S. Afrocentric Biblical Interpretation* (Atlanta: Society of Biblical Literature, 2003), 33–59.

7. Cain Hope Felder, "The Bible, Re-Contextualization and the Black Religious Experience," in *African American Religious Studies: An Interdisciplinary Anthology*, ed. Gayraud S. Wilmore (Durham, N.C.: Duke University Press, 1989), 155–71, 155–57; also idem, *Troubling Biblical Waters: Race, Class, and Family* (Maryknoll, N.Y.: Orbis, 1989), 5–7.

8. James H. Cone, *God of the Oppressed* (New York: Seabury, 1975), 31.

9. Theophus Smith, *Conjuring Culture: Biblical Formations of Black America* (Oxford: Oxford University Press, 1994), 17.

10. Ibid.

11. Ibid.

12. Ibid., 55.

13. Albert J. Raboteau, *Slave Religion: The "Invisible Institution" in the Antebellum South* (New York: Oxford University Press, 1978), 304.

14. Smith, *Conjuring Culture*, 101.

15. W. E. B. Du Bois, *The Souls of Black Folks* (New York: Signet Classic, 1969), 47–48.

16. Smith, *Conjuring Culture*, 101.

17. Ibid., 17.

18. On this issue Smith, *Conjuring Culture*, 250, states: "The figural correspondence between the worldwide dispersal of Jews and that of African peoples has been recognized at least since the early nineteenth century. The word 'Diaspora' itself derives from the Greek word for dispersion and was typically applied to the 'scattering' (as in Nehemiah 1.8) of the Jews among Gentile nations beginning with the fall of the Northern Kingdom to Assyria in 721 B.C.E. The dispersal of Jews in the Hellenistic world of the Roman Empire sets the scene for the appearance of the word in the Christian Scriptures (for example, John 7.3-5). According to this view, Diaspora

configures a people's eschatological (end of the age) dispersal from every earthly homeland."

19. C. Shelby Rooks, "Toward the Promised Land: An Analysis of the Religious Experience of Black America," *The Black Church* 2/1 (1972): 1–48; quoted in Smith, *Conjuring Culture*, 249.

20. Smith, *Conjuring Culture*, 249.

21. Delores S. Williams, *Sisters in the Wilderness: The Challenge of Womanist God-Talk* (Maryknoll, N.Y.: Orbis, 1993), 147.

22. Ibid., 144, 148.

23. Ibid., 149.

24. Ibid., 144–45.

25. Ibid., 146.

26. Ibid., 144.

27. Randall C. Bailey, "'And They Shall Know that I Am YHWH!': The P Recasting of the Plague Narratives in Exodus 7–11," *Journal of the Interdenominational Theological Center* 22 (1994): 1–17; 16–17.

28. Ibid., 17.

29. Ibid.

30. Randall C. Bailey, "'Is That Any Name for a Nice Hebrew Boy?' Exodus 2:1-10: The De-Africanization of an Israelite Hero," in Randall C. Bailey and Jacquelyn Grant, eds., *The Recovery of Black Presence: An Interdisciplinary Exploration: Essays in Honor of Dr. Charles B. Copher* (Nashville: Abingdon, 1995), 25–36; 36.

31. Clarice J. Martin, "The *Haustafeln* in African American Biblical Interpretation: 'Free Slaves' and 'Submissive Wives,'" in Cain Hope Felder, ed., *Stony the Road We Trod: African American Biblical Interpretation* (Minneapolis: Fortress Press, 1990), 206–31; 227 (emphasis in the original).

32. Cheryl Townsend Gilkes, *If It Wasn't for the Women: Black Women's Experience and Womanist Culture in Church and Community* (Maryknoll, N.Y.: Orbis, 2001), 125.

33. Evelyn Brooks Higginbotham, *Righteous Discontent: The Women's Movement in the Black Baptist Church* (Cambridge: Harvard University Press, 1993), 120.

34. Karen Baker-Fletcher, "A Womanist Ontology of Freedom and Equality," *Journal of Religious Thought* 49/2 (1993): 60–71; 61.

35. Higginbotham, *Righteous Discontent*, 121.

36. Baker-Fletcher, "Womanist Ontology," 61.

37. Ibid., 70–71.

38. Ibid., 62, 67.

39. Jacquelyn Grant, "Womanist Theology: Black Women's Experience as a Source for Doing Theology, with Special Reference to Christology," in *African American Religious Studies*, 208–27; 210.

40. Jacquelyn Grant, "Womanist Jesus and the Struggle for Liberation," in *Recovery of Black Presence*, 129–42.

41. Ibid., 138.

42. Ibid.

43. Williams, *Sisters*, xiv.

44. In this section I have benefited from Stanley Stowers's critique of Gal. 3:28 in "Paul and Slavery: A Response," *Semeia* 83/84 (1998): 295–311; 302–10.

45. Ibid., 303–4.

46. Ibid., 304.

47. Ibid., 303.

48. Ibid., 303–4.

49. Peter J. Paris, *The Spirituality of African Peoples: The Search for a Common Moral Discourse* (Minneapolis: Fortress Press, 1995), 1–18.

50. Molefi Kete Asante, *The Afrocentric Idea* (Philadelphia: Temple University Press, 1987), 3–4.

51. Cf. Felder, "The Bible, Recontextualization."

52. Cf. Randall C. Bailey, "Beyond Identification: The Use of Africans in Old Testament Poetry and Narratives," in *Stony the Road*, 165–84, and "Is That Any Name for a Nice Hebrew Boy?"; Clarice J. Martin, "A Chamberlain's Journey and the Challenge of Interpretation for Liberation," in *Semeia* 47 (1989): 105–35.

53. J. Deotis Roberts, *Africentric Christianity: A Theological Appraisal for Ministry* (Valley Forge, Pa.: Judson, 2000). The word *Afrocentric* has currency in a wide range of activities and events among African Americans, and the word *Africentric*, now often used instead of the word *Afrocentric*, "seems to be gaining ground because of the former's more etymologically correct connection to its root, 'Africa'" (Roberts, *Africentric Christianity*, vii–viii).

54. Ibid., 3.

55. Nathaniel S. Murrell, "Wrestling the Message from the Messenger: The Rastafari as a Case Study in the Caribbean Indigenization of the Bible," in Vincent L. Wimbush, ed., *African Americans and the Bible* (New York: Continuum, 2000), 263–64.

56. Ibid., 264–65.

57. Irene Monroe, "The Struggle for Human Acceptance," *The African American Pulpit* 4/3 (2001): 65–69; 67.

58. Victor Anderson, *Beyond Ontological Blackness: An Essay on African American Religious and Cultural Criticism* (New York: Continuum, 1995), 11–12.

59. Ruether, *New Woman, New Earth: Sexist Ideologies and Human Liberation* (Boston: Beacon, 1995), 116.

60. Ibid.

61. James H. Cone, *For My People: Black Theology and the Black Church* (Maryknoll, N.Y.: Orbis, 1984), 122–39.

62. Garth Baker-Fletcher, *Somebodyness: Martin Luther King, Jr., and the Theory of Dignity*; HDR 31 (Minneapolis: Fortress Press, 1993), 175.

63. Pauli Murray, "Black Theology and Feminist Theology: A Comparative View," in *Black Theology*, 1:304–22; 307.

64. Clarice J. Martin, "Womanist Interpretations of the New Testament: The Quest for Holistic and Inclusive Translation and Interpretation," in *Black Theology*, 2:234.

65. Samuel Bacchiocchi, *Women in the Church: A Biblical Study on the Role of Women in the Church* (Berrien Springs; Mich.: Biblical Perspectives, 1987), 26.

66. Ibid., 24 (emphasis added).

67. Susan T. Foh, *Woman and the Word of God: A Response to Biblical Feminism* (n.p.: Presbyterian and Reformed Publishing, 1988), 238–39.

68. Murray, "Black Theology," 308.

69. Deborah White Gray, *Ar'n't I a Woman? Female Slaves in the Plantation South* (New York: Norton, 1985), 27–28.

70. Ibid., 27.

71. Ibid., 28.

72. Ibid.

73. Emilie M. Townes, ed., *A Troubling in My Soul: Womanist Perspectives on Evil and Suffering* (Maryknoll, N.Y.: Orbis, 1993), 78.

74. Delores C. Carpenter, "Black Women in Religious Institutions: A Historical Summary from Slavery to the 1960s," *The Journal of Religious Thought* 46/2 (1989–1990): 7–27; 26.

75. John W. Kinney, "God with Us," *The African American Pulpit* 5/2 (Spring 2002): 60–63; 60–61.

76. Nelle Morton, "Preaching the Word," in Alice L. Hageman, ed., *Sexist Religion and Women in the Church: No More Silence!* (New York: Association Press, 1974), 34.

77. Francis E. Wood, "'Take My Yoke upon You': The Role of the Church in the Oppression of African American Women," in *A Troubling in My Soul*, 37–47; 46.

6. Women, Word, and Witness

1. Susan D. Johnson, *Wise Women Bearing Gifts* (Valley Forge, Pa.: Judson, 1988), 16 (emphasis in the original).

2. Sheron C. Patterson, *New Faith: A Black Woman's Guide to Reformation, Re-creation, Rediscovery, Renaissance, Resurrection, and Revival* (Minneapolis: Fortress Press, 2000), vii.

3. For statistics see Bettye Collier-Thomas, *Daughters of Thunder: Black Women Preachers and Their Sermons, 1850–1979* (San Francisco: Jossey-Bass, 1998), 280.

4. Cheryl Townsend Gilkes, *If It Wasn't for the Women: Black Women's Experience and Womanist Culture in Church and Community* (Maryknoll, N.Y.: Orbis, 2001), 210.

5. C. Mackey Daniels, "A Letter from the President of the Progressive National Baptist Convention, Inc.: Introducing the PNBC," *The African American Pulpit*, 4/3 (Summer 2001): 10–11; 11.

6. Collier-Thomas, *Daughters of Thunder*, 26; Sandy Dwayne Martin, "The African Methodist Episcopal Zion Church and the Women's Ordination Controversy, 1898–1900: A Case Study on the Value of Racial Inclusivity in Religious Studies," *Journal of the Interdenominational Theological Seminary* 21/1–2 (1994): 105–26; 107.

7. Felton O. Best, *Black Religious Leadership from the Slave Community to the Million Man March: Flames of Fire* (Lewiston: Mellen, 1998), 154.

8. Elaine J. Lawless, "Not So Different a Story after All: Pentecostal Women in the Pulpit," in Catherine Wessinger, ed., *Women's Leadership in Marginal Religions: Explorations outside the Mainstream* (Urbana: University of Illinois Press, 1993).

9. H. Carlyle Church Jr., "The Accommodation and Liberation of Women in the Church of God in Christ," *The Journal of Religious Thought* 52.2/53.1 (1997): 77–90.

10. Best, *Black Religious Leadership*, 154–55.

11. Church, "Accommodation and Liberation," 88.

12. Gilkes, *If It Wasn't,* 210.

13. Evelyn Brooks Higginbotham, *Righteous Discontent: The Women's Movement in the Black Baptist Church* (Cambridge: Harvard University Press, 1993), 3.

14. Ibid., 122.

15. Henry H. Mitchell, *Black Preaching* (Philadelphia: Lippincott, 1970).

16. William L. Andrews, ed., *Sisters of the Spirit: Three Black Women's Autobiographies of the Nineteenth Century* (Bloomington: Indiana University Press, 1986), 35.

17. Ibid., 2.

18. Ibid., 36; emphasis added.

19. Ibid.

20. Ibid.

21. Ibid.

22. Ibid., 36–37.

23. Ibid., 82.

24. Collier-Thomas, *Daughters of Thunder*, 46–47.

25. Paula Giddings, *When and Where I Enter: The Impact of Black Women on Race and Sex in America* (New York: Bantam, 1984), 49.

26. Marilyn Richardson, *Maria Stewart, America's First Black Woman Political Writer: Essays and Speeches* (Bloomington: Indiana University Press, 1987), 5.

27. Giddings, *When and Where,* 52.

28. Richardson, "Lecture Delivered at the Franklin Hall," *Maria Stewart*, 19, 45; the Franklin Hall was the regular site of the monthly meetings of the New England Anti-Slavery Society.

29. Ibid., 66.

30. Ibid., 67.

31. Ibid., 22.

32. Gilkes, *If It Wasn't*, 110.

33. Richardson, *Maria Stewart*, 68.

34. Ibid., 69.

35. Ibid., 70 (emphasis added).

36. Manning Marable, *How Capitalism Underdeveloped Black America: Problems in Race, Political Economy, and Society* (Boston: South End, 1983), 79–80.

37. Angela Y. Davis, *Women, Race, and Class* (New York: Vintage, 1983), 60.

38. Ibid.

39. Ibid., 61.

40. Ibid.

41. Ibid., 61–62.

42. Ibid., 62.

43. Collier-Thomas, *Daughters of Thunder*, 57–59.

44. Andrews, *Sisters of the Spirit,* 208–9 (emphasis added).

45. Ibid., 227.

46. Gilkes, *If It Wasn't,* 111.

47. Higginbotham, *Righteous Discontent,* 125.

48. Ibid., 131–32.

49. Ibid., 133.

50. Ibid., 135.

51. Ibid., 133.

52. Collier-Thomas, *Daughters of Thunder*, 126.

53. Ibid.

54. Ibid., 173–74.

55. Ibid., 180–81.

56. Ibid., 177.

57. Ibid., 211–14.

58. Ibid.

59. Ibid.

60. Ibid., 213.

61. This notion is central to Elisabeth Schüssler Fiorenza's work; cf. Elisabeth Schüssler Fiorenza, *Searching the Scriptures*, 2 vols. (New York: Crossroad, 1993–94), 1:11–12.

62. Collier-Thomas, *Daughters of Thunder*, 221–23.

63. Ibid., 224.

64. Ibid., 253.

65. Prathia Hall, "Beyond Eden," *The African American Pulpit* 6/1 (2002–2003): 46.

66. Ibid., 46–51.

67. Ibid., 47.

68. Ibid., 50.

69. Ella Pearson Mitchell, *Those Preaching Women*, vol. 1: *Sermons by Black Women Preachers*, vol. 2: *More Sermons by Black Women Preachers* (Valley Forge, Pa.: Judson, 1985, 1988), 1:12.

70. Ibid.

71. Ibid., 14.

72. Ibid., 16.

73. Cynthia L. Hale, "Women Transformed by Christ . . . Filled with Power," in Ella Pearson Mitchell, ed., *Women to Preach or Not to Preach? 21 Outstanding Preachers Say Yes* (Valley Forge, Pa.: Judson, 1991), 91.

74. Ibid., 107.

75. Ibid., 142.

76. Judy L. Brown, *Women Ministers according to Scripture* (Kearney, Neb.: Morris, 1996), 2–3.

77. Gilkes, *If It Wasn't,* 123; from Charles H. Pleas, *Fifty Years Achievement (History): Church of God in Christ* (Memphis: Church of God in Christ Publishing House, n.d. [circa 1975]), 35.

78. Church, "Accommodation and Liberation," 88.

79. Gilkes, *If It Wasn't,* 124; from Pleas, *Fifty Years,* 36.

80. Gilkes, *If It Wasn't,* 124.

81. John W. Kinney, "Surprise! Surprise! Surprise!" in *Women to Preach or Not to Preach?* 25.

82. Ibid., 28.

83. See also Kinney's "God with Us," *The African American Pulpit* 5/2 (2002): 60–63.

84. W. Franklyn Richardson, "Faith that Denies the Context," in *Women to Preach or Not to Preach?* 31.

85. Ibid., 34–35.

86. J. Alfred Smith Sr., "Surprise: Guess Who's Coming to the Pulpit," in *Women to Preach or Not to Preach?* 64.

87. Ibid., 65–66.

88. Gardner C. Taylor, "Three Women and God," in *Women to Preach or Not to Preach?* 86.

89. Samuel H. Proctor, "The Four Daughters of Philip, the Deacon," in *Women to Preach or Not to Preach?* 102.

90. James A. Forbes Jr., "Ministry on the Eve of a New Millennium," in *Women to Preach or Not to Preach?* 123.

91. G. Daniel Jones, "E.R.A.," in *Women to Preach or Not to Preach?* 137.

Conclusion: "We've Come This Far by Faith"

1. Jacquelyn Grant, "Black Theology and the Black Woman," in James H. Cone and Gayraud S. Wilmore, eds., *Black Theology: A Documentary History*, 2 vols., 2nd ed. (Maryknoll, N.Y.: Orbis, 1993), 1:327.

2. Peter J. Paris, *The Social Teaching of the Black Churches* (Philadelphia: Fortress Press, 1985), 16; cf. Elsie Johnson McDougal, "The Double Task: The Struggle of Negro Women for Sex and Race Emancipation," *Survey Graphic* 6 (March 1925): 691, quoted in Gerda Lerner, ed., *Black Women in White America: A Documentary History* (New York: Vintage, 1992), 171: "The feminist efforts are directed chiefly toward the realization of the equality of the races, the sex struggle assuming a subordinate place. . . . The wind of the race's destiny stirs more briskly because of her striving."

3. Cone, *Black Theology,* 1:281.

4. Bettye Collier-Thomas, ed., *Daughters of Thunder: Black Women Preachers and Their Sermons 1850–1979* (San Francisco: Jossey-Bass, 1998), 279; cf. Cheryl Townsend Gilkes, *If It Wasn't for the Women: Black Women's Experience and Womanist Culture in Church and Community* (Maryknoll, N.Y.: Orbis, 2001), 125.

5. Grant, "Black Theology," 328.

6. Quoted in Evelyn Brooks Higginbotham, *Righteous Discontent: The Women's Movement in the Black Baptist Church* (Cambridge: Harvard University Press, 1993), 148.

7. Manning Marable, *How Capitalism Underdeveloped Black America: Problems in Race, Political Economy, and Society* (Boston: South End, 1983), 103.

8. Theresa Hoover, "Black Women and the Churches: Triple Jeopardy," in *Black Theology*, 1:303.

Selected Bibliography

Allison, Robert W. "Let Women Be Silent in the Churches (1 Cor. 14:33b-36): What Did Paul Really Say, and What Did It Mean?" *JSNT* 32 (1988): 27–60.

Bailey, Randall C., and Jacquelyn Grant, eds. *The Recovery of Black Presence: An Interdisciplinary Exploration: Essays in Honor of Dr. Charles B. Copher.* Nashville: Abingdon, 1995.

Bartchy, S. Scott. *ΜΑΛΛΟΝ ΧΡΗΣΑΙ: First-Century Slavery and the Interpretation of First Corinthians 7:21.* SBLDS 11. Missoula, Mont.: Scholars Press, 1973.

Betz, Hans D. *Galatians: A Commentary on Paul's Letter to the Churches in Galatia.* Hermeneia. Philadelphia: Fortress Press, 1979.

Collier-Thomas, Bettye, ed. *Daughters of Thunder: Black Women Preachers and Their Sermons 1850–1979.* San Francisco: Jossey-Bass, 1998.

Cone, James H., and Gayraud S. Wilmore, eds. *Black Theology: A Documentary History.* 2 vols. 2nd ed. Maryknoll, N.Y.: Orbis, 1993.

Felder, Cain H. *Troubling Biblical Waters: Race, Class, and Family.* Maryknoll, N.Y.: Orbis, 1989.

Giddings, Paula. *When and Where I Enter: The Impact of Black Women on Race and Sex in America.* New York: Bantam, 1984.

Gilkes, Cheryl Townsend. *If It Wasn't for the Women: Black Women's Experience and Womanist Culture in Church and Community.* Maryknoll, N.Y.: Orbis, 2001.

Higginbotham, Evelyn Brooks. *Righteous Discontent: The Women's Movement in the Black Baptist Church.* Cambridge: Harvard University Press, 1993.

Keener, Craig S. *Paul, Women and Wives: Marriage and Women's Ministry in the Letters of Paul.* Peabody, Mass.: Hendrickson, 1992.

Kraemer, Ross S. *Her Share of the Blessings: Women's Religions among Pagans, Jews, and Christians in the Greco-Roman World.* New York: Oxford University Press, 1992.

Lincoln, C. Eric, and Lawrence Mamiya. *The Black Church in the African American Experience.* Durham, N.C.: Duke University Press, 1990.

MacDonald, Dennis R. *There Is No Male and Female: The Fate of a Dominical Saying in Paul and Gnosticism.* Philadelphia: Fortress Press, 1987.

Martin, Clarice J. *Tongues of Fire: Power for the Church Today.* Louisville, Ky.: Presbyterian Church (U.S.A.), 1990.

Mitchell, Ella Pearson, ed. *Those Preaching Women.* Vol. 1: *Sermons by Black Women Preachers.* Vol. 2: *More Sermons by Black Women Preachers.* Valley Forge, Pa.: Judson, 1985, 1988.

———. *Women to Preach or Not to Preach? 21 Outstanding Preachers Say Yes.* Valley Forge, Pa.: Judson, 1991.

Paris, Peter J. *The Social Teaching of the Black Churches.* Philadelphia: Fortress Press, 1985.

Patterson, Sheron C. *New Faith: A Black Woman's Guide to Reformation, Re-creation, Rediscovery, Renaissance, Resurrection, and Revival.* Minneapolis: Fortress Press, 2000.

Schüssler Fiorenza, Elisabeth. *In Memory of Her: A Feminist Theological Reconstruction of Christian Origins.* New York: Crossroad, 1983.

Smith, Theophus. *Conjuring Culture: Biblical Formations of Black America.* Oxford: Oxford University Press, 1994.

Williams, Delores S. *Sisters in the Wilderness: The Challenge of Womanist God-Talk.* Maryknoll, N.Y.: Orbis, 1993.

Williams, Demetrius K. "The Bible and Models of Liberation in the African American Experience." In Randall C. Bailey, ed., *Yet with a Steady Beat: Contemporary U.S. Afrocentric Biblical Interpretation*, 33–59. Atlanta: Society of Biblical Literature, 2003.

———. "Paul's Anti-Imperial Discourse of the Cross: The Cross and Power in 1 Corinthians 1-4." *Society of Biblical Literature Seminar Papers 2000*, 796–823. Atlanta: SBL Press, 2000.

Wire, Antoinette Clark. *The Corinthian Women Prophets: A Reconstruction through Paul's Rhetoric.* Minneapolis: Fortress Press, 1990.

Index